Revolution

The Irish Clans

Book Five in the Series

Stephen Finlay Archer

Manzanita Writers Press
San Andreas, California

Revolution: The Irish Clans
Book Five in the Series

ISBN: 978-0-9986910-9-1
Library of Congress Control Number: 2021904752

Publisher: Manzanita Writers Press
manzapress.com
manzanitawp@gmail.com
PO Box 215, San Andreas, CA 95249

Contact the author at stephenfinlayarcher@gmail.com
Cover design: Stephen Finlay Archer
Book Layout design: Joyce Dedini

Revolution: Book Five cover credits:
>   Front Cover.
>>   *Roadside Ambush*, painting by Martin McGrinder
>   Back Cover:
>>   *Book of Ballymote* folio, courtesy of the Royal Irish Academy
>>   *From Collage of Irish Civil War*, painting by Norman Teeling

Searchers: Book One - Front cover:
>   *The Sinking of the Lusitania*, Courtesy of the Everett Collection

Entente: Book Two - Front cover:
>   *Canadians at Ypres, The Belgian Front 1915*, Painting by William Barnes Wollen, courtesy of the Princess Patricia's Canadian Light Infantry Museum

Rising: Book Three - Front cover:
>   *Montage of the Irish Easter Rising 1916*, Painting by Norman Teeling

McCarthy Gold: Book Four - Front Cover:
>   *The Money Diggers*, Painting by John Quidor, Courtesy of the Brooklyn Museum

Fortunes: Book Six - Front Cover:
>   *Burning of the Custom House*, Painting by Norman Teeling

Revelation: Book Seven - Front Cover:
>   *Iona Abbey*, Painting by Reverend John Butterfield

This is a work of fiction. Any resemblance of my fictional characters to real persons, living or dead, is purely coincidental. The depictions of historical persons in these novels are not coincidental, and to the best of my knowledge, are historically sound. Some historical aspects have been augmented or adjusted for dramatic purposes.

DEDICATION

This novel is dedicated to the Irish men and women, under the command of their inspirational leaders, Michael Collins and Éamon de Valera, who desperately fought for freedom in their War of Independence against the British overlord in post-World War I Ireland.

The Volunteers
by Stephen Finlay Archer

The Irish Volunteers were brave,
Committed all to free their land.
Their heritage to finally save
From England's boot and fettered brand.

Young Collins helped the martyrs' rise,
By Plunket's side, in Pearse's wake,
Their military plan unwise,
He vowed revenge for Ireland's sake.

In Frongoch jail he formed his plans,
To drive the English off his Isle,
In keeping with ancestral clans,
Guerrilla warfare, wit, and guile.

Released, he quickly took command,
Behind closed doors he chose his Squad.
Assassins all, a fearless band
Those brutish Brits, they'd ride roughshod.

Mick snuck into the Castle dark,
He stole the names of British spies,
Coerced informers with his bark,
Those demon lords he'd neutralize.

Mick's flying columns nationwide,
Were here then gone, they'd hit and run,
They looted barracks fortified
With British bullet, bomb, and gun.

They sabotaged both roads and tracks,
They freed their comrades from caged jail.
They stole Brits gold, they paid no tax,
They clogged the courts; they robbed the mail.

Cruel Churchill sent the Black and Tans,
To bolster besieged RIC.
Ex fighters from the mud of France,
They slashed and burned, revengeful glee.

They killed or jailed the Volunteers,
They executed them for spite,
MacSwiney led the mutineers,
On hunger strike, the world incite.

Mick ordered death for British spies,
On Bloody Sunday they were shot,
The British foe to traumatize,
Upset their brutal intel plot.

The Auxies raided full Croke Park,
A football match was underway,
Murderous bullets found their mark,
Fourteen victims died in that fray.

The Irish Volunteers were brave,
Committed all to free their land.
Their heritage to finally save
From England's boot and fettered brand.

Map 1
Entrance to New York City Harbor, 1916

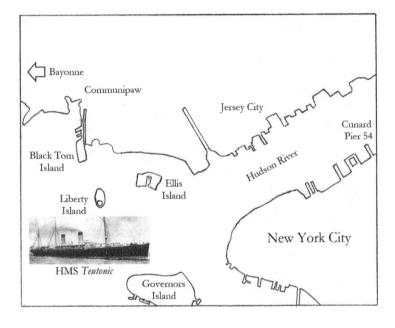

Bayonne

Communipaw

Jersey City

Cunard
Pier 54

Black Tom
Island

Ellis
Island

Hudson River

Liberty
Island

New York City

HMS *Teutonic*

Governors
Island

CONTENTS

Chapter One
Sabotage

Saturday, July 29, 1916
Onboard HMS *Teutonic*
Forty Miles East of New York City

*I*t was just before midnight. Sam strained his weary eyes, searching for lights on the western horizon. He was exhausted from shepherding his protégé Collin O'Donnell and his pregnant wife Kathy through the deadly search for Collin's sister back in his homeland, Ireland. Her rebel lover, Tadgh McCarthy, had been a handful as he searched for his ancestral treasure. Sam's mind churned as he recalled that without his intervention, they would all have died a horrible death at the hands of the Clans' wicked police adversary, Head Constable Boyle. That villain was continuing his murdering ways after he had killed both the O'Donnell and McCarthy elders in search of the same fortune.

He knew Collin was torn between wanting to stay with his sister, Morgan to continue the search for his own family's buried treasure back in Ireland and the need to appease his wife and return to Canada to save his job at the *Tely* newspaper. Fortunately, Sam's wife, Lil who was waiting anxiously back in Toronto for their return, had no knowledge of their peril in these harrowing adventures.

Amid the frightening Atlantic crossings during WWI, HMS *Teutonic*'s captain had received an urgent message from the Admiralty yesterday to divert south from Montreal to New York City, away from the mouth of the St. Lawrence River due to U-boat sightings off Prince Edward Island. The emboldened Germans had recently announced they might resume sinking Allied ships. Wouldn't that provoke the United States into the Great War? Likely the Central Powers needed to put an end to the strangling effects

11

of the British naval blockade. This deadly war had become damn inconvenient. He and the O'Donnells needed to get home to Toronto immediately.

"See anything yet?" Kathy asked, as she and her husband Collin walked over to the starboard rail to join their mentor. "I'm looking forward to this docking. It's been a while since Collin and I saw the lights of New York City."

"Not yet." Sam checked his watch. "We're still two hours out, I'd guess, lass. I'm worried about our transportation home. School starts next Tuesday."

Collin shook his head. "Not to worry, boss. That's why the captain announced he is pushing to dock tonight because of the delay. There are a dozen other passengers who need to get home to Canada. The purser is supposed to be organizing the earliest train out of Penn Station for us all."

At that same moment, in a New Jersey tenement house at the port of Bayonne, its Czechoslovakian landlady, Mrs. Anna Rushnak, peered out of an upstairs window at the Statue of Liberty across the docks, scowling. Her twenty-three-year-old boarder, Michael Kristoff, was acting suspiciously again. His going out at night was secretive, and sometimes she suspected that his forays coincided with explosions or fires in the seaport area. After these odd nocturnal wanderings, he came back with a swagger in his step, maybe carrying extra money in his pockets because they bulged and jingled as he walked.

In recent days, with America's entry into the Great War so uncertain, one couldn't be too cautious. Anna wondered whether to contact the police. People with a foreign name or appearance, especially if they were German, were under observation. A paranoia, really, but since Michael was a distant relative, she had kept silent. Tonight, he was gone again.

Just north of Anna's tenement, protruding east into the Hudson River from the town of Communipaw, the Lehigh Railroad had built a mile-long pier connecting the shore to little Black Tom Island. Michael Kristoff had studied its extensive complex of warehouses, railroad shunt tracks, and docks that stood just west of Liberty Island in the mouth of the Hudson River and opposite the southern tip of Manhattan Island off its eastern shore. This shipping port stored lucrative weapons of war funneled from neutral America to the Allies.

Despite the military sensitivity of this facility, security was generally lax, he noticed. The entry points for the poorly lit warehouses and railyards were not guarded at night. The six railroad detectives and two private night watchmen seemed more concerned about keeping smudge pots lit to ward off descending mosquito hordes than looking for intruders. The island contained a hundred loaded freight cars, and, he had found out, about three million pounds of explosives destined for Mother Russia. One of the barges moored hazardously at the wharf, the *Johnson 17,* was carrying one hundred thousand pounds of TNT, information Michael had ferreted out of a drunken dockworker. *So much the better,* he thought.

Michael deferred to his boss for orders. The German Ambassador in Washington, Count Johann Von Bernstorff, had assembled a crack team of spies and saboteurs to interrupt the three-billion-dollar supply of war materials annually delivered by America to the Western and Eastern Fronts. He didn't know all the details, but he had heard rumors that the German General Staff gave the count a hundred and fifty million dollars for the job.

Michael knew Captain Franz von Rintelen personally, one of Bernstorff's nefarious agents and a master saboteur. They had talked about his invention of the pencil bomb that would remotely ignite cargoes at sea. They rejoiced in the fact that Franz had personally hampered supplies by this method, directly accounting for about ten million dollars of loss.

It was Von Rintelen who had scoped out the Black Tom facility. They had discussed the benefits of blowing up the munitions and having them damage the symbol of liberty, that monstrous gift from France. He had put the plan in motion to address the Black Tom opportunity before the British apprehended him near the end of July when he passed through Southampton en route home to Germany. Now it was up to Michael to implement the plan.

Teutonic nosed its way northwest at about two in the morning, a couple of miles away from the mouth of the Hudson River.

"I see her!" Kathy called out. She pointed portside from the ship's bow toward the Statue of Liberty in the distance. "We'll be going right by her on our left. Isn't she beautiful all lit up like that?"

Collin motioned to his right, beyond the starboard bow. "The city lights are more spectacular, don't ye think, even at this hour?"

"Imagine being refugees arriving from Europe to a new land of opportunity. 'Tis certainly a welcoming symbol for liberty and justice."

Sam puffed on his Prince Albert pipe. "All right, you two. We need to focus on getting home before school starts and then saving Collin's job at the *Tely*. Let's go below and get our valises."

Kathy shook her head. "We're going to stay up here until docking, Sam. You can go down if you must but look at what you will be missing." Her arms waved at the vista.

"The purser just told us that our train won't leave until seven. We've plenty of time," Collin added.

Sam drummed his fingers on the rail and stayed on deck, then coaxed his compatriots aft along the port side, closer to the disembarkation point. The three of them were alone, looking north along the Jersey shoreline.

Soon, the tug drew alongside, and the port pilot transferred to the *Teutonic* to guide her into the harbor. *Teutonic*, now broadside to the Statue of Liberty, towered higher than the tip of the ship's masts, and not a thousand yards to port. The vessel would be docked at White Star Pier 54 in less than an hour.

Collin turned toward Kathy and grabbed her hand, pointing. "See those lights twinkling ahead in the river? That's Ellis Island, I think. Where the immigrants are processed."

Kathy frowned. "Where you were processed, you mean. With your Ma, rest her soul, into that den of iniquity, Brooklyn."

Suddenly, a blast rocked the vessel. A ferocious fireball erupted behind the statue blinding the trio. Collin instinctively spun to face his wife to shield her as a stabbing pain pierced his back under the ribcage. He threw his arms around Kathy, barely a moment before the explosion hurled them back from the rail. Their spinning momentum caused Collin to slam into the bulkhead. They slumped onto the deck together in a tangled heap.

The plate windows on the bridge and elsewhere on the port side imploded in a hail of glass with the blast, while the lower portholes stayed intact. The ship listed heavily starboard, then rolled sharply back to port side. The stunned couple slid and tumbled down the slanted deck, their bodies aimed precariously towards the sea.

Sam had grasped the rail with both hands when the Black Tom warehouses and boxcars started exploding, nearly bowling him over. The initial shock wave walloped and tore at him as his body flew horizontal toward the bulkhead. As the ship recoiled to port, he lost his grip and flopped down by the rail.

Still dazed, Sam felt the impact of his friends' intertwined bodies sliding past him. He thrust his arm out, grabbing at them as they slid under the railing. Sam's right hand found purchase on Collin's ankle, and he closed on it with a vise-grip, preventing his protégé from going over the deck lip into the foaming sea. Collin, in turn, gripped his wife to his chest as her legs slid out over the edge of the deck under the rail. With a violent jerk, Sam yanked them both back to safety on the stabilizing deck.

There they all lay, spent, as the roaring fire raged above the island.

Suddenly, the *Johnson 17* barge exploded at the wharf and blew more shrapnel out toward the statue and the *Teutonic*. It sounded like crashing thunder, with a deafening roar. Sam threw himself over the couple as the ship rocked once more.

The heat from the inferno roasted the side of the ship as Captain James regained his composure. The port pilot and two officers sprawled on the bridge deck, effectively out of action. Oblivious to the cuts on his face and body, the captain barked orders to his crew. Pushing the speed lever to all-ahead full, he spun the rudder controls to starboard to maneuver away from the fires before they could engulf his ship. "My God! Hop to it, lads!" he yelled into his intercom. The memory of the recent massive naval engagement in the North Sea flashed in his mind. "It looks like the battle of Jutland up here!"

Then he summoned his chief medic on the intercom. "Mercer, get up here on the double!"

Projectiles rocketed skyward and burst a thousand feet above. A sickly yellow pale glow lit a blizzard of debris falling on the Jersey harbor. The clock in the Jersey Journal's tower more than a mile away had stopped at two-twelve after being sliced by shrapnel. The skyscraper windows of lower Manhattan disintegrated. Patrons emerged from bars where rolling shock waves knocked them down. Citizens as far away as Philadelphia jumped out of bed from the vibrations, certain that it was a powerful earthquake.

Warders and immigrants waiting to be processed on Ellis Island dove for shelter trying to escape hot cinders raining down on them.

♣ ♣ ♣ ♣

Sam pulled himself up, then jerked back from the heat in the metal railing. The smoke billowing eastward over the water enveloped them like a dense fog and choked Sam's throat. His arms hurt like hell, but he wasn't bleeding. That's when he realized that his heart was pounding, as if it wanted to leap out of his chest. Not good—especially with his medical condition. He had to calm down.

"This war is becoming more than inconvenient," he muttered, kneeling to check on the O'Donnells, still prone on the deck.

Kathy groaned and rolled off her husband. He lay face up, not moving, with his head resting in a pool of blood.

"Collin's hurt!" Kathy cried. "Help me, Sam!"

As they gently turned Collin onto his stomach, he moaned. Protruding two inches out of his back, a few inches below his right shoulder blade, was a jagged piece of shrapnel. No telling how badly it had affected his internal organs.

Kathy touched the end of the metal piece, her eyes wide with panic. "Should we pull it out?"

Sam grabbed her wrist. "Don't! You'll cause more damage."

Kathy yanked her hand free. "We must do *something*!"

Sam pulled off his sweater and placed it gently around the spike.

"Press down on my sweater to help stop the bleeding. I will get help."

"Don't leave me, Sam." Kathy had learned to tend to her baby's minor medical needs before they left for Ireland, but this was a frightening nightmare. Collin's life was at stake, and she didn't know how to save him. "Oh, God. We need his sister Morgan. She'd know what to do."

"I have to go. Just do as I've said, lass." He guided her hands in pressing on the wound, then stood up. "Be right back."

Collin moaned.

Alive! Kathy thought. She obeyed instructions as Sam took off at a trot toward the Bridge.

Sam found the ship's medical team administering to the officers. The captain, wiping blood from a cut on his forehead, seemed focused on getting his ship away from the disaster and directed him to the ship's medic. Inside the Bridge, Sam peered through the shattered window and the area's dissipating smoke and realized that they were now north of Ellis Island, entering the Hudson River, and approaching the piers on Manhattan's southwest side. He took stock of the situation. Behind them now, the Statue of Liberty stood silhouetted against the orange conflagration rapidly consuming Black Tom Island. The port pilot he'd observed boarding the ship earlier was being ministered to on the deck below him. At least they were clear of further danger as long as the injured captain didn't ram the pier.

Sam found the medic in charge. Unfortunately, at that moment, the man was kneeling, preoccupied with suturing an officer's arm wound. Sam ground his teeth and dug his fingernails into the palms of his hands. As soon as the doctor finished his stitching, Sam gripped the man's shoulder and tried to raise him up, urging, "I need assistance. My friend is bleeding profusely with shrapnel in his back. Please help!"

The medic pushed Sam's arm away. "We're trying to save our ship's officers and the port pilot here. Your friend will have to wait, I'm afraid."

Sam looked around. The wounded had multiple lacerations from glass cuts and bruises, but none of them seemed to be bleeding as profusely as Collin was.

"These men seem to have minor wounds, sir. My friend may die." His voice took on a desperate tone.

The captain overheard the conversation. "Take care of him, Mercer. Our passengers are our lifeblood. Send your best man to help. We can manage here." He addressed the medic. "Are others hurt as well?"

"I don't know, sir, but I imagine those below decks and on the starboard side should have been spared, except for a few bumps and bruises."

The chief medic motioned to one of his assistants, and he and his kit were dispatched. Sam quickly led the man to where Collin lay stricken. He noticed other passengers had congregated on the aft port deck, transfixed on the fiery devastation behind them.

Kathy looked up with anguished eyes. "Thank God you're here, Sam. Collin is trying to move, and I've urged him to lie still."

The medic dropped down, rolled Collin on his side, and checked his mouth and airway, then gave a cursory examination of his head. "There's no bleeding here. That's a good sign."

He checked Collin's pulse. "Rapid," he frowned. "Collin, is it? Can you hear me, lad?"

"Y–yes," Collin murmured.

"Take a deep breath if you can."

Collin obeyed and abruptly coughed. "Buggers, hurts like hell," he croaked.

Sam saw the medic's dour expression as the man examined the dirty, jagged metal protrusion and then said to Collin, "I expect that it would hurt a mite. You have a rather large piece of shrapnel imbedded in your back. Please lie still." He rolled Collin back on his stomach, turning to Kathy. "Are you his wife?"

"Yes, sir. Will he be all right?"

"He will if we get him to hospital soon. He may have a collapsed lung. I'm going to cut away his coat and shirt to examine his back. Then I'll know if he has a sucking wound." The medic extracted a pair of scissors from his kit.

Whoomph! Another freight car in the distance exploded, reinvigorating the inferno, and the deck rocked. The medic froze, scissors in hand. The rocking subsided. The medic cut the clothing around the wound area and stripped it away. Sam brought over a blanket.

The bleeding had stopped, and the medic acknowledged Kathy with a nod, "Good job of triage, my dear. I'm going to use the battlefield antiseptic bacteriophages," he said, as he pulled a tube from his kit. "Then I'll apply some petroleum jelly around the wound before I bandage it closed. That way the cavity opening should be sealed, which will help his lung expand when he breathes in."

Kathy looked relieved now that a medical professional had taken charge.

Fifteen minutes later, Sam was relieved when the *Teutonic* docked at Pier 54. He saw five motorized Model T field ambulances marked "Presbyterian Hospital," standing idling, their red lights flashing at the bottom of the gangway. They must have been alerted by new-fangled ship-to-shore radio. Thousands of New Yorkers had rushed to the western docks to catch a glimpse of the fiery destruction on the opposite Jersey shore.

The medic and Sam carefully carried the litter holding Collin down the gangway and into one of the ambulances. Kathy jumped into the back of the vehicle and sat holding Collin's hand.

"I'll get our belongings and meet you at the hospital," Sam told her as he turned with the medic to re-board the ship.

"We're just ten minutes away," the ambulance driver announced, then sped away from the pier, swerving among the crowded streets of observers.

The hospital wait stretched through the early morning until Sunday afternoon. Sam gave up any hope of returning to Toronto in time for the opening of school on Tuesday. *I'll have to call the administrators*, he thought.

Finally, the doctor emerged from the operating room. "We have repaired Collin's punctured right lung. Fortunately, the projectile missed his spleen and his heart." He grasped Kathy's hands. "I believe that your husband will make a full recovery. We were able to remove the shrapnel, suture the lung penetration and the exterior wound, pump out the pleural air, and re-inflate his lung. I placed a tube into the cavity between his lung and ribcage temporarily to remove residual air and any remaining blood. Your husband will remain with us for at least a week, though, until we know he is out of danger of infection."

Kathy thanked the surgeon, but as the good doctor was about to leave the waiting room, Sam asked, "Could you arrange a checkup for Collin's wife here? She was thrown against the bulkhead in the blast and thinks she may be with child." He stole a glance at Kathy, and she proffered him a grateful look in return.

"Certainly. Why didn't you tell us sooner, young lady? Come with me."

Sam said, "You took quite a tumble last night, lass."

Kathy cradled her belly and obediently followed the doctor.

Two hours later Kathy appeared in the waiting room, all smiles.

Sam jumped up and put his arm around her. "What did they say?"

"Oh, Sam. The doctor confirmed that I am indeed in the family way, and it's a blessing our baby was not hurt in my fall. We are incredibly lucky, given what happened."

"Collin likely saved you and the baby by making himself a human shield. You know he hit the bulkhead first."

Kathy gasped. "He saved my life more than once! And his sister Claire's, I mean Morgan's, as well."

Sam nodded, wanting to press the point while it was raw in Kathy's mind. "Is there any question in your mind now about Collin's commitment to you and your family, lass? I recall you had your doubts about his loyalty. Remember that business with the newspaper reporter and your worries about an affair?"

Kathy hugged her mentor. "No doubts now, none whatsoever."

Later that afternoon, Sam sent a telegram home to his wife Lil. He assured her that they were all safe but asked her to contact the school principals for Kathy and for himself, letting them know what had happened. Then he would make it a point to notify Mr. Robertson at the *Tely* of Collin's predicament. Kathy said she wanted to stay overnight with Collin in the hospital, but Sam convinced her to rest at the nearby temporary lodging he secured for her.

Next morning, Sam was relieved to find out that Collin's condition had improved. Kathy agreed that she would be content staying with him on her own until he was released to go home. Sam organized their train transport and arranged to return home himself on Wednesday. All was in order.

Anna Rusnak confronted her boarder Michael Kristoff in her tenement that Sunday morning. He sat on his bed, head in hands, lamenting, "What I done, what I done?"

He had no alibi when questioned by the police she called.

The fires burned through Monday evening, leaving Black Tom Island without viable storage facilities or railyards. Over a hundred railroad cars and thirteen warehouses had been destroyed. The intense heat had melted and warped the metal, and all the charred remains gave new meaning to its name, "Black Tom." It would be confirmed later, after thorough review, that the Black Tom series of explosions that night was the largest man-made detonation at that point in world history. After a close examination of the Statue of Liberty, engineers found shrapnel damage to her uplifted arm to be so serious that from that day forward visitors were prohibited from walking up into her torch. Sam later discovered all this had happened. Four people were known to have died from the blasts, including a barge captain.

Meanwhile, from the German embassy west of Thomas Circle at 1435-41 Massachusetts Avenue, NW, Ambassador Von Bernstorff sent a coded message home to Berlin while drinking champagne. Then he contacted John Devoy, the New York head of the Irish Clan na Gael.

Chapter Two
Home Fires

Friday, August 4, 1916
RIC Barracks, Cork City

*D*istrict Inspector Maloney had a problem. It had been three weeks since his men had reported in. Head Constable Boyle, and Constables Jackson and Simpson, were now missing, the latter two assigned to Boyle after Gordon James was murdered by the McCarthy brothers. Much as he hated Boyle and Jackson, the inspector couldn't procrastinate any longer.

Constable Angus Ferguson knocked on the door, then burst into his boss's office. "You want me, sir?"

"I need you to go and check Head Constable Boyle's residence at Number Eighty-One Concord Street. I want to make sure he is all right after his near-death shooting. Then go to Records and find out where Jackson and Simpson live and try to locate them.

"Yes, sir. I haven't seen them around the barracks recently."

"That's why I want you to find them."

Angus arrived at Boyle's flat to find it locked. Flashing his badge, he got the landlady to open it. Remembering Boyle's gruff nature, the constable was surprised to find Boyle's digs to be neat and tidy, as if he had gone away on holiday. But running his finger across the kitchen counter, he found that dust had settled, indicating a period of disuse. In the bedroom, he stepped on a squeaky floorboard, but thought nothing of it.

Had he had decided to pry it up, he would have found Boyle's copy of the Clans Pact and other materials related to Boyle's attacks on the McCarthys and O'Donnells.

Two days later, in the District Inspector's office, Ferguson issued his final report on the matter. "It's as if they just disappeared off the face of the earth, sir. I checked their residences, talked with their landlords, and all the men here in the barracks. No one has seen them."

Maloney suspected foul play. At least Simpson would have checked in. He needed another head constable and knew the brawny, red-haired Ferguson could be trusted and manipulated. *A welcome change from that bastard Boyle. I hope to hell that tosser never shows up again!*

"Head Constable Ferguson, I want you to put out 'missing person' bulletins on all three men."

The new head constable gaped, wide-eyed. "Head—Do you mean—?"

"Yes, lad. You've been promoted. On probation, mind you."

Ferguson saluted, turned on his heel, and left the office.

Maloney liked being saluted. Boyle had never done that. Maloney decided the McCarthys must have been involved, so he made a note to add his men's disappearances to the list of illegal McCarthy activities that were based on circumstantial evidence. After all, hadn't the McCarthy boys tried to murder Boyle on two occasions?

Collin gazed over the rail of the Beaches boardwalk at the foot of Balsam Avenue and out onto Lake Ontario. It was October 5, the occasion of the Finlay and O'Donnell Thanksgiving Day picnic, and a fine, balmy one in Toronto. Now, two months since they had returned home, he thanked God for their many blessings. His lung had healed, yet it still hurt when he coughed.

Being back with their child, Liam, had settled Kathy's nerves, a good thing. Her pregnancy, at nigh on to three months, was progressing nicely. Sam had come through for them once again in

Ireland, but Collin worried about his mentor's health. It seemed that their ordeal had taken its toll. Sam seemed more out of breath these days, even though he tried hard not to let it show.

Collin had scooped the other papers with his first-hand account of the Black Tom attack, gaining him international recognition. Although he didn't know it when he was abroad, his insightful reporting of the aftermath of the Easter Rising and its impact on the population of Ireland had already assured his place at Robertson's *Toronto Evening Telegram*. As a result, he had been elevated to national and foreign correspondent. The publisher had even started talking about a potential assignment for Collin in Europe covering the Canadian offensives in the Great War.

Kathy happily returned to her classroom, at least until the new year. Collin prayed every night that their second child, expected in April, would be a girl they would name Claire, after his sister.

Collin acknowledged that all was not sweetness and light. Kathy was unhappy and fearful he might get assigned overseas again, especially with another child on the way. Having been so obsessed and secretive about his search for his long-lost sister to the point of almost losing his wife, he now agonized over hiding his commitment to support gun acquisition in the USA for the Irish Cause. Damn, this new Clans Pact with Tadgh would surely test his marriage once again and quite possibly lose him his job and put him in jail. Yet their ancestral McCarthy and O'Donnell Chieftains had banded together over three hundred years ago for the cause of freedom, and he wasn't going to let them and his McCarthy brother-in-law down at such a critical juncture.

"Come back down to the blankets, Collin. Lunch is ready," Kathy called, pulling Liam back from crawling out onto the compacted white sand. He was particularly rambunctious for his tender age of six months.

Collin returned to the group and hoisted his son high up onto his shoulders. Then he danced around, splashing his feet into the shoreline water, oblivious of the chilly temperature of the lake. Liam giggled with glee, so Collin held him up by his ankles and dangled him upside down with his dark brown curls dipping into the water.

Sam's wife Lil called out, "Collin, you're going to hurt the lad. Turn him right side up."

"Nonsense. A son of mine has to learn straightaway that this world can go topsy-turvy."

Collin thought that world events, and even Labor Day, had taken on a somber, almost grisly, turn in Toronto. Since the tradition began in 1872, with printers striking for a shorter workday of nine hours, the parades on this day had demonstrated solidarity in the struggle for workers' rights in an evolving industrialized society. Now, almost two years into the war, the male population was decimated, both in Canada and elsewhere, due to belligerent nations fighting a bloody stalemate war. The government talked of the likelihood of conscription. Women were allowed to work on war materials under grievous conditions, and if they had a husband actively involved in the war, they were allowed to vote in the federal election. Otherwise, women were relegated to the home without representation. Foodstuffs and other essentials were becoming harder and harder to come by.

"Why won't you tell me all the details of what happened to you in Ireland, Kathy?" Lil asked again, after numerous unanswered inquiries since their return, as she doled out bully beef sandwiches to her daughters. This staple of the Canadian army had become a tinned delicacy back in Canada. They were lucky to get it with the devastating war overseas taking a terrible toll at home as well.

Kathy saw the warning gestures from Sam and then Collin behind Lil's back. She hated to keep the truth from her best friend, but she bit her lip and answered, "I told you all the good things like how Collin showed that he loves me and how we discovered Maureen is my cousin and all." Kathy hoped her reply appeased Lil's curiosity. Her mind flashed back to the doubts she had about her husband's loyalty at their reunion, their ordeal of finding Collin's sister Claire who had been renamed Morgan, and who had bonded with her rescuer and beau, the rebel Tadgh. She flashed back to that harrowing time, the discovery of the McCarthy treasure, the death defying firefight with the constables. How could she keep that all from Lil? Her stomach churned.

Lil saw Kathy's reaction and pressed, "But what about the dangers?"

"I don't like to think about that, so please don't ask me. We're safe now. That's all that matters," Kathy sighed.

Kathy's glance found Collin's. He had overheard the women's conversation and was proud that his wife had kept her silence. Relief flooded their communal facial expressions. They had rid the world of Collin's father's killer, a corrupt policeman back in Ireland by the name of Boyle, in a fiery turn of events that had nearly taken their lives. Yet in the dead of night, they continued to be hounded by the frightening events that had almost gotten them killed.

Lil looked at Sam for answers.

He lied to keep the peace and to honor their agreement with Tadgh. "Don't ask me, my dear. Collin hasn't shared the gripping details of their adventures with me, either. Just look on the bright side and let it go. Claire was found and has married a strong, capable young Irishman, right, Collin?"

"Yes, boss. We had our set-to, but in the end, I highly approve of Tadgh being with Claire. I mean Morgan." He chuckled. "That is her chosen name now. Let's all just move on with our lives." Collin handed little Liam back to Kathy, took his own sandwich, picked up one of the three O'Keefe ales that they had brought, and dunked in the lake to keep cool. It was a rare treat in these days of austerity.

Lil grumbled but let it drop and went about tending to fair-haired Ernie's nappies. Younger than Liam, he was still not crawling, so the lad wasn't full of sand yet. She decided she would interrogate Sam further in private and get the truth out of him.

"Hello, Finlays and O'Donnells," a now familiar masculine voice rang out from the other side of the boardwalk.

"Father, Mother. Come join us, we've already started lunch," Kathy sang out.

"Are you taking good care of your wee one to come, Kathy?" Fiona plopped down on the blanket with the O'Donnell tartan on it.

"Yes, Mother. It's still early yet."

"I remember the trouble you had with Liam, lass. Don't you be drinking any alcohol."

"Really, Mother. When have you known me to drink such a libation?"

"I just worry, you know."

"Now, Fiona, leave the girl be. She knows what she is doing, don't you, daughter," Ryan said, accepting a beer offered to him by Sam.

"Yes, Father," Kathy droned. "Have a bully beef sandwich."

"We brought a hamper of food, Lil. Some fruit, cheese, crackers, and apple juice. All we could muster."

"Thank you, Fiona. A real feast it is for these dark days." Since Sam had returned to teaching art at Riverdale with an increased salary, the Finlays were set, without worries about finances in these troubled times.

They sat down to what in the past would have been a lean Thanksgiving meal. But not this year. They were happy to have what they could gather up for their time together on this abnormally warm autumn afternoon.

"Lil, I understand that you are expecting again, just like Kathy."

"Yes, Fiona, Sam is incorrigible." She lowered her eyes and blushed. "But four children will be enough, for heaven's sake, right, dear?" Lil looked mock daggers at her husband and then broke into a laugh.

"We only had one, you know. Couldn't have any more, really," Kathy's mother looked away.

"But the one you had, Fiona, is a star shining in the heavens, don't ya know," Collin grinned.

"That's why I worry so about her."

"There's a lot worse things to concern yourself, woman," Ryan gruffed.

"What's that, Father?"

"Whether I'll be fed each night when I come home from teaching." He frowned in ersatz anger, then broke into a broad smile. "Just teasing. I'd be more concerned whether the government will enact conscription, requiring Sam and Collin to go to war in Europe."

Kathy looked ashen at this discussion of her dreaded worry, especially coming from her father. "They couldn't force them to go, could they?"

Before Collin could defuse the situation by offering the man his grandson to hold, Ryan took his daughter's hand and answered, "The allies are not making progress in the trenches and there is terrible loss of life requiring replacements. They may change their criteria for acceptance. Collin's hearing, for instance. I'm sure that most of the men are nearly deaf after a few days in the trenches anyway."

"Oh, Father. Don't talk that way. I don't think I could stand Collin being away from our family again."

"Steady, Daughter. There are millions of wives living with the reality of their husbands in peril in the European trenches as we speak. We live in a treacherous world, I'm afraid."

Collin placed his son into Ryan's arms and said, "We're all aware of the situation and talking about it will only aggravate your daughter, sir."

"They wouldn't enlist you, would they, love?" Kathy picked at a soft spot on her apple.

Collin saw an opening. "No, darlin.' If they needed me over there, it would be as a war correspondent. I wouldn't likely be in the trenches." Collin was stretching the truth there. If he went, he would be down in the muck photographing the agony, but Kathy need not know about that.

"But they wouldn't send you, would they? With my being pregnant and all?"

"I haven't been told anything of the sort, so don't worry." Collin cringed at the fib and hoped his wife would not notice it.

Lil wasn't worried that Sam, with his heart condition, would be conscripted. She took her best friend's hand and sat her back down before saying, "You've heard me say this before, but it bears repeating. No use in worrying until there is something to worry about, Kathy. Come and help me with the children."

Ryan went on anyway. "Do you think that the Americans will join the war, Sam?[3]"

"I hope so, to help our boys." Sam had tuned in to Collin's responses but kept it to himself.

Collin had been researching the situation south of the border as an assignment from the paper and for personal reasons. He knew that if he were going to organize the acquisition of guns for Tadgh, it would have to be before the Yanks declared war on Germany, if indeed they did.

He set his empty beer bottle aside. "It's not clear yet what the Americans are going to do, Ryan. Their government has maintained a position of neutrality despite the sinking of the *Lusitania* last year with a hundred and twenty-eight American lost souls on board."

"I wish they'd just join the Allied forces and get the war over," Kathy sighed, taking a squirming Liam from her father's awkward arms, and setting him down on the blanket, where he promptly crawled beyond the boundaries of the cloth.

"It's not as easy as that, love." Collin grabbed Liam by the feet and pulled him back onto the blanket. "Easy there, lad." He tickled the toddler's feet and set him to laughing. "There are so many different groups, for and against. The Irish, German, and Scandinavian communities are not in favor of joining, along with women's groups and church leaders. Then there are the non-interventionists like the former Secretary of State William Jennings Bryan, Henry Ford, and

William Randolph Hearst, who feel both Britain imperialism and German militarism are corrupt."

"Then it sounds like they will stay out of it," Ryan said, grabbing a piece of cheese.

"It's not that one-sided. The Atlanticists have been pushing for military preparedness and Entente with Britain and France since last year after the *Lusitania* tragedy, men like former President Theodore Roosevelt and Henry Cabot Lodge. They're concerned that the American military force is too small compared to the Germans'."

Ryan chewed thoughtfully, pausing. "How small, Collin?"

"About two hundred thousand men, including the National Guard, or one-twentieth the size of the German force. The American government finally enacted the National Defense Act to double its land forces as a direct result of the Black Tom explosions."

Kathy shuddered. "Don't remind me of that frightful night."

"We survived, my love. It's all right, now."

Kathy raised her voice. "Collin, you could have died. We all could have. We'd have been swept overboard if Sam hadn't grabbed us."

Lil's hands shook, and she dropped her sandwich in the sand. "What?" Her voice was strident. "You didn't tell me about *that!*"

Sam reached down, picked up the bread, and started brushing the sand off. Then he gave it back, gently touching his wife's hand. "There, there, *astore*. There was no need to worry you. The threat had passed."

Lil decided that she would grill Sam on this as well when they were alone later on that evening. The look on Sam's face showed he knew what was coming.

Kathy spoke for all of them. "We're lucky to be safe at home with our men and children by our side. We need to keep it that way, right, Collin?"

Her look spoke volumes, so Collin nodded and changed the subject, resuming his discourse. "After the Battle of Jutland last

June, the U.S. government decided they needed a strong navy, and this act authorized a rapid three-year buildup of naval systems.

Ordinary U.S. citizens in the South and Midwest, where most of the immigrant families are located, do not want war. Whereas industries like Bethlehem Steel, and now Atlas and Hercules Powder Companies—they make gunpowder and dynamite, among other things—and banks like J.P. Morgan, are all staunch supporters. They have given massive loans to belligerent countries like Britain and France."

"Seems reasonable," Ryan said, taking another draught of his beer.

Collin continued, "Industrial production is up thirty percent and the American market value of all goods and services produced has increased twenty percent since the war started."

Sam folded up one of the blankets. "Isn't this just American propaganda?"

"No, boss. I have this information directly from the publisher of the *Washington Post*, under Ned McLean. It's a reputable paper."

"The paper has fallen into dubious practices of late since his father died in July, I dare say, Collin, so take that with a grain of salt," Sam replied. "Then what is the upshot? Are they going to war, or not?"

"I don't know. There is a group that President Wilson leads, calling themselves Liberal Internationalists. They are in a tough spot, what with such a divided nation. They are reluctant to go to war believing the United States is the only country that can promote post-war liberal democratic values to end wars once and for all."

"Now, there's a mouthful." Ryan coughed. "Collin, how will America's decision affect the push for Irish independence?"

"I expect that the Irish rebels, those who are left, anyway, will still be trying to woo the Germans. If that is the case, then America's entry into the War would hamper the Irish cause."

After clambering to her feet, Lil's eldest daughter Norah tugged at her mother's hem. "What is Unca Collin talking about, Mommy?"

Lil scowled, too much talk of war. "Adult things, Norah. Collin, go take the girls down the beach for a walk with Fiona, will you?"

Collin took the not-so-subtle hint, picked the squealing young girls up under his arms, and the four headed east towards the Balmy Beach Canoe Club.

Kathy looked up from tucking cheese squares in between saltine crackers and smiled at her best friend Lil, silently mouthing the words "Thank you."

Sam and Ryan retreated to sit on the edge of the boardwalk out of earshot of their wives, where the smoke from their pipes wouldn't disturb the babies. The two Belfast men were of different generations, Ryan being almost twice Sam's age and half a head higher. Yet they both had similar Irish features—round facial curves, a pronounced cranial skull, and receding central hairline. But Sam's face still seemed cherubic with a dimpled chin, and his eyes sparkled. And Ryan's showed the tension lines around his eyes and jowls. The nature of the men was further on display by the clothes they wore, with Sam loafing in his colored cardigan, and Ryan always wearing his white shirt and black tie no matter the venue.

Ryan sniffed. "Smells like Prince Albert."

"You've got a connoisseur's nose there. Smoked it since I was in art school back in the homeland." The gray smoke curled up into the offshore breeze.

"Tell, me, Sam, you were just over there. I read Collin's reports. Will there be a real revolution in Ireland, do you think?"

"I think Collin is right. Only a matter of time."

Ryan tamped more tobacco into his pipe as its coal had gone out. "Whatever happens in this war, I'm glad that we are here in Canada and not back in Belfast."

"I fear that at least the northern part of Ireland will have troubles for a long time to come, Ryan, no matter what. Too many Protestants and Catholics in close proximity."

"Aye, lad, I know what you mean."

Sam glanced behind him to where the women were packing

up. He wondered what they were saying, but they were too far away to hear them any better than they could hear his conversation—he hoped, anyway.

Lil put the remaining fruit in her hamper. "I saved you from another hour of politics, so tell me more about your adventures in Ireland. Let's have it."

Kathy glanced over at Sam while she hoisted Liam into his pram. He seemed lost in discussion with her father, so she decided to confide in her best friend. "You should have seen the jewels and old money that we found in the McCarthy treasure chests."

"What? Treasure? You never told me about that. My God, girl."

"You must promise not to tell a soul about this, Lil."

"My lips are sealed. Spill everything about the treasure."

"Keep your voice down." Kathy tucked a blanket around Liam while she described the treasure, wedding, and the clan chieftain ceremony. She left out the deadly trauma at the Rock of Cashel as Sam had requested of her before they left Ireland, and she hoped that Lil could not decipher the look of terror that must be surfacing in her eyes. The events remained burned into her brain.

Lil quietly absorbed her best friend's information and pondered what remained unsaid. Her eyes narrowed as she searched Kathy's face for emotion. After a moment of silence, Lil said, "What blarney, girl. Rocks don't talk," referring to the Blarney Stone spoken about.

"Well, the Blarney Stone did. Three times. I was there and it was spooky, I can tell you."

"What were you drinking?"

"Nothing, you know—because of the baby." Kathy hugged her best friend and then called out to Collin on the strand, "Come on back, love. There's a chill in the air, and I don't want Liam to catch cold. We'd best be on our way home."

Despite the protests of the girls, the picnic was over. The three linked families headed back to their abodes and the realities of wartime life.

♣ ♣ ♣ ♣

The first of December brought Collin exciting news from Tadgh. The telegram read:

> 'How would you like to become a real uncle and godparent in April? Stop. Heaven help us. Stop. Have assessed value available for merchandise. Stop. Three-Hundred-Fifty. Stop. Contacts ready and willing. Stop. Urgency. Stop.'

This reminded Collin of the responsibilities and commitment he had agreed to before he left Ireland months before, part of the new McCarthy/O'Donnell Clans Pact. This missive from Tadgh meant that there was an equivalent of three hundred and fifty thousand U.S. dollars available from the McCarthy treasure to purchase weapons. The Clan na Gael leaders, Joseph McGarrity in Philadelphia, and John Devoy in New York City had been contacted, and they were prepared to support acquisition and shipment of the armament.

But it was the other unexpected news that fascinated him. A child? His brother-in-law was in for it now.

That night at dinner, Kathy was preoccupied in breast-feeding Liam. It seemed a good time to share information with her, so Collin said, "I heard from Tadgh and Morgan today by a telegram delivered at work."

"Why did they send it to the paper, do you know?"

"I don't know why they sent it there," Collin told her. *A white lie.* He cringed, wondering if she would detect the falsehood in his voice or eyes once more.

Kathy put the baby over her shoulder to burp him. "What does it say?"

"The news may interest you. Would you like to be a real aunt and godparent?" He left out the part about the other plan, thinking that omission was as much of a lie as any, if you leave the bulk of the message out. He hoped he could justify it someday.

"Really?" she squealed, lifting Liam over her head, and smiling at him. "You're not fibbing me, are you, love?"

"God's honest truth, lass. Claire—uh, Morgan—seems to be in the family way."

"Why, that's wonderful news! We must send our congratulations right away."

Collin echoed his reservations aloud. "I wonder if it is such good news for Tadgh, given his commitment to the revolution."

"Our children are our future, Collin. Morgan will be ecstatic over this. Send them a telegram tomorrow."

"Will do, lass." He watched her intently as her eyes searched out his. "I've seen that look before, that's certain. What are you thinking?"

Kathy twirled her hair behind her ear.

Collin knew that couldn't be good.

Still holding Liam with one arm, she swept the other over the cramped kitchen. "Our Lee Avenue house won't be big enough for the four of us. With my job and your new higher paying assignment, we could afford a proper home like Lil and Sam's."

Collin stood up from the table, squeezing his serviette into a ball in his hand. "This second bedroom should be large enough for both babies for a few years yet, surely." He reached out his arms. "Come here with Liam, lass. You both warm my heart, so you do."

"I would love a larger house with a proper kitchen and a real electric icebox, like Lil has. Will you at least think about it?" She batted her eyes at him, turning her chin up, inviting him closer.

Collin kissed her sensuously on the mouth, his arm cradling her back and pulling her and Liam in. She yielded briefly and then backed off to adjust the baby's mussed blanket.

Collin was frustrated. Kathy's pregnancy and her attention to Liam had consumed her, with not much left for him and he ached for her, his need rising. Her game of flirting and then resistance was driving a wedge between them.

Kathy stepped back, put the baby down in his tableside bassinette and asked, "Will you?"

Collin winced and answered, "Yes, darlin'."

Later in bed, Collin pulled Kathy towards him under the covers.

She drew back, sat up and asked, "I've been wondering, with Claire coming and all. Can't you just imagine us being in a bigger bedroom with glorious windows and drapes?"

Collin sat up and put a finger to her lips. "No talk of such things now. I've been needing to kiss you."

Kathy resisted at first and then succumbed. She wrapped her arms around his neck and allowed him a lingering kiss.

Collin realized that she was using her femininity to try to persuade him. He lifted her nightdress, but she pulled it back down, smoothing the fabric against her body. "Kindly take off that flannel thing. It's getting in the way," Collin said, his voice hoarse.

Kathy pushed him away and reached to turn off the light. "It's late, and I'm tired. You know I've school in the morning, and Liam is going to wake us up later."

Collin decided he wasn't to be denied tonight. He grabbed her hand and pulled it down, saying, "I need you, lass. Don't you need me, too?"

Kathy's eyes teared up. "You were gone so long, and left me alone with the baby, not knowing whether you were alive or not. I've grown cold."

Collin remembered. This wasn't the first time his neglect had come between them at a sensitive moment since they returned home from Ireland, and it wouldn't be the last, he feared. They had conceived in Ireland, but the pain she still felt here in this house was a problem. Could this just be a tactic to get a new house? No, her pain was real, and he still needed to make amends. Maybe they did need a change of scenery.

"I'll be forever sorry for the hurt I caused you, Kathy, but can't we focus on the present and our future?" he asked, pulling her in and pressing his chest against her breasts. "There now, lass. Isn't that better?"

He could feel the anxiety draining from her body, at least temporarily, as she shuddered, then relaxed into him.

Kathy gently pushed his hands away, sat back up, and peeled off her nightgown. She shivered and flung her arms around her bare breasts before diving back under the covers. "Brrr. It's getting colder these nights, and there's no insulation in these walls. Lil's home is much warmer than ours, her walls—"

Lying on his back, Collin pulled her down until she was facing him, skin to skin. "Now, where were we?"

"There! Did you feel that?" Kathy took his hand and put it on her belly.

"Is that the first time Claire kicked you?" he whispered.

"I think so. The miracle of life."

Collin kept his hand there and waited for the next movement. She warmed to his touch as the baby moved again.

Collin nuzzled her and explored her body. Even after a long day, her hair still smelled like lilacs. How did women do that? "You smell wonderful, darlin'."

"You really think so?" Kathy took the lead now, kissing him urgently. She wrapped her arms around his neck and rolled sideways until she was on top of him.

Nature took her course.

Spent, the two of them lay there quietly, breathing in harmony.

Collin thought, *Maybe unborn baby Claire is the key to revitalizing our marriage.* Then he remembered his commitment to the new Clans pact with Tadgh and the secret he was hiding from his wife.

On the way to drop off Liam at Lil's for the day that Monday, December 3, it was then, in their old Hudson, that Collin threw out a comment. "I need to go to Philadelphia later this week for two days of business. Will you be all right alone, here, you and Liam?"

"Why do you have to go? The *Tely* says that we're supposed to get the first snow of the season later today. It's coming in from Hudson's Bay, they say."

"I have to meet an Irishman to give him a message from Tadgh, darlin'."

"I don't understand. Why can't Tadgh just telegraph him directly? Why do you have to be involved? I don't want you entangled in Tadgh's war." She rolled down the window to get air.

"It's not a matter that should be put in a telegram," Collin answered obliquely, maneuvering around a car stopping to turn in the intersection.

"Then how did you hear about it? Was it in the telegram?" Kathy pried.

Maybe she suspected that he wasn't telling her everything. "It's something that Tadgh and I discussed before we left Ireland."

Kathy dug into her husband's thigh with her nails. The car swerved right and almost smashed into a tree before he could bring it under control. Liam, his basket strapped into the rear seat, began crying.

Collin's eyes flashed. "Bollocks, Kathy! You could have gotten us killed."

His glance was met with an icy stare.

"Hear me. I don't want you getting mixed up with Tadgh's revolution, Collin. Heavens, we were almost killed in Ireland and in New York harbor."

"There is no revolution, at least not now, and no real danger on my part, to be sure. But my job for Tadgh is important and I can't talk about it." He stared ahead, setting his lips into a firm line.

"Well, you can't go anywhere unless you tell me why," she pouted. "Besides, this old car of ours is not very reliable in cold weather, and you're not willing to get a newer one, let alone a better house." She folded her arms and stared him down.

Collin hoped she couldn't read any more into his thoughts. She was good at that.

Arriving at the Finlays' home at Number Ten Balsam Avenue, Kathy got Liam out, bundled him in an extra blanket, and headed for Lil's front porch. The sky was gray, and the wind was whipping in from the lake. The parlor beyond the front bay window in the two-story white clapboard home looked cheery and inviting against the backdrop of the impending gale. But Kathy didn't notice because of the gathering storm clouds in her brain.

Lil greeted her best friend at the door with a hot cup of tea. Taking her daycare charge from Kathy's arms, she asked, "What's wrong? Where's your husband?"

"He's in the car, waiting," she blustered, "and nothing I have time to talk about now. I'll be late for school. I'll tell you later."

"I know that look, dear. It's not *nothing*." Lil took her best friend's hand. "Stay a minute."

Kathy's eyes burned. "Collin needs to go away again. To the United States, this week."

"For work, I presume."

Kathy brushed her hair out her eyes with her gloved hand. "Not work, but for his brother-in-law, Tadgh. He won't tell me why."

Lil patted her hand. "All right. I'm sure that there is a good reason. Why don't you and Collin come for dinner this evening when you come for Liam?"

Kathy looked down at her boots. "Thanks, Lil. I'll ask him."

Kathy fretted all day as she taught her thirty-five students in the Kingston Road one-room schoolhouse. By four o'clock, as she was cleaning the chalkboard of numerical fractions, that old feeling of being left behind returned.

Sam came to pick her up after his school day ended. He sensed that Kathy was loaded for bear, her emotions boiling over. He could see the old look of anxiety etched in her face as he opened the passenger door for her. *Here we go again*, he thought, another turn at playing referee with the young couple, like before. He started the conversation, hoping to ward off trouble. "Lil told me about Collin's trip. How long will he be gone?"

"Two days, plus travel time, I guess, but that's not the point."

"What is the point then, Kathy? You're clearly upset."

"He won't tell me why he's going except that it's for Tadgh. We're not supposed to keep secrets from each other. You and Lil don't play cat and mouse, do you?"

Sam couldn't lie. "Generally, no."

"What do you mean, 'generally'?"

"There are times when I am told something confidential at the school that I can't share with Lil, so I just keep quiet about it. But that's part of my job. And then there's Ireland. She worries so about my health, as you know." He gripped the wheel tightly as he drove and could feel the tension inside the car thicken.

"Ah, yes, I know about that. What would you do if Lil wanted to know what it was that was so secret in your life?"

"She's been trying to pry the details of what happened in Ireland from me, so she has. It's best that she not know. It's over and done."

"You realize that Lil will extract it out of me eventually if you don't tell her, Sam."

"But you promised me, lass."

"So I did, but you know that wife of yours. What do you do to smooth her feathers when you have to keep something from her?"

"I bring her flowers to let her know I love her and have her best interests in mind."

"That's a nice gesture. But you realize that men treat women like underlings, don't you?"

"I'd like to think that I don't, Kathy. We're equals, Lil and I."

"You treat Lil well. I can see that with you and my best friend. You have been like an older brother to me, looking out for and counseling me every step along the way." She touched his shoulder.

"I'm not mad at you." Her teeth set and she could feel the ache in them from trying to keep still about things.

"I think that you should give Collin the benefit of the doubt, lass. It's not as if he's leaving for three months like the last time. Only for a few days on this side of the ocean."

"You're right, I suppose, Sam, but that man makes my blood boil."

"But you love him, right?"

"That's what is so maddening." She smiled, imagining the night they just luxuriated in and his loving ways. Maybe that was the problem. She wanted more of him, without interruption.

"Come stay with us while he's gone, if that will help." He shot her a grin, holding the wheel firm and threading expertly through the streets.

Kathy loved that about her friend. Steady as a rock.

When they arrived at the Finlay home, Collin was already there, sitting in the comfortable parlor, carnations in hand. Their family living room was inviting with its soft chesterfield and high-backed wing chairs that faced the crackling stone fireplace.

"Come and sit down in your chair," Lil said to Sam, rushing in from the kitchen with his slippers. "Relax before you start talking international politics. How's your heart been today, my love?"

"Thinking of you and the children, astore, as always." Sam said, as he removed his coat and galoshes.

"That's not what I'm talking about."

"I'm fine, dear. Where are the girls?"

"In their room, playing house."

"Well, I have something for them at dinner."

"Aren't you thoughtful," she teased. "And something for me?"

"Later this evening, when the children are asleep," he promised, with a boyish grin.

While Lil was concerning herself with her husband's heart, Collin tensed, stood up, and presented the bouquet of flowers to his wife. "These are all I could find today, darlin.' At least they are red to match your hair."

Kathy's narrowed eyes belied her mood as she took the gift. "Thank you. I'm surprised that you could find any in December."

In reality, the news desk secretary had gone out searching for the flowers on her lunch break while Collin had met with his boss, Jim Fletcher. There he had gained his approval to go to Philadelphia to research a story about the League to Enforce Peace, a group that had been created in Independence Hall under President Taft's leadership the year before. It was a valid story pertaining to whether the United States would enter the war.

"Why are you going to Philadelphia, Collin?" Sam asked.

Collin's bushy eyebrows twitched as held up his hand and said, "Give us a minute, boss," before turning back to address his wife. Taking her coat, guiding her down into the chair and raising her face towards him, he said, "I realize that I shouldn't have sprung this trip on you out of the blue this morning on the way to work."

Kathy avoided his stare and picked a petal off one of the flowers before responding. "It wasn't blue. It was threatening gray this morning."

Collin knelt in front of her. "I really have to go, my love. Consider it a clan duty as well as a business assignment. I'll be leaving on the train on Wednesday morning and coming home on Sunday morning. I promise. I won't just disappear. Not like before. All right?"

Kathy returned his gaze with earnest eyes. "I don't begrudge you the trip, Collin. I just don't like you keeping the reason from me."

"Please answer my question, lad," Sam said, once his Prince Albert pipe was lit.

Collin stood up again, went to the fireplace, and tossed in another log. The flames flared up. It made him think of the terrible fires in the warehouse and the Cashel cathedral. He remembered when he had first met Sam who had saved him from a disastrous fire as a young man. *Had it been over five years ago?*

He squared his shoulders and faced Sam outright. "I have two reasons for going to Philadelphia this week. As I told Kathy this morning, Tadgh McCarthy gave me a task we discussed during his wedding reception. This is not a dangerous assignment at this time, but one I must not divulge to anyone in the room. So yes, it is one of those familial secrets that cannot be betrayed." Collin knew after what had happened in New York, if he mentioned munitions, Kathy would forbid him from going.

"Secondly, Jim Fletcher is sending me to Philadelphia as part of my research regarding whether America will join the war. He explained to me the story about the League to Enforce Peace and its connection to the Liberal Internationalists."

Collin stretched out his hands like a minister preaching to his flock, and continued, "Rumor has it that after the war, they want an international agreement of nations to jointly use their economic and military forces against any one of their number that goes to war or commits acts of hostility against another. This could end wars as we know them. I might meet Alexander Graham Bell, you know. He's a supporter, so he is." Collin smiled at the thought. He hoped that this smoke screen would resolve Kathy's concerns.

Sam exhaled. The smoke from his pipe curled up toward the stucco ceiling. Right above his chair, its color had changed over many years from white to a smudged light gray. "I don't see how this league for after the war can affect whether America joins the fighting."

"It has President Wilson's blessing and that might unite the country to go one way or the other." Collin thought that his explanation should satisfy them. He hoped so.

Kathy went to the fireplace near Collin to warm her hands. "I'm sure that these things are too weighty for me, Collin. I talked to Sam, and he assured me that you must have my best interests at heart for not confiding your other reason for going."

Collin looked at his mentor and mouthed *Thank you*. "Aye, lass, 'tis true. Suffice it to say that it is best you all aren't bothered with the matter."

"And do you promise that it is not illegal?"

"That much I can assure you, Sam, from what I know at this point." *A fib, yes, but they didn't need to know that.*

"But at some future point?"

"I'm going to make sure that it doesn't become illegal, either." Collin hoped that his face had an earnest appearance. "Look, I know that the scars of my absence in Ireland run deep. You know how sorry I am for causing that necessary pain. But consider this—I could have just told you that I needed to go to Philadelphia for a work reason. However, I didn't. I told the truth. I just can't explain the details of my reason for going to help Tadgh." *Sin of omission,* he thought. *So be it.*

Norah and Dot came bounding down the stairs. "Unca Collie! Auntie Kaffie!" They ran to their godparents. Collin grabbed Norah in his arms and swung her around. She kicked with glee just at the wrong time and her foot dislodged Sam's pipe from between his teeth, sending it flying across the room into the cushions on the chesterfield. Lil sprang to action and rescued Prince Albert before he could set the furniture on fire.

Sam was checking the condition of his teeth with his fingers, adjusting his jaw. "Be careful there, my boy. I only have two daughters and one set of choppers."

Collin set the whirling Norah down gently at her father's feet.

Dot was laughing uncontrollably. "My turn, my turn," she cried, throwing her arms in the air in front of her declared uncle. Collin raised her up, turned her, and dangled her by her feet. When her hands touched the ground he said, "Hold it, Dot."

He let her take the weight while he supported her feet. Then he let go. She held the pose for a second and then fell forward in a ball, completing a half somersault.

"Again, again!"

"No, me now, me now!" her sister clamored.

"I can see that we have a couple of budding acrobats here," Kathy laughed, getting into the fun.

Collin knew at that point that his trip would be accepted

without further interrogation. The icy climate had warmed.

"That's enough excitement for now, girls," Lil told them. "Come on. I have supper ready."

Kathy followed her dear friend to the kitchen seeking a flower vase.

Collin had used this distraction to gather his thoughts. His pact with Tadgh was one thing he couldn't shirk. But lying to his wife and friends to accomplish its commitments was devious at best, and cowardly at worst. He convinced himself that he was protecting them all from persecution in case things went awry. There was truth to that, to be sure.

"Where's my boy?" Collin asked, as they were going to the table.

Lil answered, "Since I don't hear crying, I'd guess that Liam and Ernie are still asleep upstairs, although with all these shenanigans going on down here, I can't for the life of me figure out why."

Chapter Three
Guns

*C*atching a glance at himself in the train window, Collin thought he looked very dapper, sporting his favorite double-breasted brown Irish tweed jacket. He stepped lively off the Pennsylvania Railroad slumber car at noon, despite the sixteen-hour ride from Union Station in Toronto. He had come a long way up in the world since his start as Sam's art assistant at the paper over five years earlier.

He had taken three railway lines passing by Niagara Falls, Albany, then transitioning through New York City. Customs border officials, skittish because Canada was at war, questioned Collin's need to enter the United States until he produced his newspaper credentials and a letter of intent from the *Tely* editor-in-chief, Robertson. While waiting for his transfer in Penn Station, he was reminded of the trip he and Kathy had taken more than a year before in Sam's Model T, named Lillie. Their torturous journey in search of Claire had taken them through this very station, over to Rhode Island, then overseas to Dublin, and beyond. He prided himself on persevering in his mission to find his sister, yet he was convinced now that a higher force was guiding his steps.

Although Collin had never seen a photograph of Joseph McGarrity, he did research him in the *Tely's* archives before the trip. McGarrity, born in County Tyrone in 1874, then immigrated to Philadelphia at age eighteen, in the year that Collin was born. He read that the man made his money in the liquor business and established quite a reputation as a cofounder of the Clan na Gael, with New York's John Devoy. Then, when Sir Roger Casement came to America in 1914 seeking aid from the Germans by way of this Irish organization, McGarrity befriended him and argued in favor of Casement's position against a skeptical Devoy.

Collin had read assembled *Tely* reports during the train ride-that McGarrity helped establish the Friends of Irish Freedom organization, or FOIF, during New York City's 1916 Irish Race Convention, which included members of the United Irish League and the Ancient Order of Hibernians. This important event had taken place just six weeks before the Easter Rising. In fact, fifteen of the seventeen positions in the FOIF executive organization were held by Clan na Gael members, which strongly pushed for US neutrality and against an alliance with Britain.

One article described how the FOIF supported the Easter Rising and raised over a quarter million dollars through the Irish Relief fund to assist dependents of those who fought and died in the rebellion. This noble and urgent effort had temporarily drained funds set aside for arming and organizing a future revolution. Collin underlined the key phrases with a red pencil and thought of the sacrifices they must have made.

Collin was bringing very good news in that regard based upon Tadgh's correspondence, and for security purposes, he had not told McGarrity the financial magnitude of his contribution to the revolution before now. He hoped Tadgh was right, that McGarrity would be supportive of the plan for munitions acquisition.

Five hours later, Collin arrived in Philadelphia. He observed the cavernous train depot on crowded Broad Street Station, with its largest single span roof in the world. A myriad of greeters met the train in the bustling railway hub, many holding up signs. It took a few minutes before Collin spied a very distinguished, middle-aged gentleman displaying a sign bearing Collin's name. The man's strong oval face had a pronounced forehead. His clean-shaven, strong, dimpled jaw, and a dark brown well-trimmed moustache, furthered an impression of dignity. He was impeccably dressed in a brown tweed suit with matching waistcoat, clearly a man of means and purpose.

"Mr. McGarrity, I presume?" Collin held out his hand and the man shook it strongly. Collin returned the grip with equal firmness.

"Yes, that's right. Mr. O'Donnell, isn't it? From Donegal, no doubt. McCarthy mentioned you in his correspondence."

"Yes, sir, pleased to meet ya, to be sure."

Once they were alone, heading out of the train station through the throng, Collin said, "I am from Donegal originally but now reside in Toronto." He handed McGarrity his card. "Although I am a newspaper reporter and photographer, I am here mostly on private business for the IRB. I appreciate your meeting with me."

"Are you, lad? From Canada, you say. You have my attention, now."

"Thank you, sir. I believe it will be worth your while."

"Call me Joseph. How about some lunch?"

"That would be grand. Can we find a private spot where we can talk?"

The older man gestured toward the parking lot. "Certainly, I have a car at our disposal. Shall we?"

Half an hour later, Collin and McGarrity were sitting in a secluded alcove of McGillin's Olde Ale House, with its arched brick façade and metal second-story railings.

Joseph pointed out the historical significance of the public house. "This establishment was built in the year Abe Lincoln became president. It's the oldest bar in Philadelphia."

Collin looked around the dark walnut Tudor interior with its huge mirror-topped open fireplace. The walls were covered in framed Irish pictures and drawings of all sorts, pastoral as well as sports figures. He peered closely at these photographs to see if they gave any indication of Irish resistance. None. Interestingly, there was one green-white-orange striped flag hanging from the ceiling just above their heads.

Joseph brought him back to the subject of his visit. "We have a rich Irish tradition here in my city."

"Yes, I've been reading up on it, so I have. I need to find out more about the Irish Convention here last year that created the League to Enforce Peace for my article."

Joseph puffed out his chest and the coat buttons threatened to pop. "I helped organize it and I take a leadership role, so I would be happy to brief you on that subject."

A wizened woman with a harsh-looking face took their order consisting of Guinness and steak sandwiches.

"She looks like she rules the roost here, Joseph."

"She is the proprietress, Catherine McGillin, who took over after her husband died six years ago, and she has raised thirteen children in the rooms on the second floor. She's been here nigh on to fifty-five years, she has."

Collin stood up and looked around the pub to see if they could be overheard. He noticed the lunch crowd was self-absorbed near the long bar. He moved his chair closer to McGarrity, sat back down, and spoke in hushed tones.

"My visit with you concerns Tadgh McCarthy, who I believe contacted you. He is a member of the IRB and fought in the Rising under Mallin at St. Stephen's, so he did. He went to school with Mick Collins."

"Word is, Mick and his mates will likely be released from Frongoch Internment Camp, Collin. That's good news."

"Yes, I imagine Tadgh will be happy that the revolution can proceed." Collin reflected that Morgan would not likely be pleased.

A waiter appeared with their stouts, set the mugs down on the oak table, and moved back towards the bar.

"Tadgh is married to my sister who is also a member of the IRB."

"Really, a woman? Not part of the female Cumann na mBan?"

"She is definitely IRB. Battle-tested and wounded at St. Stephen's Green in the Rising, I'm told." Collin winced when he thought of her lying near death on the battlefield and took a swig of the dark brown foamy liquid.

McGarrity's eyes widened. "You don't say."

Collin leaned in and spoke softly into the American's ear. "Let me come right to the point. I know you were instrumental in assisting and financing Sir Roger Casement's attempt to get German arms to Ireland for the Rising."

"We were devastated when the German ship was lost. That effort emptied our coffers, I can tell you." Joseph didn't seem worried about the secrecy of their conversation.

Collin had researched the Clan na Gael gunrunning funding efforts in the recent *Tely* archives. "I am also aware of your initiative to arm India's Ghadar Party as part of the Hindu-German Conspiracy, which also involved Sir Roger."

"Sad business. The schooner *Annie Larsen* couldn't make the trip. It is tough to get arms through customs, you know. We have two strikes against us."

"That's why I have come to you, Joseph." Collin lowered his voice further. "Tadgh wants to use his funds to purchase arms for your revolution in Ireland."

"Really?" Joseph looked askance over the top of his mug of Guinness, brows raised. "It takes a lot of money, funds that we certainly don't have at this point in time. How much?"

"Tadgh can provide three hundred and fifty thousand dollars for armament."

McGarrity got up from the table without saying another word and headed for the door, leaving his beer on the table.

Collin had expected a reaction but not this one. He hopped up and chased after the revolutionary leader, catching up to him outside on Drury Street just as he was getting into his automobile.

Collin grabbed the edge of the driver's door to stop Joseph from slamming it in his face. "Hold on there, Mr. McGarrity."

"Who are you and why are you wasting my time? Did the Atlanticists send you?"

"No, I support Tadgh and your organization against the British."

Joseph let go of the door handle of his Model T and asked, "Are you Protestant or Catholic?"

"Married in an Anglican church in Toronto, sir. Definitely not Catholic."

"Well, at least you're honest about that."

"I can assure you I am honest and accurate in what Tadgh offers. Come back inside, sir."

"I suppose I can hear you out." McGarrity stepped out and slammed the car door shut.

The waiter appeared at the doorway. "Are you coming back in, Mr. McGarrity, to pay your bill?"

"Aye, Sean," Joseph answered, as he followed Collin back into McGillin's.

When reseated with their sandwiches before them, McGarrity scratched his head.

"Where would a young Irish lad get that huge sum of money? Is he an earl?"

"No, sir, but I can tell you from personal experience that Tadgh inherited this money honestly. It was left to him from Florence MacCarthaigh Reagh, back before the Battle of Kinsale."

"How, pray tell? Money doesn't grow on trees, you know."

"He unearthed his inheritance and doesn't plan to pay an inheritance duty on this money to the British. But he wants to pay them back for all the centuries of abuse. Rifles and bullets will help accomplish that goal."

"Well said, lad. I'm having difficulty understanding where this money came from but will accept for the time being that it exists and is available to pay for arms. If true, this would be a marvelous turn of events for the prospects of a revolution."

"I believe that is what Florence MacCarthaigh Reagh intended to happen three hundred and sixteen years ago."

Joseph smiled. "I know my history, too, lad. Your friend Tadgh is a descendant of that McCarthy chieftain who solicited an army from Spain to fight the battle of Kinsale in 1602."

"Aye, sir, and I'll leave the rest to your imagination."

McGarrity looked perplexed as he took a bite of his steak sandwich. "How will the money be transferred, then? Such a considerable sum."

"I don't know that at this point."

"It's not yet illegal to buy guns in this country, but it is illegal to ship them to Irish revolutionaries, Collin. How do you propose to get arms out of the United States and into Ireland?"

Collin drained the last of his Guinness and munched on the sandwich, looking sideways at the man before him. "This steak with the cheese is very good."

"It's our city's signature dish, lad. Now, what of my question?"

Collin caught the leader's eyes and stared. "Can you get us the arms if we supply the money? I was hoping to discuss that with you because of your experience in the matter."

Their conversation was interrupted when the waiter came over. "Another round, gents?"

"Yes please. Do you have O'Keefe ale?"

"Yes sir. For you, Mr. McGarrity?"

"Another Guinness, please."

Collin took a small bite of the second half of his sandwich and bent forward, speaking lower, "Let's put first things first. We don't manufacture military weapons in Canada, or I wouldn't be here now. Where can we buy the guns and how many can we get?"

The waiter returned with the beer and disappeared back to the bar.

"I have a contact at the Remington Eddystone plant downriver. It's actually part of the Baldwin Locomotive Works. They constructed a rifle manufacturing factory there last year to supply the British, and it is up and running, making the .303 Pattern 1914 Mk 1 rifles at a rate of two thousand or more a day. This is the standard weapon used in the trenches by the English."

"How many cartridges in the magazine?"

"Five. It is an excellent sniper weapon. Soldiers can hit a man-sized target at a thousand yards with the battle sight set at infinity. The rifle comes with strap and bayonet, although there is some talk that their bayonets don't meet the English specifications."

"Would the British reject them, then?"

"No, I don't think so, Collin. They're shipping them overseas."

"Their cost?"

"They are charging the British eleven pounds, five shillings apiece."

Collin was prepared with the current exchange rate on a paper in his pocket. "That would mean that they cost about thirty U.S. dollars each, right?"

"About that."

"Ammunition cost?"

".303 ammunition costs about five cents a round when bought in bulk."

"What about Browning machine guns?"

"In development, so I've heard. Coming next year. That's what the Americans will use if they enter the war."

"What's your view about the war, Joseph?"

"Of course, we Irish are pushing for President Wilson to remain neutral, but I fear that the Germans will have to resume unrestricted submarine warfare to throttle Britain, and that may bring the United States to the brink of war."

"I see. I presume any clandestine commercial window to purchase weapons will close if the United States enters the war."

"Absolutely, and even before then. The Eddystone factory is supervised by a Colonel John Thompson, who resigned from the army to be chief engineer at the plant. He has a beady eye on the production and distribution."

Collin had been scribbling figures on his piece of paper and stopped long enough to take a long draw on his ale. Looking at his sums, he said, "It looks to me as though we could afford seven thousand rifles, a million rounds of ammunition, leaving enough extra money for transportation home and other incidental expenses, plus some machine guns later on."

Joseph whistled. "That would be more than a third of the shipment that came on the *Aud-Norge* from Germany, alas, the twenty thousand rifles that now lie rusting at the bottom of Queenstown Harbor. A sizeable shipment, that'd be."

"Florence and Mick Collins would approve. Can I meet your contact at Eddystone before I leave on Saturday?"

"I'll try to arrange it, Collin. You realize that this quantity of weaponry creates a large shipment."

"How large?"

McGarrity made a quick calculation in his head. "Let's see, that's almost four days' worth of production at the plant. The rifles come in padded boxes, three to a box, each box weighing thirty pounds. It looks to me that this shipment would occupy approximately seven railway boxcars, loaded floor to ceiling."

"Wow! I hadn't thought of the size of it."

"Well, you'd best start thinking about it. They normally ship the rifles bound for England by train to New York City, but we could ship the guns down the Delaware River from Eddystone by boat or barge. Then they would have to be transferred to an ocean-going vessel somewhere. And then there's the delivery end of the trip to worry about."

"Would it be seven separate shipments, then?"

"We had multiple deliveries with the India project."

"First things first, Joseph. Let me meet your contact."

"I'll arrange that. We will likely go to Eddystone tomorrow, and I would like you to come to my home for dinner. We will have more privacy and can discuss the real state of preparedness for inevitable war here in the United States."

"I'd like that, sir."

"Where are you staying while you're here?"

"The Penn's View Hotel on Front Street, near the Delaware River."

"I can drop you there."

"Thank you. I'd like to visit the Hall of Independence this afternoon."

"It's an easy half-mile walk from your hotel."

The two men remained silent during the short trip. This was all new to Collin, high risk subterfuge. Could he trust this self-confident liquor store owner? McGarrity had apparently done it before, or at least attempted to do it. What would Kathy think if she knew what her husband was doing? Damn, he knew exactly what she would say. And wasn't he risking his job, his family, his life? Yet he had made a pact with Tadgh and signed it in blood.

Later that afternoon, Collin toured venerated Independence Hall and admired its splendid Georgian, red brick façade. It was blustery, yet the sharp wind didn't contain snow. This historical edifice consisted of a central building with bell tower and steeple, and two smaller wings via arcaded hyphens attached to the sides. Seeing the cracked Liberty Bell displayed in the main floor rotunda struck him at that moment. The impact of liberty, the concept of freedom, resonated. There was damage, that crack, but he took comfort in the fact that history on the side of righteousness had prevailed. Perhaps this would be a model for Ireland.

While standing in the Hall's Assembly Room, Collin imagined the men drafting and signing both the Declaration of Independence and Constitution. He was drinking in the history of America's courageous patriots and their successful fight for freedom from British oppression, when he heard the Centennial Bell hanging in the cupola of William Strickland's 1828 wooden steeple chime. An attendant told him that the ringing was done each day to commemorate the first reading by Colonel John Nixon of the Declaration of Independence on July 8, 1776, at noon, four days after this momentous document was signed.

This gave Collin pause to think about Patrick Pearse at noon, reading of the Irish Proclamation of Independence earlier that year on Easter Monday. He wished he'd been outside the General Post Office in Dublin to hear it. Undoubtedly, Pearse, a Gaelic history and political educator, may have wanted to mirror the American history in their fight for freedom from a common enemy. He supposed Pearse chose the General Post Office as the most auspicious building in Dublin, similar to the hall in which he now stood.

Collin realized why the Clan na Gael used this sacred place for conducting their Irish Race Convention earlier in the year, sensing how important the Irish had been in the fight for freedom and development of this country.

As an example of this, he'd heard that the Irish Brigade from New York had led the defense of Washington at the Battle of Antietam during the American Civil War. Having been driven out of their homeland by the British overlords during the Great Hunger, they were going to fight for the preservation of their new home, America. And how ironic that the Irish were treated so badly in the New World since they were willing to work harder than the other immigrant nations and were despised for it. But that was still better than the death and oppression back in Ireland. He could understand the reluctance of Irish Americans to have their new homeland join Britain in this war for European domination. Good, for all of that.

Collin found the downtown telegraph office and sent a telegram to Kathy via Sam:

> 'Arrived on schedule. Stop. Researched Independence Hall. Stop. Love you all. Stop. Will be home Sunday noon. Stop.'

McGarrity picked Collin up at his hotel in the morning and drove him the seventeen miles south along the Delaware River to Eddystone, until recently a sleepy little town of about eight hundred citizens. As they traveled down the main street, he explained, "You can see the new shops and office buildings. The population has swollen to almost eight thousand since Remington started to build the Eddystone Rifle Works here last year."

Just outside of town, they came upon a cleared area, which housed an enormous factory and parking lot. "The floor space inside covers thirty acres," McGarrity explained, as they parked and approached the business entrance. "This facility will likely double again in size when the rifle works is running at capacity."

After a short wait in the lobby, they were ushered into a closed, glass-lined office next to the factory floor where a short middle-aged man with horn-rimmed glasses sat behind a metal desk. He didn't get up to greet them but offered his bony hand.

McGarrity leaned forward at the desk and shook the hand, saying, "Henry, this is my friend, Collin O'Donnell. We are going to need a sizeable shipment of rifles and ammunition and we're willing to pay the British going rate."

Collin extended his hand and was met with a clammy paw. "Nice to meet you, Henry—?"

"Silvermann." The man squinted. "Collin O'Donnell, is it? You Irish?"

"I'm Canadian, Henry, and I have adequate resources. Let's leave it at that." Collin wiped his hand on his pants.

"Oil, then."

"If you like. Need weapons for expansion of the Canadian West," Collin lied, noting the smirk on McGarrity's face.

"Who are you kidding?" Silvermann looked over at McGarrity and then turned back to face Collin. "They're going to Ireland, right? Not the railhead in Montreal."

Collin didn't answer.

As they walked the factory, Silvermann explained that he was the production foreman responsible for packaging shipments for customer delivery. Collin was impressed by the degree of mechanization at the various milling, boring and extruding stations, not to mention the final assembly areas. What a far cry from the Lippitt textile mill in Woonsocket. Here the myriad employees worked eight-hour days with voluntary paid overtime and supportive, non-oppressive supervision. Then he showed them the lunchroom designed to seat two thousand at a time, with hot meals served on china plates.

"When we enter the war, we will need to turn out five thousand rifles a day."

"You expect the United States to end neutrality and join the Allies, do you, Mr. Silvermann?"

"Maybe that's wishful thinking on my part, Mr. O'Donnell, but yes. I expect we will do so." Silvermann handed Collin a specification sheet for the .303 Pattern 1914 Mk 1 rifles.

Back in the production foreman's office with the door closed, they got down to business.

Collin accepted an Old Grand-Dad whisky. "Mr. Silvermann, could I order, say, seven thousand rifles and a million rounds of ammunition without affecting your contract delivery rate with the British?"

"For delivery, when? It would have to be before we declare war. After that, the military would control production and distribution and my hands would be tied."

McGarrity put down his glass on the side table and asked, "Could we do this without paperwork, like we did last year, if you know what I mean?"

"Yes, Mr. McGarrity. With the same arrangements."

McGarrity raised his eyebrows, "Meaning?"

"The same percentage extra as before, for, shall we say, expediting the process."

"I understand." McGarrity quickly shook his head at Collin as if to say, "Don't ask just now. I'll talk to you later."

Collin took a cautious sip of the Kentucky bourbon. It tasted raw and rough; he wasn't used to it. "What about ammunition?"

"You didn't see that operation this morning, but that can be part of the shipment as well, picked up at our dock on the Delaware along with the rifles."

Joseph asked, "How big a shipment would it be, Henry?"

"I would suggest seven shipments spread out over time, one boxcar each."

Collin followed up. "How often do you ship to Britain?"

"Whenever there is a convoy. Usually at the beginning of each month."

"That means approximately sixty thousand rifles. Is that right?"

"Give or take. Maybe more. Why?"

"Then about a thousand extra per month would be a very small percentage of the total shipment, easier to absorb."

"I see your point, Collin. When can you get the money?"

"Very shortly. I'll have to get back to you through Mr. McGarrity, here. How many people will know what we are doing?"

"Just the three of us."

Collin quaffed the last of his whisky and they all shook hands again. Collin thought that Silvermann's palm seemed even more slippery than before. But that might have just been the nature of the business they had just transacted.

Joseph McGarrity lived in a country home with a mansard roof at Penn's Landing on the Delaware, in downtown Philadelphia near Carpenter's Wharf. Through the living room window, even as snowflakes began to fall in the waning daylight, Collin could see the cargo ships being loaded with goods in the distance. After a dinner of striped bass and turnip prepared by Joseph's wife, Karen, the men retired to the library to talk.

Joseph began, "I did some research and Tadgh McCarthy is a transportation and communications specialist in the West Cork IRB."

Collin looked up in surprise from his upholstered leather chair, wondering who had identified his brother-in-law.

His host caught the look. "So, de Valera sent me a coded

telegram if you must know. Said he was active in the Rising. Saw him at Boland's Bakery. Care for a whisky?"

"Yes, thanks, Jameson's if you have it." Collin thought that it was uncanny how Joseph could sense what he was thinking, and how he would check out his story. It left him feeling reassured.

"It's better than Silvermann's Kentucky bourbon, isn't it. Triple versus single distilled malt is a lot smoother." Joseph handed Collin a snifter and poured himself one as well.

Collin was curious. "So, is de Valera imprisoned, then? I heard he was spared execution after the Rising because of being born in America."

"Yes. He is in Lewes Prison, but we are pressuring for his release. We have our contacts to get messages in and out."

"What kickback does your man Silvermann want?"

"It's the price of doing business in an unfair world, I'm afraid, Collin. He wants ten percent."

"That can be absorbed within Tadgh's funds, I think. What do we get with that cut?"

"Henry will accept your funds and enter it minus his fee into their books as a British shipment. He will label the boxes the same. But when the shipment is being delivered, it will get lost in transit and will show up at our designated location and time."

"How will he explain the loss?"

"The British will not have ordered those rifles, remember? They won't be expecting delivery. But the manifest will need to be doctored."

"Can Mr. Silvermann be trusted?"

"He came through for us with the Hindu-German shipment."

"The need for four separate shipments bothers me, Joseph. Each time there is a separate risk of exposure."

"We must go along with Henry. He knows best. How do you plan to get the arms to Ireland?"

Collin had no idea. "Tadgh is working on it. A sympathizer offered one of his company's freighters, but how that ship can drop out of a convoy is still uncertain."

"Remember, lad. The shipment must leave US waters before America declares war on Germany, if indeed that happens. So, time is of the essence."

"When are the Germans likely to resume unrestricted submarine warfare to starve the British of supplies?"

"We have connections with the German Ambassador to the United States, Johann Heinrich von Bernstorff. He has been helpful with the Casement activities. He thinks that his GGS will be forced to order U-boat attacks to recommence by the end of January, next month."

"I'm not sure if we can organize our shipment by then, Joseph."

"The Clan na Gael has some experience with these matters. But Devoy tells me there are stricter security and export controls at the Ports in New York and elsewhere since that terrible Black Tom sabotage. It won't be easy."

"I was there, Joseph, and have the battle scar to prove it."

"What do you mean, lad?"

Collin explained how he and his wife had a harrowing front row experience with the incident.

"Well, then, you can understand the need for better controls."

"Aye, sir. Won't submarine warfare bring the United States into the conflict?"

"That's not clear. The papers are full of speculation. President Wilson doesn't want it, nor do the financiers who are loaning lots of money to the current belligerents. I think that it would take more than that. Bernstorff says the GGS believes the United States is far behind militarily and could not mobilize fast enough to affect the outcome of the war."

"That would be a big gamble on the part of Germany, I should think, Joseph."

"It's all a risk, in my opinion, on a monstrous scale. You said you wanted more information on the convention and the League to Enforce Peace."

"Yes, for my newspaper. I won't quote you."

"That would be best, Collin. Anything to do with the Clan na Gael that I tell you is off limits. No offense, but the less there is to connect the two of us, the better."

Joseph spent the next half hour educating Collin on the various Irish organizations in the United States and the Clan na Gael's efforts to integrate them to lobby for Irish interests at the federal, state, and local levels. During this discussion, Collin learned quite a bit about the formation, actions, and members of the Clan na Gael and their influence over revolutionary planning and actions in Ireland.

When Collin was satisfied he'd learned enough information, Joseph went to his desk and unlocked a drawer. From it, he extracted a small, red notebook. Leafing through it, he found the page he was looking for.

"The codes that I was using with the IRB prior to the Rising still work. That's how I learned of you and Tadgh. It's a simple but effective cypher that you'll need to memorize."

Collin took the book and studied the page closely before handing it back. "Is this the cypher Tadgh used to contact you?"

"No, but it comes from Michael Collins who conceived it while in Frongoch prison. He got it delivered to us by messenger, and we have been using it to try to gain the release of our men there. Collins asked me to give it to you so you can communicate with him."

"Good, but how will that help me communicate with Tadgh?"

"I checked last night, and our efforts have borne fruit. Michael and most of our men are being released before Christmas. He will find your brother-in-law. Something else you need to know about communications with Europe, Collin. At the beginning of the war, the English cut the German trans-Atlantic cable. Now all communications must go coded through the English cable that passes through Britain at Lands' End in Cornwall. So we need to be very careful with our transmissions. Also, if you write about the situation south of the forty-ninth parallel for your paper, you can't talk about what we know from the German ambassador."

"That goes without saying. Based on your intelligence from the Germans, there is no time to lose."

"Agreed. We need a code name."

"How about Florence?"

"Perfect," Joseph said, clasping hands with Collin.

"Let's drink to that and to freedom for our brothers and sisters in the old country."

With the clink of their drinking glasses, the deal was struck. After bidding good night to his host and hostess, Collin walked the five blocks to his hotel in the swirling snow, pondering the fact that he was now an international spy and gunrunner. With no scarf, he pulled his woolen coat tightly around his neck to try to stop the shivers running up and down his spine. He'd made the commitment to Tadgh to carry out the wishes of their ancient ancestors Red Hugh and Florence. It was one thing to come to the U.S.A. to start discussions, but he couldn't see how he would be able to implement this gunrunning operation personally. It would jeopardize his life, his employment, his family. What would Sam think of this subterfuge, he wondered, however noble the cause? *Kathy must never know about this.*

Back at his hotel, Collin fell into a somewhat inebriated slumber, his current tasks accomplished in Philadelphia but with many unanswered questions left on the table.

Chapter Four
War Drums

Monday, December 25, 1916
Creagh, Ireland

*T*adgh was shocked when the telephone rang Christmas morning. The voice on the other end of the *IRB* line astonished him even more. *A voice from the dead.* "Mick! Is that you?"

"Right enough, Tadgh. Released from Frongoch, thank God. I'm glad you survived. Still in our West Cork?"

"Ever the same. Is it safe to talk in the open?"

"Yes, for the moment. They've let their guard down for now, Tadgh."

"How many were released from Frongoch yesterday?"

"Two thousand, give or take. I've been training them, Tadgh."

"Have you, now. For what?"

"Can you come to Dublin, lad?"

"If I'm careful, yes. I need to talk to you, Michael."

"And I need to talk to you as well, don't ya know."

"How does Wednesday suit you?"

"An Stad Hotel pub?"

"Noon."

Tadgh was excited. How fortuitous. From his voice, Michael sounded full of energy, not at all what you would expect from an inmate who had been mistreated in prison.

Morgan had overheard the conversation since Collins had a booming voice. "Divine intervention, in my opinion."

Jeffrey Wiggins showed up at Tadgh's home at six o'clock Wednesday morning in the brewery delivery lorry.

Morgan came to the door to see Tadgh off. At four months pregnant, she was already showing. "Be careful, *mavourneen*."

"I should be home by noon tomorrow, *aroon*. Right, Jeffrey?" Tadgh remembered the British roadblock that they had barely squeezed through outside Dublin when they ran the guns to *an Stad* just prior to Rossa's funeral. He hoped to hell they could get the 'McCarthy gold' delivered without incident. Florence MacCarthaigh Reagh was counting on him from the grave.

"We'd better pull it off, or I'll be in trouble with the brewery."

As previously arranged, they filled two specially marked and empty B & C stout barrels with most of the McCarthy fortune. Wiggins used the company band sealer to fasten the tops. They loaded them into the back of the lorry and covered them over with two layers of tied-off full stout barrels."

The trip went without a hitch, and the B&C lorry's engine was smoking as they pulled into the alley behind *an Stad* just before noon. Tadgh couldn't help but remember with some angst being introduced to O'Donovan Rossa's widow by Thomas Clarke on this very spot only eighteen months earlier. So much had happened since that pivotal day, and poor Tom was dead, murdered in cold blood by damn General Maxwell's goons. They would pay for this and so many other atrocities.

After the special barrels were removed and moved to a room that Tadgh had rented in the hotel, Jeffrey took his leave to deliver the brew to a few pubs on his route. "I will return for you tonight, Tadgh, and we can have supper together."

Tadgh stood in the same room that he and Morgan had occupied during the Rossa funeral, the same chamber where they had made passionate love for the first time. And now she was going to have his child. The enormity of change in his life swept over him. What if he hadn't found Morgan that fateful day as she clung for dear life to the flotsam from the *Lusitania*?

When Tadgh entered *an Stad* pub, Michael Collins was sitting alone in the corner, as fit as usual, spit and polish. Tadgh checked. There were no British police in sight. He was disappointed to see that his friend Sean O'Casey was not in his normal haunt, carrying forth with whoever would listen.

"Mick, you don't look the worse for wear," Tadgh said, as he sat down after cuffing him on the ear, almost knocking his bowler hat off his head. "Wearing civvies, I see."

Michael Collins spoke in a subdued voice, not his normal authoritative tone. "It's a different war now, Tadgh."

He had made sure that no one could hear their conversation by sitting in the shadows, away from the crowd at the bar. The noise of the rowdies would drown out a herd of stampeding elephants. During the next few minutes, Tadgh learned that Michael had led a contingent of exhausted Volunteers out the back of the GPO onto Henry Street when it was firebombed, and he almost got himself killed, like The O'Rahilly. He avoided execution by blending into the crowd of prisoners when first apprehended, following the advice he had given Tadgh in the GPO at the height of the Rising. Survive to fight another day.

"It will be different this time. Back to the guerrilla warfare that our Gaelic ancestors employed so successfully."

"When will that be, Mick?"

"After we organize, convince the population, and find the funds."

"Who do you mean by *we*, Mick? Most were executed."

"Aye, lad. By murderous British scum. But Maxwell did us a favor as Pearse knew he would. Helped our Cause, the bastard. I take orders now from de Valera, even though he's still in jail at Lewes."

"He wasn't executed?"

"No, since he's American."

"He was confused when I saw him at Boland's Bakery, Michael."

"Well, he will have the reins now. It's going to take some time to get organized but I'm going to need you, Tadgh."

"Whatever it takes. I'm committed to the Cause." Tadgh lowered his voice even further. "I have some good news that will change your planning, I think, to be sure. I'd like to show you something I've brought. It's best discussed in my room."

Michael's eyebrows raised with curiosity. He paid the bill and they trundled up the creaking staircase to Tadgh's bedroom.

Tadgh had tipped the two barrels on their sides around the small table. Once they were inside, Tadgh motioned Michael to take a seat on one of the barrels.

Collins sat down cautiously, making sure the barrel didn't roll out from under him. "Odd chairs, don't you think? I don't recall seeing them here in the past."

Tadgh ignored the comment and started in. "My ancestor Florence MacCarthaigh Reagh hid his wealth back just before Kinsale, specifically to assist with our revolution, Mick. And I found it."

"You don't say. You must tell me some time about how that came about. How much is it worth?"

"By my calculation, about eighty-seven thousand, five hundred pounds, or about three hundred and fifty thousand U.S. dollars." Tadgh had held back telling him about certain jewelry items that were keepsakes for the family.

"Christ Jesus. Did you find a gold mine?"

"In a manner of speaking. Do you remember the story of the McCarthy gold plate disappearing when Blarney castle fell to Boyle?"

"Yes. Jeffreyes spent a fortune dragging the lake and didn't find it. My God, Tadgh, where was it?"

"Under the feet of St. Patrick's Cross."

"At Cashel, your family home until Brian Boru. Well, I'll be damned. This is grand news, lad. Where is it, might I ask?"

"You're sitting on it. Coin and gold and silver plate, plus some jewelry."

Michael jumped up. "Let's have a look." He reached to right

the barrel.

Tadgh stood and put his arm on Collins' shoulder. "Best left intact until it can be transported. I have no way to re-seal it." Then he thrust out his left hand. "But look here—Florence's signet gold ring."

Michael inspected the massive inlaid gold ring and whistled loudly. "Tadgh, if the rest is like this, it must be worth a fortune."

Tadgh straightened the ring on his finger, looked up at his leader and smiled. "I have a plan, but I need your help."

"Of course you do. Name it."

"We will use my new-found providence to pay for armament. Suffice it to say that I know this is the wish of my ancestors."

Michael's eyes were dancing. "Of course, lad. You are right. This changes everything."

Tadgh continued. "We must get the weapons from America. I have an agent and the Clan na Gael, McGarrity, in Philadelphia, is excited to help."

"What agent? Is he trustworthy?"

"Remember I told you about Morgan who had been shot?"

"Yes."

"Morgan and I married."

"Did you, now? Oh, I see that from the finger with that ring on it. I've been away too long."

"Morgan and I are all yours when the time comes. But there is a complication. She's expecting our child."

Collins studied his school chum carefully before responding. "That will change things, for her, I mean. Perhaps Cumann na mBan work would be more appropriate."

"We'll see. She's saved me more than once, Mick. She's fierce about being there. Her Irish brother is Canadian, trustworthy, and on our side. He went to Philadelphia recently and checked out a gun factory there."

"Ah, that starts to make sense, Tadgh. McGarrity sent me a note to contact you and give you the code we have been using out of Frongoch." Michael pulled a scrap of paper from his pocket and handed it to Tadgh. "We'll be using this cypher in all our planning."

Tadgh memorized the code structure before incinerating the paper in the ashtray on the table. "But how will my contact—?"

"McGarrity has it. He'll give it to him, I'm sure. What can I do to help, Tadgh?"

"Fence the treasure here in Dublin. I can't do it. I am a wanted man. I will use some of the funds to rent a vacant storage building near the Queenstown docks. We'll store the rifles and ammo there."

"You are a Godsend, comrade. You have no idea what this will do for our Cause."

"That's what my ancestor Florence MacCarthaigh Reagh intended, for certain."

"Unbelievable."

"I received an encrypted letter from my brother-in-law last week, using the pre-Rising code."

"You must discard that cypher, Tadgh. It was compromised during the Rising."

"Understood. He and McGarrity met with the gun supplier. Including his cut to keep the sale quiet, they think we can get seven thousand .303 Pattern 1914 Mk 1 Enfield rifles, a million rounds of ammunition, and hopefully a hundred Browning machine guns when they are finally produced later this year."

"Incredible. That will enable the revolution, lad."

"I hope so."

"How will you transport the weapons?"

"I have another associate. He can organize freighter shipping to Queenstown where he works. Mick, this shipment takes up seven train boxcars, you know. That's why I need the storage facility there."

"You are a savior, Tadgh."

"One more thing, Mick. I need cash. We can't have any traceability for this sizeable amount of funding."

"I will deliver the money personally to Creagh, by New Year's Day. It will give me a chance to go home and see my family in

Woodfield, Sam's Cross.

They lugged the two barrels down to Collins' automobile and stuffed them into the back seat. Jumping into the driver's seat, Michael said, "I'd best get busy."

"I'll see you in Creagh, then, Mick."

With a wave of his hat, Collins, who already envisioned himself as the future intelligence leader of the revolution, drove off leaving Tadgh feeling suddenly empty. But it was the will of his ancestor, Florence.

Kathy was happy that Collin had come home from his trip to the United States in time for Christmas. He had decided not to tell her that he would be going away again soon, and for much longer, on a mission she would absolutely forbid if she knew. When the families had gotten together for New Year's Day, Collin cornered Sam alone in his studio and finally turned to his mentor for help.

"I've been hiding a secret from all of you, and it is really bothering me, Sam."

"It's about your task for Tadgh in America, isn't it?"

"Yes. I'm sworn to secrecy, but I can't keep it to myself any longer." Collin told Sam everything about the dangerous plans for gunrunning.

"You can't do this, Collin. Not after what happened to your family last year. I heard you promise Kathy when we left Ireland. You know how she feels."

"I know. That's why I am torn between two families. I made a blood pact with Tadgh, so I did."

"Tell Tadgh that it will destroy your marriage, me boyo. He'll understand."

"Then how's he going to get the munitions?"

"That Philadelphia chap you mentioned, McGarrity isn't it? He can handle it."

"I don't know. He's a politician, Sam. He uses men like me to implement his plans."

"Tell Tadgh or tell Kathy, Collin, and let the chips fall where they may. That's my advice, lad." Sam opened the door from his studio, clapped Collin on the shoulder, and led him back to the families sitting around the meager Christmas tree.

Collin had always valued Sam's suggestions, until now. They were always sound. Yet he knew that he couldn't trust McGarrity to implement this crucial plan on his own and Tadgh was counting on his blood-pact colleague. Surely, with a baby on the way, he wouldn't be able to leave Ireland himself. And telling Kathy was a non-starter. There was no way she would agree to his being a clandestine gunrunner.

The children were playing by the now-bedraggled looking tree, the only vestige of Christmas that Sam and Lil had been able to muster in this era of austerity. It was still up, due to the adverse weather. Nonetheless, they had enjoyed the celebration of the Lord's birth that had shone through the gloom of the ongoing war.

On the 2nd of January, while he was still agonizing, Collin got a coded telegram at work. It was in the McGarrity cypher, from Tadgh.

'Contacted leader. Stop. Resources being prepared. Stop. What is your status? Stop.'

Collin sent back,

'War drums sounding down south. Stop. Urgency. Stop. Dealing with problems on the home front. Stop.'

After sending that mealy-mouthed telegram, he chastised himself for not facing his dilemma resolutely. That's when he finally realized what he must do. *When the time comes, I will have to execute Tadgh's plan.*

♣ ♣ ♣ ♣

Kathy and Collin, with Liam, started for church at St. Aidan's when the blizzard descended on them, so instead they headed for Number Ten Balsam. Luckily, the Finlays were still there, having thought better of braving the storm. The O'Donnells warmed themselves by Sam and Lil's parlor fire while the blizzard howled all around them that Sunday morning the 14th. The weather forecast called for at least two feet of snow before it was all over later that night.

"I heard on the newswire, Sam, that Germany invaded Russia a week ago." Collin's news brought the gentle conversation to an end.

"Why would they do that in the dead of winter with so much trouble on the Western Front?" Kathy asked, as she grasped a cup of tea Lil offered and tried to thaw her numb fingers.

"I think it may be due to the unrest of the Russian people with the Tsar and the concern that their Bolshevik revolutionaries would invade German territory. They were hoping to make short work of Western Europe through Belgium by implementing Schlieffen's plan before this happened." Collin picked up the Sunday paper and looked at the headlines. "Allies Respond to Wilson's Peace Suggestions. League of Nations Premature!" Then he turned back to the group huddled close to the blazing parlor fireplace. "But the Belgians held the line and thwarted their plan."

"Will that affect the United States' neutral position, do you think, my boy?"

"Indirectly, maybe. Germany can't survive fighting on both fronts. They have to bring the war with Britain to an end. I've heard that they are likely to resume U-boat attacks in the Atlantic, cutting off supplies, which could bring the United States into the war."

"When did they stop it, then, mavourneen?"

Collin accepted a warming sherry from Sam and responded to Kathy. "They agreed to cease torpedoing Allied shipping last May after the Cross-English Channel Ferry, *Sussex*, was badly damaged with twenty-eight Americans killed. The United States threatened to break off ties with Germany if they didn't stop sinking civilian ships. The Germans called that the *Sussex* Pledge."

"But you were attacked on your way to Ireland."

"On May 2nd, my love. Just before the pledge went into effect."

"Well, I hope the Americans finally do join the war to get it over with," Lil stated, wrapping up Ernie's feeding and putting him over her shoulder to burp. After a few minutes, she signaled to Kathy, and the women went off to organize lunch.

Sam took Collin aside. "What did you decide, lad? Time is growing short."

"I'm going to go, and I'm afraid of telling Kathy."

Sam frowned.

Collin continued, "I got another coded telegram from Tadgh just after New Year's. He sold the coins and most of the plate. He has the money hidden in the operations center at Creagh. I'm expecting to hear from him any day now how the money will be transmitted and whether it will come to me or directly to McGarrity. Then we can set the acquisition in motion."

"I know you made a commitment, Collin, but I still think this plan is folly. You should avoid it like the plague." Sam saw Collin clench his fists before responding and cut him off. "If you must do this, you'd best tell Kathy before it's too late, me boyo."

Collin shook his head. *How would he break it to her this time?*

The men joined their families for the noon meal before returning to the parlor fireplace warmth. The girls and Collin set about building a cabin with the little wooden toy log set he gave them for Christmas. "You know, this toy is a new invention by John Lloyd Wright," Collin spoke out. "He was working in Japan with his famous father, Frank Lloyd Wright, on a similarly designed Imperial Hotel in Tokyo." He chuckled. "We are playing with history, imagine that."

"Look out the parlor window. You O'Donnells will have to stay the night since the storm's frightful," Lil said after the meal as she poked her head in from the kitchen dishes. She waved her hand, weaving them all together in the scene. "I was thinking we could have a game of whist this evening after supper, once we've put the children down for the night."

Having just finished the planks for the roof, little Norah got up and stretched. Looking out the front door window, she was fascinated by the swirling snow.

"Come away from the door, Norah. There's a draft," her father said, moving to the fireplace to stoke the logs.

"But Daddy, there's a snowman in our yard."

"Come away, Norah. You'll catch your death."

Dot rushed to the door. "I see him, too. He's coming."

"Come away," Kathy called, and crossed to the door, grabbing both girls by their hands. "Oh, my God."

"What is it, darlin'?" Collin inquired, getting up from the rug to join her.

"A ghost from the past."

The snowman materialized through the swirling blizzard and approached the door. He was dressed for the weather except for his uncovered boots.

Kathy pulled the girls away as Collin threw open the door and ushered the mystery man in.

"Sweet Brigid. How in heavens did you get here?" Collin gave the man a bear hug, snow, and all.

The snowman, carrying a beaten-up suitcase, stood in the entryway, and started to melt.

"By Jack's boat, then train, streetcar, and finally, on foot after the bloody vehicle stalled in the snow. You gave me your address. I went there only to find the house closed up. Your neighbor said because of the snow you might be here."

Collin grinned and shook the water off his own clothes like a dog. "Damn, Tadgh, it's good to see you." Relieved, he welcomed the unexpected support.

Kathy and Sam had gathered around as the newcomer's gray parka jacket became visible beneath the crust of snow.

Lil came in from the kitchen to see who was creating all the ruckus. "Land sakes." She rushed upstairs, grabbed towels from the linen closet and brought them to the front door.

Thrusting the towels into Kathy's arms, she said, "Get that coat off him before he freezes to death." She peered closely; her head tilted toward the man in her entryway. "Well, who do we have here?"

The man took off his cap and said, "Tadgh McCarthy at your service, ma'am."

Norah and Dot, who had hidden in the corner, came forward and offered to help mop up the wet floor with the towels.

"Now who are these two Irish beauties?" Tadgh bent down, removed his gloves, and held out his almost frozen hands to them.

"I'm Norah and she's my little sister Dot, sir."

Norah reached out her hand tentatively, intimidated by the burly man with the thick ice-covered moustache. "Pleased to meet your acquaintance, sir."

"Call me Tadgh, lassie."

"That's a funny name. I can't say it," Dot chimed in, brazenly taking Tadgh's other hand, and shaking it as vigorously as a two-year-old can. "Can I call you Tug?"

Tadgh laughed and winked at the child. "Certainly, young lady."

Two hours later, with Lil's wonderful potato and leek soup and slices of soda bread inside him, Tadgh started to feel human again. The adults were seated at the rustic oak dining table at the far end of the parlor, away from the front door and next to the kitchen. The girls were off for their nap upstairs. The warmth from the fireplace kept the room cozy despite the cold window panes rattling from the gale outside.

Tadgh opened his shirt collar and gave a laugh. "Thank you, Lil, for your hospitality and nourishment." Turning to Collin, he said, "I thought you told me that this was a beautiful place with great opportunities. You didn't say anything about it being the Arctic tundra."

"You came at precisely the right time to see the fury and beauty of our Canadian nature," Sam said, pointing at his painting of a snow-covered Muskoka scene on the wall. "That's about a hundred miles north of here. Don't you just love the primitive majesty of it all?"

Lil said, "Spoken like a true landscape artist, *creena*. But I'm sure Tadgh doesn't see things the same way as you do at the moment."

"Nonsense, my love. An Irishman knows the value of his land."

"Especially after it's taken away from him," Tadgh said, standing up from the table to examine Sam's painting more closely. "I do see the love in the brush strokes here. It is beautiful. I wish I could do that."

Sam stood to join him and lit his Prince Albert. "We each have our mission in life, lad."

"Aye, Sam," Tadgh said, sitting back down at the table.

"So why are you here, and where is Morgan?" Kathy asked, offering Tadgh a cup of tea.

"Well now, the answer to that question might require a little intestinal fortitude," Tadgh unabashedly replied.

Sam reached behind him to the dining room sideboard and brought a partially full bottle of Jameson down to the table. "Would this help, perhaps?"

"To be sure, Sam." Two minutes later, with four fingers of the familiar amber liquid coursing through his veins, Tadgh was ready to respond.

"Morgan is at home with brother Aidan. She's fine but her condition with child has been a hard one. She sends her love to you all. I am here to assist Collin in the task we have before us. Trying to accomplish it from the other side of the Atlantic proved to be too difficult for me."

Kathy leaned forward in her seat. "What task is that, Tadgh?"

Collin wondered how his fellow Irish Clans brother would answer Kathy.

"Collin and I agreed after my wedding that we would put the McCarthy treasure to good use, as our ancestors Florence MacCarthaigh and Red Hugh O'Donnell intended. In fact, we took a sacred oath together, just as those great Clan Chieftains did three hundred and sixteen years earlier."

Sam and Lil took notice as Tadgh spoke.

Collin saw Kathy twirling the hair behind her ear before asking, "To do what?"

Collin shook his head side to side towards Tadgh, to no avail. *She's upset now.*

Tadgh was in his element. "To use the treasure to supply weapons for our revolution."

"Your revolution," Collin corrected him.

"All right then, my revolution."

Kathy's eyes flashed. "So *that's* why you went to Philadelphia. Collin!"

"One reason. I was sworn to secrecy, darlin'."

"You mean that you are going to buy guns in the United States and take them to Ireland? Gun-running?" Kathy demanded, striking her fist against the tabletop so hard that the supper silverware rattled.

Tadgh realized that he had been too forthcoming. "I had asked Collin not to share this with you because I didn't want you all implicated in case we are caught, don't ye see. But I realize now that there was no way for us to carry out our task if I had stayed in Ireland, and if you are left in the dark, especially if it involves a trans-Atlantic crossing with the weapons. Don't ye see, Kathy?"

"You are right about that, Tadgh. I appreciate your concern for our safety, but there is no way that I can condone Collin being involved in this dangerous scheme." Kathy stood up, arms crossed and looked daggers at her husband, who cringed.

Tadgh reminded her, "You do remember what happened to us at the hands of the British when you were in Ireland, don't you?"

"Of course I do, Tadgh. All the more reason not to be involved."

Lil, who had been trying to get that piece of information out of her best friend ever since she got back from Ireland, asked, "What happened?"

Tadgh looked at his hostess and then at Kathy. "You tell her. Let's all be open and honest."

"We. . . uh . . . had some very bad men follow us and try to kill us. Sam, Collin, Tadgh, and Tadgh's brother Aidan saved us from certain death."

"My God, girl." It was Lil's turn to glare at Sam. By that point, all five of them were standing at the table.

Sam stepped over to his wife and held her close. "I didn't want to worry you, creena. It's all right. They can't hurt us anymore."

Tadgh went and stood with his back to the roaring fireplace deep in thought before returning. *These relatives cannot jeopardize our mission from over here in Canada. I need their help to fulfill our ancestors' requirements to free Ireland of the bastardly British.* Then he cleared his throat and said, "Listen, everyone. We must get the British out of Ireland and we can't do it without guns. The only source of these weapons that we can use at this point is in the United States, and only if we move before they join the war."

Kathy pleaded, "Why do you have to involve my husband? He's all that Liam, my unborn, and I have got."

"I *don't* have to, now. That's partly why I am here. It's up to you, Collin."

Collin reached out his arms to his wife who backed away. "Kathy, after what I saw from the British in Ireland, and with my ancestors looking over my shoulder, I cannot in all good conscience walk away from my responsibility to do all I can for Tadgh and the other rebels." He spread out his hands in appeal to her. "Can't you see that?"

"What about our family?"

"How can I look our family in the eye if I don't do all I can? They won't let me fight in the war, like all the other Canadian soldiers. Here, I can make a difference."

Kathy saw that Collin had traded in his obsession of finding his sister for a new crusade, saving the Irish in Ireland. "We need you, all three of us, back here in Canada."

"I can do this myself," Tadgh said, stepping between her and her husband, and putting his hands on Collin's shoulders as he attempted to get to his wife.

Firmly, Collin looked at Tadgh, "No. We made a pact and I believe in the Cause. I will help you as long as the *Tely* doesn't fire me for taking time off."

Kathy threw up her hands to Lil who looked pleadingly at Sam for a solution, to say something. But no single answer would satisfy everyone.

Sam loaded his pipe and tamped down the Prince Albert tobacco. "Look, with the blizzard outside, why don't we all bed down here overnight and sleep on this dilemma? Maybe a solution will present itself in the morning."

Blankets were brought to the parlor. Collin and Tadgh brought in wood from the protected shed out back. The household readied for sleep.

While they were alone, after everyone had gone to bed, Collin couldn't contain his curiosity. "How are the funds getting to McGarrity?"

"Sewn into the lining of my beat-up suitcase in thousand-pound British bank notes, Collin, eighty-eight of them. I didn't ask Michael how he got them but it's ironic that we will be paying the enemy back using their own coin."

"Aye, Tadgh, but that was a huge risk you took getting through Customs."

The Irish rebel laughed and pulled on his moustache. "And we will still have that to look forward to when we cross into the U.S."

"So that's equivalent to three hundred and fifty thousand U.S.

dollars, Tadgh?"

"Yes. McGarrity and his liquor business will have to figure out how to get it converted without attracting suspicion."

Remembering the risks and his pain of separation from Kathy a year earlier, Collin asked, "Is Morgan angry with you for coming to America without her? Especially now that she is with child?"

Tadgh's eyes did not make contact. "I'm not sure, Collin. This has to be done for the revolution, and she let me go."

Collin knew that his independent sister would be more understanding than his own more-needy wife.

The storm raged, unabated. The families settled in for the night.

Monday dawned sunny and frigid. Sam got the call on the telephone. School was canceled due to the snow load, which had totaled almost three feet. The weatherman had been wrong. Toronto businesses ground to a halt under the silent blanket of white.

The girls were drawing stick figures in the condensation on the inside of Sam's studio windows when three-year-old Norah exclaimed, "Look, Daddy. The squirrels are jumping off the branches into the snow. They sink right in."

"Where to?" Dot cried. "They must be freezing. Will they die in the snow?"

Sam chuckled. "No, dear Dot. Didn't you see their bushy black coats? They're just digging to find the entrances to their acorn larders."

"What's a larder, Daddy?"

"It's like our own food cupboard. It's where they stash their nuts for the winter."

Lil called them to breakfast. She made do from her meager

pantry to feed them porridge and tea. Unfortunately, the supply of brown sugar was almost gone, but there were some raisins to sprinkle on the oatmeal.

"I have a suggestion," Sam said, while they sat at the dining table after their meal, and after the girls had been sent to their room to play. He stood up, pulled out his pipe, and loaded it with Prince Albert.

They all turned to look as he stood and tamped down the tobacco.

"Collin, I will lend you my Model T to drive Tadgh to Philadelphia when the roads are clear."

Lil stopped eating. Kathy started to object.

Sam held up his hand. Then he struck a match and drew his breath in. The tobacco caught fire. Sam puffed. Its pungent smoke wafted out over the table. "Hear me out, lassies. Collin can introduce Tadgh to Mr. McGarrity and the gun plant manager, and then come home."

Lil beamed.

Sam continued. "Collin can help the most here at his newspaper. He can get up-to-date intelligence on what the United States is doing with regards to the war. Tadgh can do what he does best, organizing and transporting the weapons. Together, you can accomplish your common goals."

Lil thought to herself, *my brilliant husband.*

"I can certainly live with that," Collin said, standing up and coming around the table to shake Sam's hand.

Tadgh stroked his moustache. "Works for me, sir."

Kathy stood up and kissed Sam on the forehead, saying, "Ditto. Right, then. What's your plan, boys?"

Collin looked at Tadgh who nodded and said, "Thank you all. We'll let you know, that's certain."

Norah and Dot heard the adults' intense talk coming to an end and came bounding down the stairs.

Norah blurted out, "Can we make a snowman, Daddy?"

Dot added, "Can we, please?"

They tugged at the pant leg of their father.

Sam checked the front window. The storm had abated completely. "If your uncles will help."

This broke the tension. Lil made sure the girls were bundled warmly and sent them off with a warning to her husband, "If they get too cold, bring them in right away."

The men hustled the giggling girls out into the snow, leaving the women to tend to their crying baby boys upstairs.

While they changed Liam and Ernest's nappies, Lil said, "Are you sure you agree to this plan Sam suggested? No matter how you cut it, it's still gunrunning and it's quite illegal."

"What are my choices, Lil? Any alternative I might think of is worse. I never thought I would be saying this, but if you had seen what it took to get the ancestral treasure, you would understand how important it is to our men to use it wisely."

"But international arms trafficking?"

"Listen, Lil. At least Collin will be safe at home when the guns are being shipped."

"Aye, lass. There is that. These are hard times we live in."

That said they opened their waist-shirts and let their little laddies feed.

On Thursday, January 18, once the road from Toronto to Niagara Falls had been plowed, Collin and Tadgh set off, complete with bully-beef sandwiches and apples for the trip supplied by Lil. Sam was left to figure out if Collin's Hudson would run in the frigid weather, while the other O'Donnells were firmly ensconced at Number Ten Balsam.

When Collin finally reappeared without his brother-in-law a week later, Kathy and the Finlays pumped him for information at the front door even before he could remove his overcoat and galoshes.

Collin chose his words carefully. The cat was out of the bag, but there was no sense risking his relatives' lives more than was necessary. "Mr. McGarrity took charge with the Eddystone manager. The money Tadgh brought sealed the deal. Tadgh is off to New York City to organize the freighter through our Irish contact with Mr. Devoy. He might be there for a while."

Even though it went without saying, he hugged Kathy and added, "You can't breathe a word about any of this."

The listeners nodded before Kathy asked, "Jack?"

"Yes, my love, via coded telegram."

"How will they manage to get the . . . ah . . . shipment to New York?"

Collin winced—he had said more than he should have. "First, let me come in and sit down." He bent to unbuckle his galoshes. "Sam, your Lillie performed even better than your older Model T did on that trip Kathy and I took to New York years back."

Once he was finally seated by the fireplace in the parlor with a Jameson in hand, Kathy prodded her husband once more for details.

Collin said. "Let's leave the story at that. My job in the United States is done." He pulled Kathy down onto his lap and gave her a big kiss. "I'm so happy to be home again, darlin'."

Kathy gave him Liam to hold while she clung to her husband tenderly.

Later, when they were alone, Sam queried Collin for the full story. Since his mentor had saved them all from the clutches of Boyle at the Rock of Cashel, Collin felt obliged to keep him informed. "The process they've chosen is clever, really. To get the armament out of his factory, the manager will include it with a much larger shipment to Britain, which will be sent by train to New York overnight. Then, at a train stop between Eddystone and Philadelphia, Ridley Park Station, I think, our first boxcar, the last in the line will be shunted off to another train. At that point, the manager will change the manifest for our shipment to go to Queenstown. The top layer of boxes on every pallet will contain farm implements—shovels, rakes, and such. The new manifest will state their destination of a fictitious company in County Clare."

From his wallet, Collin produced a small piece of paper that had been folded several times. "You can see here the costs involved."

Sam perused the document:

Item	Qty	Unit Cost	Total Cost
Rifles	7,000	$30	$210,000
Bullets	1,000,000	$0.05	$50,000
Farm Implements	840	$20	$16,800
Pay Off	10%	$26,000	$26,000
Transportation	1	$10,000	$10,000
Expenses	1	$5,000	$5,000
Total			$317,800

The enormity of the operation astounded him. "But how in the world is all this money getting to the United States, Collin?"

"We smuggled it. Sewn into the lining of Tadgh's suitcase, boss."

Sam gasped and slowly shook his head in disbelief. "Don't you *ever* tell the women about that, my boy. Not one word." He rubbed his receding hairline, still not entirely able to grasp the machinations Collin had described. "This all fits into seven boxcars?"

"Three rifles to a box, nine rifle boxes to a pallet, and forty pallets fill up a boxcar. Eight hundred and forty boxes of farm implements form the top layer of all pallets. It all works out, with pallets of bullets in the last boxcar shipment." Collin folded and slipped the paper back into the inside pouch of his wallet.

"What if the inspectors want to look lower in the pallets?"

"Unlikely, Sam. Each pallet will weigh three-hundred and sixty pounds, and they will be roped down."

"I see. It sounds like you have it all figured out."

"Yes, Tadgh is on top of the process."

"When will they start with the first shipment?"

"Tadgh's waiting for confirmation that the storage facility in Queenstown is available."

Collin didn't hear anything from Philadelphia for over a week. Presumably, they were acquiring the farm tools and still waiting on the Irish end for the details of sea shipment and clandestine storage.

On Wednesday, January 31, the international newswires lit up. As predicted, Germany announced that it was resuming unrestricted submarine warfare on all classes of sea traffic in the war zone. Collin learned from the *Tely's* Washington journalist that the U.S. government was waiting for an American ship to be sunk in order to sever diplomatic ties with Germany. He telegraphed McGarrity. By return message, Joseph stated that Tadgh was still in Philadelphia but would soon be going back to Eddystone to try to get the shipments accelerated.

True to their word, Germany sank an American cargo ship, the *SS Housatonic*, carrying non-military grain and flour on its way from Galveston to Liverpool three days later. The German U-boat captain allowed the American crew to disembark in lifeboats before he blew the ship up with charges.

That humanitarian act did not placate the U.S. Government. They notified the German Ambassador Bernstorff that they were breaking diplomatic ties.

Worried about Tadgh and the gunrunning timing, Collin conferred with his boss, Jim Fletcher, who told him, "This doesn't mean the U.S. will declare war on Germany, Collin. Not yet. It will take some further threat to their country."

Collin relayed this information in a coded telegram to McGarrity, who wrote back in their agreed cypher:

'Bernstorff asked to collect all sensitive papers for disposal. Stop. Tadgh wants all 7 shipments combined and ready by March 1. Stop.'

Two weeks went by without any word from Tadgh. Then, on Friday, February 23, Collin was called, along with Jim Fletcher, into the office of the publisher, Mr. Robertson.

"Our friend Jack Healy telegraphed some confidential information to me today. He is not publishing it in *The Irish Times*—not right away, at least—and asks us not to divulge it, either. Seems the British intercepted a coded telegram via Western Union from the German foreign minister, Arthur Zimmermann, to the German ambassador in Mexico, von Eckhardt. Germany is requesting that Mexico join them in battle if the United States enters the war for the Allies. In exchange, they will return Texas, New Mexico, and Arizona to the Mexicans when the United States is defeated. British authorities are going to tell the U.S. ambassador in Britain, Walter Page, tomorrow. We need to be ready to get this scoop when Jack clears it for publication."

Collin realized the implications even before his boss said it.

"This threat will undoubtedly cause the United States to enter the war, Collin."

"How did they intercept this message, sir? Do we know?"

"Jack has an inside source. Room 40 at the British Admiralty has had the German code for several months from a captured U-boat. When the German trans-Atlantic cable was cut by the Allies early in the war, the Germans were forced to use the English cable via Norway through Lands' End, Britain. When this Zimmermann telegram is divulged openly to the public, as it undoubtedly will be, the trick will be to find a way to convince Germany that the leak was on their side. That way they won't know that the Brits have cracked their code."

Collin chuckled before responding. "I see. The German foreign secretary is a fierce mouser, that one, but he will have his come-uppance now with this *faux-pas*, I'd say."

"This should be good news for our Canadian boys in the fight, Collin. The question is, how quickly can the Yanks mobilize? That will be your assignment, Collin. I want you to focus on this story, boy, just as you did on the post Easter Rising Irish affairs. Now go out and do us proud, but remember, mum's the word for now."

"Understood, sir."

That afternoon, Collin telegraphed McGarrity in code:

> 'New aggression. We believe United States declaration of war likely imminent. Stop. Notify McCarthy. Stop. Keep me informed. Stop.'

Chapter Five
Gunrunning

Monday, February 26, 1917
Eddystone Rifle Works

*H*enry Silvermann kept Tadgh waiting in the lobby for three hours. Finally, he appeared, looking exhausted. "It's been hectic. Come with me outside where we can talk."

They stood in the cold rain.

"You won't believe what's going on with our management. We're having to do contingency forecasts and plans to greatly expand our production rate at once."

"In case the United States goes to war?"

"It's not *if* anymore, Mr. McCarthy. It's *when*."

Tadgh noted that the plant foreman seemed agitated, his eyes darting around the yard before returning to meet Tadgh's stare.

"That's why I need you to accelerate the shipments, Mr. Silvermann."

"Our government just authorized merchant ships to add armament starting today. I'm not sure I can fill your order. It will take too long to bury it in with our other shipments. I'm being watched like a hawk."

"We need the arms. How long before you go to war?"

"I don't know. Maybe a month. But we have to gear up, in any event."

Tadgh decided to push the issue. Although highly risky, it was the only way under the circumstances. "I want you to deliver my whole order when you send your next shipment to Britain. When is it going out?"

"What? Impossible! That would be almost fifteen percent of

the shipment. I'm not even sure we will be honoring our British commitments in future."

"I'm willing to increase your fee to twelve percent."

"I'll have to see. I highly doubt I can hide that big a consignment."

"Fifteen percent and that's high as I'll go. That's almost forty-thousand dollars. It's highway robbery."

"All right. I'll try."

Tadgh debated using a forceful approach then decided against it. He had to get the weapons clear of New York before it was too late. "Shake hands on it. When's the next British shipment date?"

"Monday, April 2nd,"

"Why not March?"

"We have to make the guns and wait until a transport ship is available in New York City. Convoy, you know." Suddenly, Henry grabbed Tadgh by the arm and pulled him around the corner of the building.

"What—?"

"Quiet." Silvermann peered back around the edge. "Good, he's gone."

"Who's gone?"

"That bastard, Thompson."

Tadgh remembered that Joseph had told him about the plant supervisor, a stickler.

"Your boss, I presume."

"It wouldn't do, my being seen with you, Tadgh. He's the biggest obstacle."

Tadgh brought them back on track. "You'll get the money on delivery."

"I need fifty percent now to pay for materials."

"I can give you seventy-five thousand tomorrow, cash. The rest on delivery."

Silvermann figured it out in his head. "Three hundred and fifteen thousand, eight hundred total will leave two hundred and forty thousand, eight hundred on delivery."

Tadgh shrugged his shoulders, nonchalant. "Sounds about right. I'll let you know at the end of the week." His insides churned.

Silvermann turned away as he said, "Come back Friday with the money."

Tadgh reported in to McGarrity on Wednesday at his home away from his liquor warehouse. They sat alone in winged chairs around the fireplace in his high-ceiling library overlooking the river.

"We had the same problem with Silvermann on the Hindu-German shipment. He will come through," McGarrity reassured, pouring Tadgh a second sherry.

His guest accepted the liquor even though he would have greatly preferred stout or Jameson. "That was before a declaration of war was on the table, sir."

"Mark my words, Tadgh. Henry will deliver the arms."

Tadgh wasn't so sure. The foreman had appeared frazzled and afraid of his boss, the colonel. "I'm uncomfortable giving the man even seventy-five thousand dollars without anything in writing, Joseph. What happens if he just walks away with the money?"

McGarrity fidgeted in his chair before responding. "Let's just say that he knows things would not go well with him in our Irish community. Your money will be recorded as a sale to the British so that he can get the arms released from the factory but the paperwork he gives you will reflect your desired procurement path."

"I'm still not convinced."

"This is the way it must be done in the gunrunning business. Remember the guns we shipped you on the freighter *Talmooth* at the time of O'Donovan's funeral passage. Same process. You got the weapons, yes?"

"Yes, sir, we did."

"Whatever happened to our lad who brought them to you, Driscoll? I heard he disappeared."

"Murdered, sir. We heard him call out by name up on the deck of the freighter just before they lowered the pallet of arms precipitously in an attempt to sink my hooker. Then I heard a splash, just before I was knocked over the gunnels of my ship. I think he was likely clubbed and dumped overboard for the fishes."

"It's a wicked business, Tadgh, but essential."

"Aye, sir, but you don't know the half of it."

"Someday you'll have to tell me all about the revolution. I'm stuck here on the other side of the Atlantic."

Tadgh smiled and finished the last of his sherry from a vintage Bohemian crystal goblet, setting the glass on the mahogany fireside table. "Someday, once we've driven the bastards off our island for good. But you must take pride in the efforts and finances that your Clan na Gael have provided to fuel our Cause."

McGarrity got up and stretched his legs, then bent and warmed his hands by the roaring blaze in the fireplace before responding. "I suppose, but do you realize how painful it was to expend all that time and money only to have the German arms on the *Aud-Norge* sunk at the mouth of Queenstown Harbour last April just before the Rising?"

"Yes, I do, sir. I was there on the Cunard dock lamenting that scuttle event and its likely impact on the Rising. And I was in that rath on Banna Strand with your man Casement when he was caught by the blighters."

McGarrity raised his eyebrows and sat back down, looking at Tadgh with newly found respect. "It seems that you have a lot to tell me someday soon, then, Tadgh. But I have my own news for you."

The rebel turned in his chair to face his host.

McGarrity said, "I have a contact for you regarding the Browning Automatic Rifle. Browning himself demonstrated the weapon yesterday, I'm told, in Southern Washington at Congress Heights in front of senators and military officials. They were so impressed that they are awarding a contract to go into production on the spot in case of a declaration of war."

Tadgh perked up and took notice. "What are its specifications?"

"The BAR, as it is called, weighs about sixteen pounds and has an effective range of fifteen hundred yards. Its firing rate is five hundred shells a minute, and it is gas operated. I think it would be best for guerrilla warfare."

Tadgh whistled. "Where can I contact Browning?"

"The gun will likely be manufactured at several plants, but the most obvious selection will be the Winchester Repeating Arms Company in New Haven, Connecticut. They would be the right organization to contact. The best estimate of when these weapons will be available is June of next year. If you won't need them until then, I might be able to work a deal with this contact at Winchester. It may be difficult if the war isn't over by then."

Tadgh was enthused about the automatic weapon order. His rebels could do with some of those.

McGarrity saw Tadgh salivating and said, "Once you are sure that Silvermann will deliver the rifles, I suggest that you head up to New Haven and check out the BAR with my contact, Mr. Isaac Spaulding. He already has the drawings."

"I'll do that. It will give me the opportunity to finalize the shipment plans out of New York City."

"By the way, Tadgh, how's your wife doing?"

"I had a telegram from her a few days ago at my hotel via my contact in Queenstown. She's coping, but this being her first time with child, it's causing her some pain. She's a nurse, so I'm sure she will be all right. I'm anxious to get back to Ireland, though, don't ya know."

"Soon enough. lad. Just make sure you and the guns are safe and sound at home."

"Aye that, Joseph."

Tadgh entrusted the bulk of the money to McGarrity who promptly stored it in his home safe behind a series of books about the American Revolution. "I'll have it, ah, *converted* into U.S. dollars for you tomorrow. You can pick up what you need for Henry's down payment at the end of the day back here."

Tadgh realized he was outstaying his welcome, so he shook Joseph's hand and headed for the door. "That's fine, sir. I'll see you then."

Two days later, Silvermann committed to delivery of the total shipment of rifles and ammunition on the night of April 2. He had convinced his suspicious supervisor, Thompson, to increase immediate production of rifles for Britain since the future priority would likely be for United States troops. That way, the extra seven boxcars would not be so conspicuous.

In early March, Tadgh went to New Haven by train and contacted Remington. Without needing to know the destination of the machine guns, the plant manager seemed amenable to providing a small quantity of the Browning machine guns in future after development, and if the war needs were to abate. Tadgh resolved to tell Mick about this offer since he hoped to be using the rifles to free Ireland by the time that the machine gun was in production.

While he was away, the *New York Times* was full of news about frenzied U-boat activity in the Atlantic and elsewhere. More than ten ships a day were being sunk or scuttled, most with loss of life. Four U.S. vessels had already been sunk in the English Channel to Irish Sea corridor in March: the *Algonquin* and *Vigilancia* cargo ships on the 12th and 16th respectively, the *City of Memphis* passenger ship on the 17th, and the *Illinois* tanker on the 18th. The people and government of the United States were up in arms over the situation.

When Tadgh arrived back at the Cunard Pier Fifty-One in New York City on March 19, there was a coded message in a telegram awaiting him.

> 'Have booked passage, freighter *Pretoria*, part of the April 4 convoy, Pier Forty-Six, headed for Queenstown before Southampton. Stop. Contact Captain Josephson, a friend from Cunard. Stop. Jack. Stop.'

Tadgh knew he could trust Jack Jordan, the manager of the Cunard Line port in Queenstown. After all, he had saved Morgan when the *Lusitania* was sinking and had endured the funeral pyre in the Rock of Cashel cathedral ruins with the rest of the Clans.

Tadgh immediately hunted down the *Pretoria*. She was undergoing repairs from a minor collision at sea during a U-boat attack of her convoy on the last crossing. Josephson had great things to say for his former boson colleague. He agreed to load Tadgh's shipment on April 3 after the rest of his cargo had already been packed on board, making it easier to offload first in Queenstown. As per Silvermann, there would be forty, three-hundred- and sixty-pound pallets of boxes in each boxcar. The top layer of each would contain farm implements that the bill of lading manifest would designate for the entire shipment. Tadgh did not divulge the true nature of his cargo to the captain.

Josephson informed him of the twelve thousand dollars transport charge, to be paid up front in cash upon loading.

Tadgh lied. "I'm sorry, Captain, but I was told it would be eight thousand."

Josephson eyed this Irishman carefully. The Irish were not well liked in New York City and elsewhere. And they could be brutal. He needed the money since commercial shipping would soon be curtailed. "Ten thousand, then."

Tadgh had met his target. "Done, sir." Tadgh and the captain shook hands on the deal. "Can you recommend a place to stay nearby tonight?"

"I like the American Seaman's Friend Society Sailors' Home and Institute. It's within walking distance east of here."

"That's a mouthful, sir. Sounds like a place where old sailors go to die."

"On the contrary, Mr. McCarthy. It is a grand six-story stone hotel recently designed and built by William Boring."

"Never heard of him, I'm afraid."

"He designed the immigrant station on Ellis Island, lad. The rooms at the hotel are unique; they look like cabins at sea, they do. There's a fine café in the hotel named The Old Rose. Many of the *Titanic* survivors stayed at the Institute during the inquiry and the remaining ship's crew held a memorial service there four days after the sinking. Truly historic for its young age."

Tadgh turned to leave the well-worn bridge, thanking the captain for his recommendation.

"Don't be late on the third, lad. The tide waits for no man, as they say."

Tadgh understood the consequences. "Aye, captain."

Tadgh met with the aging Clan na Gael leader John Devoy the next day over lunch at his home. In his seventies, Devoy talked about his long-standing love for Ireland and its freedom. He explained that he had been incarcerated along with O'Donovan Rossa and was finally released to be exiled from Ireland, ordered to never return. He said that these two patriots were part of the "Cuba Five" who departed their homeland in exile in 1871 to establish a funding organization for Irish revolution in America.

Tadgh thought of his ancestor Florence who had been similarly incarcerated and kept from returning to the land he loved, from 1601 until his death in 1640. This elder statesman with his long unkempt beard was clearly suffering from isolation away from his true home.

"I understand that you are a journalist, sir, at *The New York Herald*, like my brother-in-law Collin."

"Aye, Mr. McCarthy. For many years now. But most of my energy goes into the Clan now."

Tadgh saw a man etched with decades of strife, yet still standing tall, eyes ever burning with the passion for freedom.

The old man jumped to the matter at hand. "Have you seen the papers today, lad? Wilson's cabinet has just voted to go to war. Now it's up to Congress. You'd better get the rifles here in the next few days or the port authority may stop commercial shipping."

"The next convoy leaves on April 4, sir. I can't accelerate the process, I'm afraid. I'll be heading back to Pennsylvania to make sure the transport goes smoothly."

"What can I do to help?"

"What about a backup plan, Mr. Devoy?"

"Call me John. What do you have in mind?"

"We need a safe storage facility here near the docks in case our guns can't be shipped overseas right away."

"I see what you mean. Let's work on that starting tomorrow morning."

Back at the Institute for the night, Tadgh sat down alone in the Old Rose café for supper. Oh, how he hungered to be back in Creagh with his loving wife. He'd been gone now for almost three months and preferred his home in the country to the noise and confinement of big cities like Dublin. So he hated what he called the monstrosity of New York.

It took Tadgh and Devoy five excruciating days to find and secure an old storage building in the derelict part of the docks. War talk raged through the metropolis. Tadgh read in the newspapers that the moneymen on Wall Street were salivating.

Tadgh took John to meet Josephson and left the Clan na Gael leader the ten thousand dollars shipment money in case something happened to him prior to the munitions reaching Dock Forty-Six.

On the 27, Devoy saw Tadgh off at Penn Station.

"Let's keep our fingers crossed, then. We're counting you, son. Thank you for everything."

"Don't thank me, sir. Thank my ancestor Florence MacCarthaigh Reagh. You remind me of him."

The patriots, two generations apart in a land far away from the country they loved, locked eyes, and reached out to shake hands.

"Someday, Tadgh, you'll have to tell me that tale of how you came upon your inheritance. It is truly a Godsend."

"Someday, after we have rid our homeland of the English beast, John. I promise to return to New York with the guns on the third. Then we can fuel the revolution!"

With that said, Tadgh headed back to the Penn Hotel in Philadelphia.

McGarrity had bad news. A telegram had just arrived from Collin in Canada.

> 'Morgan telegrammed me. Stop. Get home as soon as possible. Stop. Pregnancy. Stop. Jack. Stop.'

Tadgh was torn. Damn. What did that mean? *To hell with the rifles. I've got to get home now.*

He settled down when he realized that his soonest transit home would be on the *Pretoria*, leaving New York harbor eight days hence and arriving at Queenstown seven days later, if all went well. His mind raced. He had to make sure that freighter sailed with him on it.

Tadgh telegraphed Jack asking for clarification, and Jack responded that he would go to Creagh, himself. Tadgh reasoned that Morgan would have had Aidan go to Skibbereen to send a telegram, but she would not take the risk of having the telegraph office deliver a response to the house at Creagh.

Joseph said that Silvermann demanded an extra five hundred dollars to pay off the switchman in the Ridley Park train station.

"He can pay it out of his already outrageous fee."

"You'll have to talk to him, Tadgh."

Two days later, Tadgh had a talk with Silvermann that involved some physical persuasion, just enough to negate the demand but not enough to make him bolt.

On April 2, Silvermann sent a message to McGarrity telling Tadgh not to come to the rifle works. Instead, he could inspect the shipment in the rail yard at Ridley Station after his boxcars were separated from the main train. There would be an hour to spare before the northbound Zephyr would pick them up on its route to New York City. Silvermann would accompany the shipment with the switched paperwork and pallet labels, and Tadgh could pay him then.

Tadgh spent the day with McGarrity at his liquor store, uncharacteristically anxious as he paced the floor, avoiding the booze. He knew McGarrity trusted Silvermann, but this change of plan sounded like a trap. He hated waiting and not being in control.

Meanwhile, in Washington, the debate over whether to go to war raged on. That day, President Wilson addressed Congress, finally recommending war with Germany, but not against United States citizens of Prussian descent. Jeannette Rankin, just sworn in that day as the first woman in Congress, threatened to vote against going to war.

House Majority Leader Claude Kitchin from North Carolina declared his opposition with a speech to the Congress. "I implore my colleagues to preserve America's place as the last hope of peace on earth, good will toward men by opposing the war measure."

But most members of the House seemed to support the President. The vote could come at any time.

McGarrity drove Tadgh down to Ridley Station, some ten miles south of Philadelphia after supper. The building was almost deserted by ten o'clock after the last passenger train had departed. Only the station master and one switch worker remained on site in the yard.

The two Irishmen sat quietly on the wooden bench just outside the main door, under the roofline of the station. A soft rain could be seen drifting down through the one light shining at the end of the platform, hardly enough to illuminate the first few feet of the weathered wood deck.

"We're counting on you, Tadgh."

"That's what John Devoy said last week. I sense that I am

fulfilling my destiny as set in motion by my ancestors. It is God's will, and He has provided Divine intervention in the affairs of man to make my life's journey possible."

"How so?"

"The sinking of the *Lusitania*."

"You think God caused the sinking to shape your destiny?"

"No, I think God made sure that my Morgan was on that ship, that she survived the sinking, that the German U-boat nearly collided with my hooker, that they suggested I look for survivors and that my path would intersect with Morgan lying almost dead on the wreckage."

"That's a tall tale, lad."

"True tale, so it is. Without Morgan, my link between the McCarthys and the O'Donnells would not exist and the acquisition of these arms for our revolution would not have been possible."

"So, you and young Collin are . . ."

"Yes, brothers-in-law and the two remaining Clan Chieftains."

Joseph looked quizzically at his bench partner but didn't pursue that line of conversation. Tadgh didn't want to go there anyway.

A couple of times the yard worker came close to the station and Tadgh fingered the Luger in his pocket. The bag at his feet contained two hundred and forty thousand, eight hundred dollars, and he wasn't taking any chances. The remaining almost twenty-five thousand dollars plus freighter shipment charges were sewn into the lining of his trench coat.

At the same time, the station master, on duty until the two freight trains went through, loaded seven cartridges into the Commander magazine of his Colt .45 1911. He slid the magazine into the gun, racked the slide, and thumbed the manual safety. The pistol was now "cocked and locked." He grinned. *This heist is going to be like taking candy from a baby.*

The 11:45 freight rolled to Ridley Station on time and made an unusual stop, with the last seven cars lined up in front of the building. The Irishmen watched as the yard worker disconnected the boxcars from the train, then walked forward and disappeared into a compartment opening of the freight train's locomotive. A few minutes later, he returned, and the 11:45 continued its journey, fifteen minutes behind schedule.

The yard worker backed a single locomotive off a sidetrack until it sat idle just in front of the cars.

Silvermann emerged from the back boxcar, clipboard in hand. He waved at the Irishmen who stood up to greet him.

"There's been a change of plans, boys. This locomotive will be taking your shipment to New York City."

Tadgh gripped the bag and put his other hand in his Luger pocket. "Why?"

"The 12:45 freight has been diverted to Pittsburgh."

Tadgh detected a hesitation in the man's speech. "Show us the weapons."

Silvermann led them to the back car and slid open its side door. "It's all here, as you can see."

The rows of pallets were arranged with enough space to slip sidewise along them. Tadgh examined one of the pallets and counted the rest. He opened one of the top boxes in the pallet to find a small shovel and rake. "All the top boxes in the top pallets . . ."

"Contain farm implements, in all the boxcars," Silvermann stated.

Tadgh undid the rope fastening of the pallet and removed the top box that he had opened. Then he pried open the next box down and the box below that. Rifles, and good ones, to be sure.

Silvermann showed him the contents, boxcar after boxcar, until Tadgh had satisfied himself that the shipment was whole. The last boxcar contained the ammunition, carefully hidden in boxes that looked identical to the rifle containers. He opened two and estimated the quantity by counting rows and height. As with the rifles, the top pallets also had farm implements stacked on the top row.

McGarrity warned, "If there is any discrepancy, Henry, we know where to find you."

Silvermann met McGarrity and Tadgh's stare and nodded his head. "It is as we agreed, I assure you. You will note that the pallets and boxes are labeled as weapons for delivery to the English. I needed to do this to get them out of the plant. Here is a set of duplicate label sheets that define farm implements to your "company" in Clare. There are sufficient quantities and binding tape for all pallets. You can change them out *en route*. Finally, here is the manifest that you will need to show to the ship's captain and the custom officials in New York. As you can see, it shows an adjusted price associated with the cost of the farm tools."

McGarrity flipped through the paperwork. "It looks like you have thought of everything, Henry, just like before."

"This one was more difficult, because of the size of this single shipment and the proximity to war. One day later and the shipment might have been stopped by the colonel."

The yard worker approached the men and Silvermann introduced Fred Larson. "This is my man. Experienced train engineer. He'll see you safe and sound to the freighter dock in New York City. All right lad, let's get the locomotive connected and then these gentlemen can be on their way."

Fred padded away into the mist toward his locomotive.

Silvermann produced a second invoice with the agreed price of the armament less the down payment of seventy-five thousand dollars. "I presume you have the money, McCarthy."

"Yes, two hundred and forty thousand eight hundred dollars as agreed." Tadgh handed him the bag.

Silvermann opened it and shuffled through the thousand-dollar bills. "It looks like it is all there. This will square me with my management for the weapons."

"Plus, a hefty sum for your efforts."

"That, too, Mr. McCarthy."

"Hands up, gents." The stationmaster had materialized out of the mist with his drawn Colt. He was accompanied by two thugs also brandishing handguns. "I'll take that bag and we'll confiscate this train."

"George! What are you doing? You'll get your cut; you know that."

"Shut up, Henry."

Tadgh could see the thieves head-on not twenty feet away. They had spread out to limit their exposure. Joseph had his back to the thieves and was in Tadgh's line of fire. He could get George, and maybe one other, but not likely all three.

"Give me the bag, Henry."

The plant foreman to Tadgh's right hesitated and George fired a warning shot that whizzed past Silvermann's head.

Tadgh realized that these goons were not going to leave anyone alive who had witnessed the transaction. He motioned to Joseph with his eyes to drop to the ground. "Don't you want to see the merchandise?" he asked as he flung his left arm out towards the last boxcar, while snatching his Luger from his right pocket.

Joseph dove to the ground just before Tadgh's nine mm bullet, which would have otherwise struck him, instead thunked into George's skull. Tadgh dropped to the ground to present as small a target as possible and rolled left, away from Silvermann. He fired again, hitting one of the goons in the heart. The third thief fired wildly in Tadgh's direction, but the bullet missed and clanged off a boxcar wheel.

Tadgh pulled the trigger on his Luger once more. Nothing happened. *It's jammed!* Smiling wickedly, the thief took a bead on his adversary. He was in no hurry. Now the loot could be all his. Seconds later, he was dead on the ground after a crescent wrench, swung by Fred, crushed his skull. The engineer had heard the commotion and had crept up behind the thieves in the mist.

The entire shootout took less than half a minute. Luckily, the would-be thieves hadn't been expert marksmen.

"Thank you, Fred. Everyone all right, comrades?" Tadgh asked, as he stepped forward to clap the engineer on the shoulder.

"Yes, thanks to you," Joseph said, picking himself up and dusting off his pants. "Henry, you should be glad to pay your train engineer his cut. And Tadgh, I see that these weapons will be in good hands."

"We're trained, to be sure."

Henry Silvermann had turned pale. "B-b-but how am I going to explain the bodies? George was well-known around here."

Tadgh reached down and grabbed the dead stationmaster's shoulders. "No problem. Fred, help me put these bodies on the train. We'll dispose of them somewhere between Philadelphia and New York, far from here."

Tadgh turned to Silvermann. "Not a word of this. Understood?"

The plant supervisor swallowed and nodded his head.

"I suggest we get this train moving before the police arrive. Someone must have heard the shots even at this late hour."

"I left a car here earlier this afternoon," said Silvermann. "Over in the parking lot."

"I think you'd best hightail it, now," Tadgh told him.

"I'm on my way." Silvermann picked up the satchel of money, gave his engineer his cut, and disappeared into the mist.

"God protect you, son," McGarrity said, then headed for his Model T on a run.

The bodies were loaded, and the train got underway. By that time, Silvermann and McGarrity were long gone. When the police arrived, they found some hastily covered up bloodstains on the train platform, but that was all.

The trip to the docks of New York City went smoothly with no interference. They dumped the bodies in the Delaware River when they crossed it north of Burlington before dawn. They had to stop four times for Tadgh to move between boxcars so he could replace the pallet marking sheets.

Fred backed the train down the siding to Pier Forty-Six just before noon. Captain Josephson stepped away from what looked to

Tadgh to be frantic loading operations, and he lumbered up to the train.

"Thank God you're here. Our departure has been moved up to tonight from tomorrow. There's word they're going to shut down commercial operations at midnight."

Tadgh summoned Fred and explained the situation. Together they commandeered six of the *Pretoria*'s dockworkers and began offloading the pallets onto seven larger metal platforms on the dock beside the ship. By four o'clock, the boxcars were unloaded. Fred and his train had departed.

Devoy finally showed up with the transport money after Tadgh called him to hurry.

Josephson came down off the bridge and checked the manifest. "Farm tools, are they?"

"Yes. That's right." Tadgh paid him half his transport fee.

"I guess it's none of my business, long as you pay, boy."

"The rest when we dock in Queenstown."

"I'll be needin' it all, now, lad. We may get torpedoed at sea."

Reluctantly, Tadgh paid him the rest. Without immediate payment, the weapons were not going to be loaded onto the ship.

Devoy stared the captain in the face. "I'm counting on you to get this man and his machinery safe to Ireland, Josephson."

"Come hell or high water, sir. We'll have our cargo loaded in an hour, then we'll hoist your shipment on board last. I've got to be battened down by nine to clear the harbor. Anything not on board by eight, we'll have to leave on the dock. It's going to be hell to get a tug when we need it. Half the ships at the docks are trying to get out."

Tadgh could hear ship sirens going off all down the line.

At six-thirty a customs inspector visited the *Pretoria*. After he checked the ship's manifest with Josephson on the bridge, he descended back onto the dock where Tadgh was standing.

"The captain says you are shipping farm tools to Ireland. Seems a mite frivolous to be shipping such implements overseas during this damn war. I've a mind to hold your shipment until we decide if we are indeed going to war. Lots of better things to send overseas."

"We're providing food for our soldiers, sir. An army marches on its stomach, they say."

"You've got a point there, but how many tools does Ireland need? Let me inspect the shipment."

Tadgh wished he had come after the guns were aboard the *Pretoria*. Tadgh opened one of the top boxes on the top pallet to reveal a shovel and trowel.

"Fine. Let me see the box below it."

Tadgh's stomach turned handsprings. He thought frantically. Should he go for his Luger? He had cleared the jam during the train ride. There were five bullets left. *No. Stall for time.* Tadgh started to pry up the top of the next box down, pretending to struggle with it. Then a familiar voice called down from above.

"Inspector, I have a manifest question for you. Could you return to the bridge?"

Josephson! Thank God! Tadgh would have slumped and sighed in relief, but he knew that would rouse the inspector's suspicions past the point of no return.

Twenty minutes later, the inspector rushed off the ship, late for his next inspection.

Tadgh looked down at Josephson, who was watching the dock below, and saluted.

The captain returned the salute. He had many Irish longshoremen to thank in his job, and they had been given a raw deal on the docks of New York City.

By nine o'clock, the shipment had been successfully hoisted aboard and battened down. The crew of the *Pretoria* waited for tug support. By ten-forty-five, the bow and stern lines were still firmly secured to the dock cleats. Josephson paced the bridge.

Tadgh raced off the ship and sprinted for Pier Fifty-One where the White Star troop carrier *Teutonic* was just being loosed from its moorings. He leaped off the dock barely grabbing onto the stern of the tug *Bronx Beauty* just as it was beginning to nose the liner out into the Hudson River. Thirty seconds later, he was in the wheelhouse.

Swiveling in his chair, Captain Jim McAllister demanded, "Who in blazes are you and what are you doing on my boat?" His second in command picked up a longshoreman's hook.

"I'm Tadgh McCarthy, sir, from Skibbereen. Do I detect an Irish accent?"

The captain motioned his man to lower the hook and leave the bridge. "My father by name of James McAllister came from Cushendall, lad, in sixty-four."

"Did he, now. County Antrim, sir?"

"Aye, lad. You've a strange way of dropping in, I have to say."

Tadgh agreed.

"Skibbereen," the captain mused. "That's great hunger country."

"To be sure, a travesty. What's your politics?"

"I hate the English if that's what you mean. Give us a minute." McAllister steered the tug about until it nudged the troop liner's bow out into the river. Then he circled around to nudge the stern. A squall was blowing in from the west.

Tadgh checked his watch. Eleven-fifteen.

"Enough to support her fight for freedom, Captain McAllister?"

"Aye, if I could from over here."

"You can assist me to help our Cause. I need to get back to Ireland and my ship must leave in the next hour. Trust me that it will fuel our fight for freedom."

"They're shutting down commercial traffic at midnight, lad."

"Don't I know it. Can you give us a tow?"

"What ship and which pier?"

"The *Pretoria* at Pier Forty-Six. It's a matter of life and death, literally millions of lives."

"Is it, lad? Well, now. I will have *Teutonic* out of here in ten minutes, and we can go see."

"Much obliged. Ireland thanks you."

The *Bronx Beauty* arrived at Pier Forty-Six at quarter to midnight. Tadgh could see the *Pretoria* still tied to the dock, and an official was in a heated conversation with Captain Josephson.

McAllister pointed. "He's a member of the Board of Embarkation for the U.S. government, Tadgh, obviously here to stop your ship from leaving."

"You know him?"

"I don't normally run my ships, but with the workload tonight, I took the helm of the *Beauty*. I serve on that Board."

Tadgh thought and genuflected, *Lord be merciful. Divine intervention.* If there was ever a time he needed God, it was now!

McAllister blew his whistle and pulled his tug up against the pier just forward of the freighter. His man jumped out and secured the stern so that the captain and Tadgh could disembark. In the distance, a ship struck eight bells.

When they reached the inspector he said, "Captain McAllister, I was just telling Captain Josephson here that his ship will be detained pending our wartime status."

"I see, Tom. But the deadline is midnight, is it not?"

"Yes, and we just had eight bells."

"I understand from my friend Tadgh that there are supplies on the ship that are vital to the war effort against Germany and therefore important for our country. I am here to steer this ship on its way. I ask you to let her go."

Tadgh had told him about the farm implements being necessary for food supply and McAllister had been smart enough not to mention Ireland.

Tom checked his watch. "I don't know. I could get into trouble."

Tadgh fingered the Luger in his pocket.

"I'll cover for you, Tom. This is important. No one will see the delay in this squall."

"No. I can't allow it. A deadline's a deadline. What about all the other ships now being held?"

Tadgh felt in his left pocket. The extra five hundred dollars in case Silvermann or his man balked.

He pulled out half of the bills and thrust them into Tom's hand. "Would this help?"

McAllister slapped the inspector on the back. "C'mon, Tom. Be a sport."

"Well, all right, Jim. But you better have them out of here in the next fifteen minutes."

"Right you are." But Tom didn't hear McAllister. The inspector was already racing down the pier. He didn't want to be anywhere near the freighter when it left the dock.

Tadgh shook McAllister's hand as he turned quickly to board his tug, placing the remaining seed money into his palm. "Thank you, Captain. You don't know how much you've helped our Cause, to be sure."

McAllister looked at the bills and handed them back. "Your thanks is enough, lad. You keep the cash. You'll need it. Just go save Ireland."

They shared salutes and Tadgh dashed for the gangplank on the *Pretoria*. Captain Josephson was already on the bridge barking orders. His deckhands loosed the stays from the dock cleats and jumped back on board. Tadgh hardly had enough time to leap onto the stairs, covering three feet of the Hudson River in doing so.

From his automobile on nearby W. Street Service Road, John Devoy had watched the desperate efforts to get the *Pretoria* under way. He saw Tadgh dart away and come back with the tug minutes later. He heard the midnight ship bells and was now breathing a sigh of relief as the ship cleared the harbor to join the convoy. His job was money and politics, not hand-to-hand operations. *Thank God for the likes of Tadgh McCarthy. If anyone can get these munitions through, it's him. All we need is ten thousand more like him!*

Chapter Six
Reunited

*M*organ was worried. Now in the second trimester, her pregnancy had not been an easy one. At first, she laughingly passed off the nausea and severe cramps as the forming fetus being a rebel's child, but in these last few weeks she had been bleeding off and on. At one point she went to a doctor's office in Skibbereen but left without seeing him because of all the information they wanted her to divulge. She was on her own, although Tadgh's brother Aidan offered to help if he could.

Morgan remembered poor Angie back at the orphanage. Only fifteen, she had been raped by one of the guards. They all lived in fear of that fate. There was no recourse. The one doctor that Fredricson employed only came around when there was a death or near-death situation, and he had turned a blind eye to sexual misconduct of the staff. If the girls could work, so be it. That was why Morgan had taken up the science of nursing on her own, to help those children afflicted from various accidents and illnesses.

It was Angie's situation that taught them about pregnancy, and in her case miscarriage. The terror of the night when Angie died haunted Morgan still. She couldn't stop the bleeding after the fetus and placenta were expelled from the young woman's body. Her good friend died in Morgan's arms, and she couldn't do anything to stop it.

Of course, now, having worked as a nurse at Rotunda, the Dublin Women's Hospital, Morgan knew the symptoms and the treatment for the agony of miscarriage. And that is why she was now worried. In the past two days, the pain in her lower back had intensified, and she felt weak.

Michael Collins had telephoned and talked to Aiden yesterday in code. Devoy had reported that Tadgh had facilitated the *Pretoria*'s departure from New York Harbor on the eve of America's entry into WWI. He was now steaming homeward to land in Queenstown on the tenth. Five days away. Tadgh had sent oblique telegrams telling of his exploits in America, but she hadn't seen him in three long winter months. God how she needed her husband here beside her now, and his convoy needed to successfully navigate through the U-boat infested waters of the Northern Atlantic. Morgan wondered whether the anxiety of Tadgh's crossing could be causing the pains she was feeling.

On the night of the ninth, it happened. Morgan's water broke and her tiny baby boy miscarried while she was lying in bed. There were no contractions, just the silent loss of a life, her son's life. And like the case of her friend Angie, she couldn't do anything to save him.

Morgan was devastated. He had just started kicking the week before, and now he lay lifeless on the sheets beside her. Morgan was not used to feeling helpless. There had always been something she could do to take charge of her life, even in the depths of her separation from Tadgh in Belgium during the war. But not now. She had failed to save the little one, Tadgh's child. Her body had failed her. There was no excuse that could relieve her of the guilt she felt in her brain, in her heart, in her soul.

The next morning, Aidan, bless him, made a simple wooden coffin and that afternoon they buried her son at sea just off Cape Clear Island, befitting an officer of naval rank. It was a radiant day with the sun beaming down through wispy clouds to the west.

Morgan was lost in her reverie, but Aidan noticed something out at sea, tiny at first, on the southern horizon. A freighter convoy of several ships. As they got closer, he counted ten, no, sixteen ships in all, steaming east.

He gently prodded his sister-in-law who was seated with him at the helm. "Morgan, dear, look."

Morgan paid him no mind.

Aidan shook her and pointed to the southern horizon. "Look. I think that's Tadgh's convoy coming!"

Morgan looked up and squinted. *He's too late. We're all too late. He'll never forgive me.*

From the Cunard Pier in Queenstown, Jack Jordan eagerly waited for the *Pretoria* to round the headland. Soon this ship, with its clandestine weaponry to enable the revolution, would be passing directly over the *Aud-Norge* German cargo ship lying at the bottom of the entrance to Queenstown Harbour, with its guns meant for the Republicans rusting and useless. It was hoped that this time the British Navy would not be escorting the freighter. It was getting late in the evening. The sun had just set.

John Devoy had sent a message to Michael Collins to say that Tadgh's ship needed to leave a day early. News of the American Declaration of War on April 6, officially House Joint Resolution 169, was splashed across the front page of every newspaper worldwide, and the German submarine attacks had immediately intensified. Apparently, the Americans were not going to officially become an ally of Britain, only an enemy of Germany. They would not fight on the Western Front under British command, but under the U.S. army command of General Pershing. Devoy indicated the *Pretoria* had escaped New York City by the proverbial skin of its teeth, thanks to Tadgh's efforts.

At nine o'clock Captain Josephson signaled the pier that the convoy was fifteen miles off Old Kinsale Head, and he would be splitting off to come to Queenstown while they were going on to Liverpool. The voyage had been uneventful. The one U-boat that attempted an attack off Dingle had been thwarted.

Tadgh paced the deck. Once they were finally at sea, he had obsessed with his concern over whether Morgan was in trouble with her pregnancy. He would never be able to forgive himself if she were in serious danger, or worse, while he was gallivanting around in America. He'd wished he could just jump off and swim home after they passed the Fastnet Light just off Baltimore earlier in the afternoon. In fact, he had seen what looked like a Galway hooker on the northern horizon and wondered if it was his family coming out to meet his ship.

He had spent most of the voyage on deck where he could smell the sea air and be in his element. At least there was that. And now, he was in sight of his homeland. America had been such an industrious, and yet in its own way foreboding land.

When they passed by Old Kinsale head, with its lighthouse marking the danger to shipping, he felt a twinge in his left ankle. He had been trapped on his beloved *Republican* hooker as it went down from the second torpedo explosion. It was ghoulish to think of all those poor souls lost below him, forever entombed in the sunken *Lusitania* from the first U-boat attack at this spot. So much had happened in the two years since that tragic day in May of 1915. At least Morgan and Jack had survived that fateful day.

Pretoria docked at ten-thirty, with Tadgh being the first man off the boat. From the top of the gangway, Tadgh searched the dock for his family before leaving the ship. He had a sudden sense of foreboding since Aidan and Morgan were nowhere to be seen. Jack was waiting at the bottom of the stairs.

The two comrades embraced. "Thank God you're finally here."

"Damn, good to be home." Tadgh broke away first.

"And your cargo?"

"Safe on board, Jack. They'll offload it first before they press on to England. Thanks for all your efforts, my friend."

"Nothing to it. You've got to go home, though, Tadgh. I haven't heard from her in a week, but Morgan needs you. I brought your Kerry down, by my office. I can have your farming tools transported to the warehouse. It's just five minutes away, but you have to clear customs first. The inspector is in my office."

Tadgh called up to Josephson on the bridge wing, who waved back. His men had already opened the deck hatch and Jack ordered his longshoremen to crane the cargo out of the hold. An hour later, the large metal platforms were safely on Irish soil and the inspector was examining the shipment.

"I have two hundred and eighty pallets of farm tools destined for Counties Clare and Tyrone," Tadgh explained, handing the inspector the manifest. "Needed for production of food for the war effort, so they are."

The inspector perfunctorily opened one of the top boxes, noting it was a rake and shovel. It was late, and he was tired. "There are custom duties to be paid on the value of a thousand pounds."

Tadgh paid the duties on the spot with a portion of his remaining cash, and the inspector stamped and signed the manifest.

"Now go," Jack urged, pointing at the motorcycle.

Tadgh needed no coaxing, as the Kerry roared off into the night just after midnight. Fortunately, it was clear, with a full moon.

The light was on in the kitchen when Tadgh approached his home in Creagh at three o'clock. Morgan was up and came to the door at the sound of the motorcycle. Before she could step out into the cold, Tadgh swept her into his arms and gently carried her into the warm kitchen, kicking the door closed behind him.

"Oh Tadgh, you're back. I've missed you so," she sobbed, gripping him fiercely around the neck.

Tadgh noticed at once that something was wrong. "Your belly, *aroon*!" He touched her softly.

"I lost him, mavourneen. I'm so sorry." Her voice trailed off and the sobs came in convulsions.

"Him?" Tadgh's mouth worked, trying to contain his confusion and disbelief.

"Yes, my love. We buried him at sea."

"When?"

"Yesterday. I didn't want to bother you with my problems while you were on your mission."

Still holding her in his arms, Tadgh brushed the hair from her eyes, hollow with sadness. "Are you all right?"

"I'm in shock. Before this, I could never have imagined what it was like to carry a life inside me, one that you and I made. It was wonderful. I was so happy, fulfilled. Then something happened. I failed as a human being. Our living son perished, and I, a competent nurse, couldn't do anything to stop it. I've killed our son and let you down terribly. Can you ever forgive me?" Morgan's tears were streaming down her cheeks and splashing on Tadgh's neck as he held her fast, quivering.

"Of course, aroon. But there is nothing to forgive." Tadgh's mind spun, wondering at her sadness and strength. He looked her straight in the eye. "You did nothing wrong," and then he softly stroked her hair, her cheeks, waylaying the tears running down her cheeks.

Morgan shivered. "He just came out, so perfect but so still. I felt him kick inside of me just a week ago, you know." Her voice trailed off, and her hands trembled.

"Morgan. I should have been here!" Tadgh sensed, from a lack of response, that his wife was not going to argue with his statement. *I am such an eejit!*

"I should be able to try again someday." Morgan smiled through a veil of tears.

"Sweet Brigid. Thanks be to God."

"I am so sorry, Tadgh." Her reddened eyelids, swollen, framed the emerald orbs that he fell in love with that day when he plucked her from the sea.

Tadgh set her in a chair by the heated stove and knelt before her, holding her fast. "It must be devastating for you." He rubbed her stockinged feet.

Tadgh had been so caught up in gunrunning that he hadn't really taken the time to dwell on the imminent fact of becoming a father. These are normally women's concerns, and in due course, he would have a son. It had seemed so simple. Tadgh tried to beat back the selfish feeling that not having children, at least at this critical juncture, would free him and Morgan up to fight for the Cause. But now, seeing the look of despair in her eyes, he was filled with compassion for what she must have gone through, and was still going through. This was a critical juncture for her, perhaps the most significant moment in her already tumultuous life. Thank God for Aidan. *I should have been there for Morgan in her hour of need.*

She moaned against him and then whimpered, "His little heart just stopped beating. I couldn't get in there to save him."

Tadgh had never seen her like this before, so lost. Not even when she was delirious after being shot on St. Stephen's Green. The one time she couldn't come to the rescue. Being there, but powerless to save her own baby. Only a woman could imagine how that felt. He wondered, was there even a heart at that point in her pregnancy? He didn't know, hadn't been there, hadn't even taken the time to ponder it.

But it was too late for that now. He had made his choice. And after all, how was he to know that there was a dire need at home? Morgan was always in charge, especially where medical affairs were at stake.

Yet his feeling of exuberance with getting the arms safely to Irish soil was shattered by this most important tragedy in his wife's life, in his life.

A son to carry on his name, to become Clan Chieftain after him, what a miracle. Now dead and at the bottom of the sea.

He brushed the tangling black locks from her sodden eyes and stroked her forehead softly. "These things are God's will, aroon. I love you more now than ever, and I feel your agony. We will have a

117

son, many sons if you want them, in a bright, free future. Can I get you some tea, Morgan?"

"No, I just want to go to bed with you at last."

"Away overseas, I've longed for you these many nights and days, aroon."

"Right now, I just want my man to sleep with me and hold me in his arms."

Tadgh swooped Morgan up again and carried her to their bed. Exhausted, he laid her down and snuggled up around her, clothes, and all. In no time, they were asleep. Clouds descended and the wind came up, howling through the old casement windows, but they never heard it.

Next morning early, Tadgh awoke to the sounds of rattling pans in the kitchen below. Morgan was fast asleep with her arms locked around his torso. Tadgh gently pried himself out of her clutches and pulled the covers up around her before getting out of bed. The same bed and room where he had nursed her back from the dead after plucking her from the sea almost two years before. He had come to know her as a strong, almost invincible woman, his life partner. Now, just like before, she looked so vulnerable, yet so desirable. There would be more children when the time was right. It was God's will.

Having splashed water on his face in the bathroom, Tadgh descended the wooden stairs with its ancient carved handrail to find Aidan starting to make his breakfast of eggs and bacon on the old Stanley solid fuel stove. His younger brother, four years his junior, had also changed in these last two years, from the lost soul in trouble with the police, to a strong warrior for freedom like himself, all thanks to Morgan.

"You're home at last, world traveler." Aidan dropped the fork he'd been turning the bacon with into the pan and clapped his brother around the shoulders. "Do you know?"

"Aye, brother. She's shattered, as am I, to be sure!"

"She's been bottling it up 'til you got home, so she has, Tadgh. I'm so glad you're back!"

"I'm grateful you were here, Aidan, so capable of handling the situation. I should have—"

"Nonsense, Tadgh. You were on a critical mission for the Cause."

"That's no excuse."

"It's all right. I handled it. After all, what's a brother for?"

"And a fine upstanding one you are, Aidan, that's certain. I'm back now, for good."

Aidan turned back to his task. The bacon was starting to burn with fat splattering all over the black cast iron. He grabbed the towel and moved the pan away from the heat. "Were you successful, Tadgh?"

Tadgh rolled up his sleeves and cracked the eggs into a bowl beside his brother. "Aye, lad. We have seven thousand rifles and a million rounds of ammunition safely stored in an abandoned warehouse near the docks outside Queenstown."

Aidan let out a whoop. "You did it!"

"We all did it, brother, and got rid of Boyle in the process. I hope Florence is happy in Heaven."

"He should be ecstatic, Tadgh. I know I am. This will enable the revolution, won't it?"

"It should help, brother, that's for sure."

Morgan shambled down the stairs with the blanket wrapped around her. "Aidan, I heard you call out. Are you all right?" she murmured almost in a daze. Morgan shuffled over to the stove and gave him a peck on the cheek, almost ignoring her husband's existence.

Tadgh was miffed until he realized that they had been living together with him gone for over three months. They had a certain bond because of how she had helped Aidan out of his self-recriminating downward spiral after their parents' murder. Something that he had not been able to do. Now, he was almost an interloper at this stage until she got used to having him home again.

Tadgh turned to give Morgan a big hug. "Sit down at the table. We'll serve you breakfast, just as soon as I figure out how to cook eggs."

"Here, let me do it," Morgan said, pushing Tadgh's arms away.

Tadgh gently continued holding her and gave her a long kiss on the mouth. "You'll do nothing of the kind. Now sit down and we men will serve you."

After the meal, Aidan took his leave to tend to the hooker. The weather had cleared, and he wanted to take her out for a sail in the crisp April air.

Morgan started to apologize again, so Tadgh stopped her in her tracks taking her hands across the table. "We should mourn, my love, the both of us, but there should be no recriminations. As I said last night, these things are the Lord's will, and God willing we will have children and a good life together." He thought about adding *after the revolution* but then stopped short, knowing how she felt about the violence that lay ahead.

"I am so sad, Tadgh."

Tadgh came around the table and took her in his arms. Then, leaving the breakfast dishes and pans unattended, he carried her back up to bed. They both needed to rest, together.

Two days later, on Friday the 13th, since Morgan was still distressed, Tadgh got Aidan to accompany him, and they drove the Kerry to Beamish and Crawford in Cork City. Tadgh hoped that with Boyle and his henchmen gone, the police would not be so anxious to apprehend him. But he wasn't taking any chances, so he gave the RIC barracks a wide berth. They found Jeffrey Wiggins directing traffic in the loading yard.

"Well, if it isn't the devil himself, back from the dead. Were you successful, my Beamish boy?"

"Aye, so far, but I need your help, lad."

"Name it."

"I'll be needin' an unmarked lorry for a time to deliver my, ah, merchandise."

"Do you, now? And a driver?"

"I think I can manage that part."

"There's that Model TT covered stake bed truck by the loading dock. We just acquired it, so it doesn't have our name on it yet."

"*Ta*. That's some swank lorry. When do you need it back?"

"I'll need to put her in service in a couple of weeks. You'll find the key in her."

"Thanks, lad, I'll get 'er back."

Aidan drove the truck while Tadgh followed on the Kerry. Their first stop was to visit Jack. They found him talking to Irish soldiers, so they waited until he finished.

"How's Morgan, Tadgh? I never got out to see her. I've been worried."

"She lost the baby, Jack. But she's all right now. Aidan took care of her for me, didn't you, brother?"

"She pretty much took care of herself."

Jack looked hurt. "I would have helped, if I'd known."

Aidan held up his hand. "You couldn't have gotten there in time, even if I had a way to contact you."

"I know, Aidan, but I care, you know."

Tadgh cut him off. "We all know that, Jack. Can we inspect the warehouse?"

"Certainly. We can drive there in one minute, walk there in five."

The warehouse was an unused, rundown, windowless, wooden import building, set back in from the docks just off Lynch's Quay. A throwback to the time of tall sailing ships. At least the door locked securely. Jack opened the creaky barn-type door, lit the kerosene lamp for light, and handed Tadgh the key.

Tadgh gave it back. "You keep it safe, Jack, in case of trouble. You are on-site."

Stepping inside, the McCarthy brothers were excited to see in the dim light this antiquated warehouse full of pallets of weapons boxes neatly organized in rows.

"This is grand, so it is, Jack," Tadgh marveled. "Nobody would think of looking in here."

"I rented it under an assumed name, no trace, based on Mr. Collins' requirements. Your equipment is safe here, I should think for a month or two."

"Not longer, Jack?"

"The longer the shipment stays here the higher the risk, Tadgh."

Aidan was salivating. "Let me see a rifle, brother."

Tadgh opened a top box and pulled out a bright new shovel.

Aidan gasped. "What goes on here?"

"Part of the subterfuge, brother. To get past customs. There are over eight hundred of them in case you want to start a garden."

He chuckled and then opened the next box down in the pile and produced a spanking-new .303 Pattern 1914 Mk 1 rifle and bayonet."

"My God, Tadgh. I've never seen anything so beautiful." Aidan grabbed the weapon, hefting it, and sighting through it. "These are marvelous." He flicked the safety and squeezed the trigger. The firing pin clicked in the rifle's empty chamber. "How many bullets?"

"The magazine holds five."

"Outstanding, brother. You've done well."

Tadgh felt decidedly better now that he was refocusing on the revolution ahead. "These fine weapons should help our Cause, boys."

"How many?"

"Seven thousand, give or take, and a million rounds of ammunition."

Jack's eyes widened. "You gave up all of your treasure?"

"Except for some of the jewelry. But this is what Florence intended it be used for, don't ye see."

They nodded their heads and Tadgh replaced the rifle in its box. "All right, lads. Help me load this truck."

At three hundred and sixty pounds a pallet, it was necessary to strip off the thirty-pound boxes and place them individually into the covered truck bed. It took Tadgh and Aidan fewer than ten minutes to fill the truck with ten boxes of rifles and one box of bullets. For good measure, they brought one box of farm implements, in case they were stopped by the authorities, and put it on top of the others at the back.

Tadgh did a mental calculation. "This truck can hold thirty rifles and thirty-six thousand rounds of ammunition."

"How many trips?"

"Two hundred and thirty-three, give or take."

Jack rubbed his lower back and said, "I don't doubt it. It took all night to move the load here with large dock dollies."

Tadgh hadn't thought through the logistics. He suddenly realized what a logistics nightmare it would have been back in Tralee if the *Aud-Norge* had been able to deliver those twenty thousand German rifles.

"We'll take this load to our operations control room at Creagh and then go to Dublin to see Michael Collins. He'll give me instructions. We are going to need a larger transport vehicle, Jack."

After the McCarthy boys left, Jack surveyed the shipment. *What am I getting into?* Then he remembered that night on the Rock of Cashel and how Churchill used *Lusitania*'s Captain Turner as a scapegoat after the tragedy. And who could forget the love of his life. He closed the warehouse, locked it with his spare key, and headed back to his office, telling himself firmly under his breath, "Yes, I've made the right decision to throw in my lot with Tadgh and Morgan."

On Sunday, the 15th, Tadgh thought Morgan could do with a change of scenery.

"It's a bright sunny day, lass. Let's go for a ride."

"No, I don't want to ride in that damn sidecar ever again."

He took her hand. "I don't blame you, girl, but we have a bright new B & C lorry to ride in."

She reluctantly agreed to go, and they set off mid-morning. Tadgh and Morgan took the truck to Dublin using the back routes. He hoped that Collins still used *an Stad* as his temporary quarters.

The Proprietress Mollie Gleeson greeted them at the door when they arrived just after three o'clock. "Well, if it isn't the McCarthys. You'll be after needin' a room for a bit, will ye?"

Tadgh lifted Morgan's left hand to show the wench her ring. "Right enough, Mollie girl."

"You've made an honest lass of her, then, Tadgh."

Morgan chuckled as he responded, "Aye. 'Twas always thus, don't ya know. Where can I find Michael Collins, Mollie?"

"He's in the pub with a woman friend who I think you'll know. She's fresh from the lock-up."

Tadgh and Morgan found Michael Collins in civvies sitting in the corner with a distinguished silver-haired woman in her forties. Michael ushered them over. "Doctor Lynn, these are valiant Rising republicans, Tadgh and Morgan McCarthy, fought at the Green."

Morgan stuck out her hand. "Doctor Lynn, it's an honor. You were the Chief Medical Officer for Connolly's ICA, I believe, at City Hall."

Kathleen inspected her admirer. "Yes, lass. Call me Kathleen. I now support Michael and the poor of Dublin in our ongoing fight for freedom."

Michael clapped Tadgh on the back. "I'm glad to see you here safe and sound, lad. You and the merchandise, I presume."

"Safe and sound, Mick, in a vacant warehouse in Queenstown. It's a wonder that all four of us are here alive and together."

"Providence, son, Providence."

The two battle-tested women sat down to discuss their Rising experiences.

Tadgh took Collins aside. "Mick, I need to talk to you somewhere private."

"Come on up to my room."

Ten minutes later, with two B & C stouts in hand, they sat across the table in Michael's room.

"It is going to take some time to mount the revolution, Tadgh. The old guard are gone, bless them."

"What's your status, Mick?"

"I'm the secretary of the IRB now, since February. Kathleen and I are focused on organizing the Amalgamated National Aid Association for widows, orphans, and dependents of the Rising Volunteers. Your Morgan could help Kathleen with that."

"I'll ask her, but it'll be hard to contribute from Creagh, don't you think?"

"We need all the help we can get."

Tadgh made a quick mental note. "Where do you want the guns stored then? The shipment filled seven boxcars."

"Did it, now. How many rifles?"

Tadgh told him and he whistled.

"The machine guns will have to wait, Mick. New Browning automatic rifles."

Collins thought for a minute. "We can't bring those weapons to Dublin, certainly not now."

"I can't store them all in West Cork, Mick, even if I could get them there."

"Your contact says we can't leave them in Queenstown for more than a couple of months."

"The risk mounts the longer they're there. It's two hundred and thirty-three truck loads, unless we can find a larger lorry, that's certain. Trying to ship by train is too risky, I fear."

"Would have been better to bring them later when we're ready, Tadgh."

"Couldn't get them out after the Americans entered the war. Barely got them out as it was."

"All right. I'll find a place where we can store them indefinitely, out of the way.

Tadgh slugged down the last of his stout and turned to leave.

"You've done a great deed for freedom, Tadgh."

"Only if we get to use the guns, Mick."

At tea in a secluded part of the pub, Morgan said quietly, "Kathleen wants me to join Cumann na mBan and help with aid."

"Mick mentioned that. But you're a member of the IRB."

"There's something to be said for a women's group, Tadgh. To save lives, I mean. Can't I be in both?"

"I suppose so. Mick talked of integrating what's left of the ICA with the loyal Irish Volunteers, to be called the Irish Revolutionary Army. But there's still the IRB."

"Is there an organized effort, Tadgh?"

"Not at present. They have to wait until we can get de Valera out of Lewes Prison. And he's waiting to see if the British enact Home Rule when the blasted Great War is over."

"That could be never."

"The war? Or Home Rule."

"Both, I guess."

"The war will end sometime, but the British will never honor their commitment to enact Home Rule here in Ireland. You mark my words, lass."

Morgan smiled. "That's what Charlotte said, do you remember?"

Tadgh twirled his moustache. "That maddening woman."

"I think that she's grand and brave."

"You would."

"So what's your job then, Tadgh?"

"For the time, to get my shipment to wherever Michael says it needs to go."

Morgan frowned and tucked her black ringlets behind her ear. "When will that be?"

"Whenever he finds the safe place to put it. Mick has just replaced Padraig. We're to go home and wait. Like before."

Their good friend and playwright Sean O'Casey strode into his haunt, *an Stad* pub, announced in a loud voice that he had arrived, and ordered a Jameson at the bar. Tadgh snuck up behind him, reached around, and grabbed the glass the barkeep had just slapped down.

"What the . . .?"

"Sean, you old langer. You on the piss again?"

O'Casey spun around, now face to face with his literary protégé, the young man he mentored while Tadgh was writing his first and only play, *A Call to Arms*, back in 1914.

"I thought you were dead, McCarthy. You a ghost?" He put his hand to Tadgh's chest to see if it would pass right through.

"You were always the one for theatrics, Sean."

"When I'm in my cups. But not tonight, lad. Where is the fair colleen? Oh, I see her over there. A vision of loveliness she is. Fair Morgan, fair Morgan. Come to me, my love!"

Tadgh put his hand over Sean's mouth, thinking you never know who is present to hear your name spoken too loudly, and half dragged him to the booth where Morgan sat laughing.

Morgan got up and lavished kisses on Sean's brow, that curmudgeon with the soft heart, as Tadgh stuffed him into a seat. He had been the man that had tended to her when she was wounded and who had walked her down the aisle to matrimony.

Sean pried Tadgh's hand loose, and he let go. O'Casey asked, "Listen, what are you two doing this evening?"

"You mean, other than staying out of sight so we won't get arrested?" Tadgh said in a lower voice.

"Surely now, after the amnesty . . ."

Tadgh shook his head and whispered, "They think I murdered policemen, Sean."

"And then on your boat."

"Exactly."

Sean returned to the bar for his drink and then rejoined his comrades. Quaffing the contents, he slammed the glass down on the table and announced, "Well, I'm off to the Abbey to see Bernard's play."

Morgan took notice. "What play is that?"

"Bernard Shaw's, called *The Inca of Perusalem*."

Morgan wrinkled her nose before she spoke. "What a strange name."

Sean reached out, took Tadgh's glass of Jameson out of his hand, and drained it. "Isn't it. But the Inca is Kaiser Wilhelm II. This is opening night. Why don't you come with me? I can get tickets."

"Could we, Tadgh?"

Tadgh shook his head again. "Out of the question, my love. I had other personal endeavors in mind, if you'll remember our first stay here at *an Stad*."

Morgan teased. "What about disguises. You could go as the Kaiser with your moustache."

"Don't laugh, aroon. We'd stick out like sore thumbs."

Sean tugged at Tadgh's sleeve. "Come on, my boy. Live a little. Don't you hanker to go back to that theater where you first made your mark in life?"

"That's what got me into trouble in the first place, Sean."

"I want to go, mavourneen. We don't get to the city, hardly ever."

Tadgh could see that he was outmaneuvered. And he *had* left Morgan to deal with her own tragic medical emergency; she didn't ask for much. The opportunity to see a play may just pull her out of her depression, at least for a moment. He thought, maybe disguises would be easy, and enough time had passed that the post-Rising witch hunt would be over. *They have released the revolutionaries from jail, for heaven's sake.* "All right then, but you can't mention our names out in public, Teacher."

"Agreed."

Tadgh looked sadly at his empty glass on the table. "Then join us for tea and we will go with you."

"Thank you, my love." Morgan hugged and kissed her husband.

It was the first time since he returned that he had seen her so attentive.

"I'll stick with my Jameson if you don't mind, lad."

When the theatre doors opened at seven-thirty, Sean O'Casey led the way with a limping old man assisted by a young nurse. The aged fellow used a cane to keep him upright. Patrons politely moved aside to let them pass by.

"Look at the entrance to the theatre," Morgan swooned, as they lurched toward the ornate metal awning in front of the door. "We're only two blocks southeast from the General Post Office and north of the river, and yet this building was never touched during the Rising. That's amazing."

Tadgh realized that there was a direct line between the firing location of the *Helga* gun ship in the Liffey during the Rising to Liberty Hall, and further northwest to the GPO. The theatre was in that firing line, only a block beyond the now destroyed headquarters of the Irish Citizens Army, that hall from which they had all marched out as martyrs to start the revolution.

"Providence, my dear. Providence," the old man croaked.

Once inside, the cavernous and brocaded interior opened up before them. Sean appeared with their tickets, and Tadgh felt his way forward with his cane until they were seated dead center near the back. The balcony swung around in a horseshoe above them. A huge plaque with a gold Irish harp hung on the wall above and to the right of the arched stage.

Sean was euphoric, and in his element. "Think of it, lad. This is where your play, *A Call to Arms*, was performed, in front of those red velvet curtains."

"Yes, and amidst the shouts of derision, Teacher."

"You were speaking the truth, my boy. They just didn't want to hear it, then."

Tadgh looked around at the nearby patrons for any sign of danger, then swept his arm toward them before he spoke. "I wonder if their reactions would be different now, Sean. We can only hope that Padraig, Tom, and the others didn't die in vain."

"The citizens of our fine city and land aren't ready yet, I'm afraid, Tadgh. The British still have us under their thumb. But perhaps there can be a negotiation with the bastards now."

"The pen instead of the sword as always, Sean?"

"Aye, lad."

Seven thousand rifles should make all the difference. A real chance for freedom, Tadgh thought to himself.

The play was a single act, fairytale-like story about a fantastical Inca from a mythical kingdom of Perusalem, where every character impersonated another. The spoof was quite entertaining, and Morgan laughed throughout at the antics of the actors. In the end, the Inca did not get the girl.

"Oh, mavourneen and Sean, thank you for bringing me here tonight. I'd love to play the Princess someday on stage. This is just what I needed." Morgan acted out the princess' part in the foyer on the way out of the theatre, to the applause of several of the nearby patrons.

Tadgh made no attempt to stop her since they didn't appear to have been recognized. He realized that this outing and what it might portend was the best tonic for her melancholy.

They walked back to *an Stad* and left Sean having a nightcap in the pub. Morgan acted schoolgirl giddy.

As it turned out, Mollie had assigned them the same room as the one they had occupied during Rossa's funeral, the one where they had first made love. *She doesn't miss a trick, that one,* Tadgh thought.

Being April, the bedchamber was cold upon their arrival. Tadgh used the stacked wood in the corner to build a roaring fire in the fireplace. The chambermaid had left hot jugs of water before she left for the evening. They were still warm enough for washing, though too cool for a bath. He guided her in.

Morgan looked around the all-too-familiar cozy room with its lace curtains of Irish respectability and high feather bed. Fortunately, that hideous flaming picture of Jesus that had so disturbed her two years earlier had been replaced with a framed quote from the "Book of John," Chapter 3, Verse 16: *For God so loved the world that he gave his one and only Son, that whoever believes in him shall not perish but have eternal life.* She wondered if God intended this truth to apply to unborn children.

Tadgh saw the furrows in her forehead and grabbed her hand, swinging her about the room. "You are still the princess to me, lass."

Morgan plopped down on the bed. "Despoiled royalty then."

"No, Morgan, vibrant, beautiful woman of my dreams."

She bowed her head in her hands and moaned, "Shattered dreams, then."

Tadgh looked around the room. *What could have brought this on after such a joyous evening?"* That's when he saw the biblical verse. That brought him back to his own guilt. *Must get beyond this.* "Listen, Morgan. I am so sorry, but these things happen. We are young. We will have lots of children if you like."

"If you're not killed first. We had our chance." Maybe it was the champagne, but she was crying now.

Tadgh took the hand towel and dipped it in the water basin and wringing it out before bringing it to the bed. He sat, grabbed her hand, and dabbed her cheeks gently with his other hand. "There, lass. It is God's will. We have to believe in his mercy."

"Do you think, mavourneen . . .?"

"I am sure that our baby is already in heaven waiting for us, Morgan. Safe in God's arms."

Morgan snuggled against him. "Do you really think so?"

Tadgh wrapped his arms around her and drew her in. "Yes, and if you believe in God, you will think so too." He parted her hair out of her eyes, pointed at the framed print. "Maybe we should concentrate on the biblical verses related to the Clans Pact. Our time for a family will come once we've found your family treasure. I promise you." Now let's get you into bed, aroon."

As she moved to disrobe slowly, Tadgh realized once again that he was mesmerized by her beauty. But now with her breasts and tummy still slightly swollen from her recent pregnancy, she looked angelic. At that moment, he agonized over the loss of their child.

He tucked her in and turned down the light, kissing her forehead and wiping a residual tear from her cheek before stripping down himself. Any thought he had entertained about repeating the lovemaking they had made so passionately those years ago evaporated. Snuggling tonight seemed so much more intimate and needed. And it certainly was not the time to make another baby.

Tadgh slipped under the covers and felt her curves in the darkness. She moaned and backed up against his chest.

He stroked her hair slowly down across the pillow and pulled her toward him. "Hush, now, my love."

Morgan reached back for his hand and squeezed it.

"Sleep soundly, my princess," Tadgh whispered as he kissed her hand.

From the limpness of her body and the slowing ripples of her breathing, he realized that she already was.

Chapter Seven
Shock

Monday, April 16, 1917
an Stad Hotel and Pub, Dublin, Ireland

*T*he next morning, Tadgh decided to visit Queenstown to take one more load of rifles to Creagh while he still had use of the B & C lorry. During breakfast, which Mollie kindly sent up to their room, Morgan said she was happy at the prospect of seeing Jack again. Even though last night's tryst had wonderfully reinvigorated their intimacy after such a long absence, Tadgh was still envious of Morgan's interest in the Cunard manager. Jack had been a pivotal help with getting the arms to Ireland after throwing in his lot with their Clans Pact group, and Tadgh reasoned that cheering Morgan up would be a good thing at this point.

After breakfast, they bade farewell to Mollie and headed southwest.

Jack was at his office desk when they arrived at midday. Morgan ran over and gave him a friendly hug, which he returned, too long for Tadgh's comfort. Jack started to say, "I'm really sorry—"

Tadgh cut him off. No need to stir up Morgan's melancholy. "Jack, we'd like to see our goods. I'll be taking another truckload with me today and then my boss in Dublin will decide where this shipment should go."

Morgan backed off and the Cunard manager grasped Tadgh's outstretched hand in salutation.

"Within two months, I hope."

"That's what I told him, Jack."

"Good. Do you have time for lunch?"

Morgan's eyes looked pleading, like that afternoon at Temple House, but this time Tadgh declined for them both. "I want to get home before dark, if possible, Jack."

"I'll leave you to it, then. I'll get the key."

Jack swiveled in his chair to hooks behind his desk where he had hidden it amongst a myriad of other openers. "Funny, that key was here yesterday."

Tadgh shot a look of concern at his friend.

Jack looked confused for a moment. "I may have left it in my flat in my other trousers. I'll pick it up tonight."

"You should keep it safely in your office, Jack, near the warehouse. Just in case."

"I know, Tadgh."

Jack turned and opening his desk drawer rummaged through its contents. "Aha, here it is."

Tadgh sounded relieved. "You found it."

Handing his compatriot the key, Jack said, "No, this is a spare that I had made for you."

"That's fine, but you must find your misplaced original, lad."

"All right. I'll let you know when I've found it. When will I see you next?" Jack looked directly at Morgan.

Morgan looked at Tadgh and finding no response answered, "I don't know, Jack. That will depend on Tadgh's boss."

"He's your boss too, Morgan."

Morgan frowned. "You know what I think of the violence ahead, Tadgh."

Tadgh knew all too well that his mate favored O'Casey's *the pen is mightier than the sword*, yet he also believed she would follow him into the jaws of hell if she thought she could save him. "Aye, lass."

"Can you spare a longshoreman to help me load the boxes, Jack?"

Jack came around his desk, almost without any limp now after his *Lusitania* ordeal, and headed for the door. "I'll send William to the warehouse. He's the one who transported the pallets there with me the night your ship arrived."

The McCarthys drove the short distance to the warehouse. When they got out and approached the door, Tadgh looked around to make sure they weren't being watched. Then he opened the door and ushered Morgan inside.

He lit a kerosene lamp just inside the door. "Come into my parlor said the spider to the fly. Isn't this a beautiful sight?"

Morgan shuddered at the vision of so many boxes of guns. So many more men, women, and children to be killed. Before she could reply, the longshoreman named William walked in and Tadgh added, "So many boxes of farm implements."

Tadgh checked out this brawny dock worker with arms the size of fence posts, noting the standard hook hanging from a loop on his belt. He asked the fellow, "William, is it? Give me a hand, will you?"

The men carried two boxes and hefted them into the bed of the Model TT while Morgan looked on.

When they returned to the warehouse and while Tadgh was reaching to grab the next box, William, standing behind him cried, "*Traitors!*"

Tadgh spun around to see the man facing him and pointing a handgun against Morgan's right temple as she looked at him wide-eyed. William was holding her in a vise grip with his other arm.

Tadgh let go of the box. His right hand crept for the Luger hidden in his right pocket. The safety was off.

"I wouldn't try that if I were you. Hands up."

"What's the meaning of this, William? Let her go."

"Not in a million years. I know what you have here, and I want it."

"Do you, now? Put down the gun and let's talk about it."

"I borrowed Jordan's key and checked it out. Them's very fine rifles you have there."

"Your boss will know of this soon enough."

"He'll be dead soon enough."

"We can work this out." With arms up, Tadgh angled slightly

to his right, blocking the thief's vision from his right pocket. He caught Morgan's eye and nodded his head down.

Morgan's mind raced. *God, these guns are causing death already.* She thought of the gunfight in the B & C brewery loading area on the river. She blinked back at him.

Tadgh knew she understood. This would be the second time he had to fight off a thief.

He dropped his right hand, went for his gun, and darted to his right. A shot rang out. Tadgh pitched to the floor to avoid the bullet. Hot lead grazed his thigh. The gun flew out of Tadgh's hand.

"I warned you."

In the split-second the gun was off her neck, Morgan squirmed free, spun around as she ducked her head, and brought her right knee up into the assailant's groin. He threw back his head, shut his eyes tightly, and cried out in agony. His gun hand opened. The pistol fell to the ground.

As William lunged forward to recapture Morgan, she scampered away.

Tadgh scrambled for his Luger and reached it just before William came to his senses. The rebel's hand tingled from shock but was unharmed.

Spinning on the ground, Tadgh fired, but William dove sideways, and the bullet just grazed his forearm.

Tadgh got off another shot before William could fire and the longshoreman's gun went flying, Tadgh's bullet having splintered his right shoulder.

"Damn you!" William shouted, and before Tadgh could fire again, the thief was on him brandishing his longshoreman's hook. He knocked the Luger out of Tadgh's hand.

"Go, get Jack," Tadgh yelled, as he grappled with William.

Morgan couldn't get to the guns located under the fighting men. She looked around for an implement to attack. There wasn't enough time to open a box even if she were strong enough to do so. And it wouldn't be loaded.

"Get Jack!" Tadgh screamed, and Morgan darted out of the building.

Even with mostly his left arm, William was stronger than Tadgh imagined. He knew how to use his hook and it was all Tadgh could do to keep from being brutally slashed.

William cursed and slashed, bloodying Tadgh's left arm, which he ignored. *It's just a scrape.*

Tadgh grabbed the brute's left wrist just as he was slashing again and stopped the blow. They were standing now arm to arm. Tadgh slowly bent the left wrist back until the hook dropped to the ground.

His longshoreman's weapon lost, William wrenched his left arm free and dove for his gun, coming up with it just as Tadgh reached the hook and swung it at the thief.

The shot rang out.

The point of the hook entered William's neck just below the Adams apple. It severed the jugular vein. A bright scarlet fountain sprayed from his neck, He dropped, gripping his throat. He would drown in his own blood.

The bullet ripped through Tadgh's shoulder and shattered the kerosene lamp, spraying the flammable liquid on the wall, hay-strewn wood floor, and the nearest wooden boxes, lighting all on fire.

The warehouse was a tinderbox. The flames spread quickly.

Exhausted from the struggle, Tadgh had been driven to the ground by the bullet and lay there in agony trying to regain his senses. The most overwhelming problem was breathing in the thick smoke that was rapidly filling the old structure as it burned.

Morgan and Jack raced back towards the warehouse and saw the flames shooting out of the roof and wall nearest the door.

"My God, Jack. Hurry!" Morgan was frantic. "I should never have left him."

Without warning, bullets started shooting out of the inferno in all directions as the fire reached one of the ammo boxes. Jack hurled himself on top of Morgan to shield her. The fire threatened to engulf the Model TT that stood not fifteen feet from the warehouse door.

"Stay down," Jack ordered as he rushed towards the side door and disappeared inside. Seconds later, he reappeared, smoke-smudged, dragging a body behind him.

Morgan let out a cry of relief realizing that Jack had rescued Tadgh, and not the thief. She didn't know how Jack had done it. He had been almost paralyzed just a year before. But there they were. Jack collapsed to his knees, breathing heavily in exhaustion. He pointed to Tadgh's motionless form. She knelt by his side and saw her husband's shoulder bleeding, the same shoulder wounded in the B & C gunfight. He was not breathing on his own, so she administered chest compressions. It made her think of the Germans on their U-boat dinghy. So long ago now, before their adventures in the Belgian trenches.

Tadgh coughed but didn't regain consciousness.

Jack panted and swallowed. "Help me move him!" He slipped his arms under Tadgh's armpits.

"He's still not breathing, Jack!"

"We've got to move him before we all end up not breathing!"

Morgan took hold under her husband's knees. She and Jack lugged him back at least a hundred yards from the conflagration to save them all. Jack watched the end of Tadgh's dream while they dragged him. The warehouse would be a total loss.

Morgan continued to work on her man. Jack headed for the truck to drive it out of harm's way, as flames billowed out of the door. The Model TT exploded as the fire found its gas tank. The blast flattened Jack to the ground near Morgan's feet.

Morgan ripped out the lining of her coat to apply pressure to Tadgh's wound. He was now breathing on his own but still not conscious. She looked at Jack while he climbed to his feet. Good. It meant his back was probably not damaged.

A pumper fire engine drove up, bells clanging. Firefighters jumped down and rushed to set up the hoses. But the fire was completely out of control.

Jack saw an RIC lorry arriving from the docks, right behind the firemen. They'd be on them in a few seconds. In the open space, there was no time to get Tadgh out of sight.

While the firemen were occupied, he quietly said, "Take Tadgh's ring and locket off and give them to me, along with your ring. Hurry."

"What?" Morgan was intently ministering to her man.

Jack stepped in and ripped Tadgh's locket from his neck, breaking the chain. "Give me your ring, girl."

Morgan complied, looking dazed. "Why?"

"Police are here."

Jack removed Tadgh's ring. He checked and found U.S. dollars in Tadgh's left trouser pocket. "Listen to me, Morgan. You are my sister, Bernice. Do you understand?"

"What? No!"

"Yes! Your life may depend upon it. You can't help Tadgh if you are in jail."

Morgan saw the lorry come to a halt near the pumper, not fifty yards away and grabbed hold of Tadgh. She looked wildly around for some place for them to hide. There wasn't time.

Initially the police were intent on the fire. Jack madly scraped a hole in the sand under a bush behind him, and threw the jewelry and money in.

Then, as an RIC sergeant turned and advanced on the threesome, Jack stood to meet him and kicked sand back over the hole with his left foot.

"I'm so glad you're here, sergeant. We need an ambulance for this man."

"One should be along presently. They usually come when there's a fire. What happened here?"

Jack explained that the warehouse had caught on fire and that he had rescued one man from the blaze.

"It looks like there was foul play here," the sergeant said, noting Tadgh's shoulder wound. "What happened? Who are you three?"

"I am Jack Jordan, the manager of the Cunard Pier down below. I came running with my sister here when we saw the flames."

"And you, young lady?"

Morgan looked a fright with blood spattered on her white waist-shirt, Tadgh's blood.

Jack realized that she needed to say it.

"I, ah, this man needs a doctor."

"He's coming. Who are you?"

"Jack?" She looked for help, dazed. Then the reality sank in. "I'm Bernice."

"Bernice who?"

Jack stared at the love of his life. What she would say now would determine the course of the rest of her life.

Morgan answered shakily, "Bernice uh, Jordan."

Jack sighed with relief. He loved the sound of it coming from her mouth.

Another RIC constable had been examining the wreckage of the truck. "Sergeant, will you come look at this?"

"What is it?"

"This used to be a truck, and there's molten metal in what's left of the bed. I can see what looks to be part of the butt of a rifle, I think."

The sergeant poked his head into the mass of charred metal, still sizzling from the blast, then glanced back at the three persons, one in a pool of his own blood. "Definitely foul play here. Returning to the trio he announced, "You will all be coming in for questioning, now."

Late that afternoon the RIC identified Tadgh McCarthy and wondered if the woman tending to him was the one Head Sergeant Boyle had identified as his accomplice before his disappearance. They couldn't be sure of the woman as Boyle was the only one who could have identified her, and he hadn't been seen since he was released from hospital in Tralee months before. The Cunard manager, Jack, insisted that Morgan was his sister Bernice. He stated that the woman he had reported seeing on the motorcycle with the Irishman after the *Lusitania* was sunk didn't look anything like his sister.

Unbeknownst to Morgan, Jack's sister Bernice was traveling back to Europe on that fateful May 7 day and was lost at sea when the *Lusitania* sank. She bore more than a passing resemblance to Morgan in height, age, and hair color. In fact, when Jack first spied Morgan on the aft port deck trying to help the stricken, he'd thought she was his sister. He had often wondered whether his strange attraction to this woman amounted to a case of grief-transference.

Morgan bit her tongue and stayed quiet. In the end, the police couldn't hold her. Jack's dog-eared signed photograph of his sister that he showed them satisfied the authorities of her identity.

Jack managed to avoid arrest, showing the police the manifest for the incinerated shipment of farm implements. The rental of the warehouse could not be traced back to him. Captain Josephson was located in Liverpool and his manifest confirmed farm tools.

Still in shock, Morgan stayed with Jack that night while he tried to get a message to Aidan in Creagh. He felt terrible about what had happened, especially since one of his own longshoremen who the firemen found as a charred corpse had been the cause of this travesty. Yet he couldn't help thinking sinfully that the love of his life might become available as a result of this development. Then he erased that thought from his mind and returned to being the perfect platonic gentleman, showing Morgan all the privacy and amenities of his humble abode. It was wonderful to have her staying under his own roof.

The shipment of guns and ammunition was molten metal, ironically as useless as those rusting German weapons lying on the bottom of Queenstown harbor not two miles away. The fact that both shipments had been lost almost a year apart to the day in the same location was highlighted in the newspapers.

Tadgh was taken to hospital where his shoulder wound was attended to. Three days later, he was transferred to Mountjoy Prison in Dublin to await trial for murder.

The next morning, Morgan announced that she wanted to stay near Tadgh. Jack cautioned her to stay away for fear that she would be identified and incarcerated like her husband. In the end, she agreed to stay at his home while he drove for help. He had been contacted by Michael Collins for the warehouse, but he didn't have the code to get him a message. So Jack left Morgan at his flat and drove a Cunard vehicle to Creagh. Aidan was shocked upon seeing Jack. He came running.

Late that afternoon, in Jack's flat, they discussed what to do. Aidan was terribly upset. Jack thought Morgan was keeping a sane presence of mind given the circumstances.

"My God, Sis. How could this have happened?"

"A rogue employee of Jack's held us up and tried to kill us to steal the guns."

Jack tried to hold her hand, but she withdrew. "I feel responsible, Morgan."

"Nonsense, Jack. You did everything you could. You saved Tadgh, for heaven's sake. That's what matters. Now we have to find a way to save him again."

"So the body they found in the ashes?" Aidan asked.

Morgan answered. "Yes, it was the thief. Tadgh must have killed him in self-defense. All of the killings Tadgh is charged with were self-defense, although we'll never be able to prove that."

"So, what can we do?"

Aidan argued that he should take some of the guns at Creagh and storm Mountjoy Prison to get Tadgh out.

"Don't be daft, Aidan. That would just get you arrested or worse."

"What do you suggest then, Morgan? We can't let him die in prison."

Morgan thought for a moment. "We won't. I think we should

go to Dublin and talk to Michael Collins."

Jack couldn't think of anything better. He had gone to the warehouse ruins before he headed to Creagh, and fortunately, the jewelry and money were still buried where he left them. He had been leery of going there when they came home from the police station the night before, in the event they were followed. Tadgh had been carrying eight hundred U.S. dollars around with him. Jack decided to store the jewelry in the safe in his house, but he gave the money to Morgan. She was going to need it.

Two days later, on Saturday the 21st, Aidan and Morgan reached *an Stad* just after noon on the Kerry. There was a message there at the front desk for her from Kathleen Lynn.

"Oh, my poor girl," Mollie lamented, when Morgan came through the door. "We've been after sick with worry about you and dear Tadgh. Any word, lass?" she said as she handed her the note.

Morgan opened the paper and cried.

Aidan reached for the note. "What is it, sis?"

"Kathleen says that Tadgh has just been arraigned for murder this morning."

Mollie broke in. "Michael asked to be contacted if you showed up, lass. He's in a meeting in his room. I'll fetch him down."

Collins bounded down the stairs and hugged Morgan to his breast. She clung tightly for a minute and started to speak.

"Hush, lass. Come with me."

Morgan pointed. "Aidan, Tadgh's brother. One of us."

"Yes, I remember. Come with me, lad." Michael ushered them upstairs and into his room where Kathleen sat at the table.

"We were just talking about what to do," he said a moment before Kathleen rose, came over to them, and took over consolation duties. She led Morgan to the bed and sat her down.

"Tell us what happened." Michael seemed more interested in Tadgh than the guns. Morgan realized that he led pragmatically, not one to cry over spilt milk.

Maybe it was the presence of another woman, one with whom she had fought in the Rising, because the floodgates of emotion broke through Morgan's veneer of self-control. Kathleen held and rocked her for several moments, while Morgan managed to get the story out between sobs. They waited in silence until Morgan composed herself.

Michael spoke. "The doctor and I have been talking and we have some questions only you can answer. First, who saw Tadgh kill the policemen in Cork and Kerry?"

"Only the rogue RIC sergeant Boyle and his henchman Gordon James knew about the killings of their two RIC cohorts in self-defense at B & C at Cork in 1915. And they're both dead."

"How do you know this?"

Morgan looked over at Aidan. "We were all there. Boyle tried to burn us all alive."

Kathleen cringed but Michael urged her to her continue with the question, "No one else saw?"

Aidan answered. "No one who would say anything."

Morgan thought for a minute. "Hold on, Aidan. When Gordon James died near Tralee, there was another policeman that Boyle killed. He blamed it on us."

"Did he, now. And who saw that?"

"When the police picked up Mr. Casement, they saw me with Tadgh before our fight with Boyle."

Kathleen said, "So there was a policeman who could identify you with Tadgh."

"Yes, I guess so. He only saw me for a minute or two before Tadgh and I were stuffed into Boyle's police car."

Michael concluded, "All right, we'll assume that the stupid RIC will remain ignorant."

"There were two other RIC officers with Boyle when he died. They both burned with him."

Kathleen glanced at Michael and then gave Morgan a glass of water from the table, helping her hold it while she drank.

Aidan paced the room. "I say we stop talking and find a way to break him out."

Michael put his hand on Aidan's shoulder and sat him down at the table. "Calm down, lad. Your time for action will come, just not now."

Morgan offered, "Aidan trained at Rathfarnham under Pearse before the Rising, Michael. He saved Tadgh and me during both of our battles with Boyle."

"I don't doubt his loyalty and capability. It's his hot head that needs to cool. Go on with your story."

"There are two other incidents that could be a problem. Tadgh told me that he shot a soldier who was trying to detain him during the Rising and several more outside the College of Surgeons."

"We all shot soldiers during the Rising and they gave us amnesty." Michael assured her. "Since Tadgh was not a commandant, he would likely not be executed because of that."

Kathleen noticed Morgan shivered at that word and sat down beside her, grabbing her hand. "What is the other incident?"

"The day before Mr. Rossa's funeral, a DMP officer recognized Tadgh on the street, and then Tadgh beat him up pretty badly."

"Did he die?"

"I don't know. He wasn't dead when we left him."

"Is that all?"

"Yes, I think so."

Michael rubbed his brow and asked, "All right, tell me about this fellow Boyle."

"He comes from a long line of murderers, as I understand it, Michael. He was after the McCarthy gold, as were his ancestors before him. He killed my father, and both of Tadgh's parents. He was an evil, malicious, immoral man who would not have shared the truth with his superiors." Morgan could have told them even more.

Michael and Kathleen paused and went over by the window to converse quietly.

After a minute, they came back to Morgan. Michael told her, "We think there is a case to be made that will save Tadgh from a firing squad. We'll need to get a reputable barrister to represent him. It will take some time."

The doctor said, "In the meantime, I'd like you to come to Dublin and live with me until we can sort this out, Morgan. I have an extra bedroom in my flat."

"Oh, Doctor. I couldn't."

"You must, my dear. Tadgh will need you here."

"All right, that's sorted," Michael said, lifting Aidan up onto his feet. "Now then, lad. I want you to go home and manage your safe house until we get your brother free."

"But I want to—"

Michael cut in. "If you want to help your brother, then this is what you must do. Go home and let us handle his defense."

"But—"

"No buts about it. First things first. We must save his life. Later, we can then figure out how to get him out of jail. You'll be a part of that, to be sure. Right now, Aidan, promise that you'll steer clear?"

"I'll make sure he will," Morgan said, giving her brother-in-law a hug. "When can I go and see him, Michael?"

He hesitated. "My dear, I'm afraid the answer is never, while he's incarcerated. You're Jack Jordan's sister, remember."

Morgan had not thought about that. She was crestfallen.

"We'll save him, Morgan," Kathleen said reaching out to hold her hand again. "You'll be together again, soon enough."

"So, we have a plan, lass, or at least the start of one," Michael said, showing them to the door. He had other plans to make.

Knowing that Collin would be keenly interested, *The Irish Times* publisher, Jack Healy, contacted Collin's *Tely* publisher,

Robertson, as soon as the story broke about the rebel guns catching on fire. Collin initially wanted to head back to Ireland. The joyous birth of their second child, a beautiful black-haired girl with tiny ringlets, who they named Claire, had just occurred on April 6, by coincidence on the same day the United States entered the war. Since his boss was more interested in him reporting on the wartime activities south of the forty-ninth parallel, and because Kathy needed him on the home front, Collin refrained from suggesting going to his homeland. Besides, with his previous obsession for finding his sister, he couldn't break his promise to put his family first. And baby Claire, with her luminous green eyes, was so cute!

Instead, he sent a telegram of condolence to Morgan via Michael Collins, and pictures of baby Claire to the home at Creagh. He hoped that would cheer his sister up.

The word came by telegram from Jack on May 1 that Morgan was safe and unharmed, but Tadgh was injured and in jail. For murder.

In the weeks that followed, the story of Tadgh's trial was thoroughly reported by several Irish newspapers, including *The Irish Times*. Healy assigned Maureen O'Sullivan to cover the proceedings, and she kept Collin and Kathy informed of some of the unpublished details by telegram.

In June, during Tadgh's trial, the British declared amnesty for many of the detained Republicans incarcerated in Lewes Prison. *The Irish Times* said that the government was bowing to the protests from Irish citizens. After Éamon de Valera's release, Éamon took charge of the IRB and Volunteers. He counseled Michael Collins to act as if the Republic was a fact. He would often say, "We defeat the British by ignoring them. As the American John Adams once said, 'Revolution starts in the hearts and the minds of the people'."

It was reported that Tadgh had brought the guns from the United States just before the Americans declared war. The American papers tried to find out where he acquired the arms but there was no provable traceability back to Eddystone. Collins heard from McGarrity that the Clan na Gael members were devastated at the news.

Michael Collins personally paid for the defense barrister, Mr. Shamus McCormack, a well-respected Dublin attorney. In court, he argued that there was no proof that Tadgh had killed any of the men involved. It was Head Sergeant Boyle's word against McCarthy, and Boyle was nowhere to be found. District Inspector Maloney from Cork testified that he was always suspicious of Boyle's motives and stories. Even Inspector General Sir Neville Chamberlain of the RIC admitted under McCormack's questioning that he wouldn't trust Boyle as far as he could throw him. McCormack even brought in the nurse from the hospital in Tralee who confirmed that Boyle had been a nasty patient with little regard for anyone but himself.

The DMP officer whom Tadgh had roughed up in Dublin had survived but didn't remember much of the incident, including what the woman with McCarthy looked like.

As Collins expected, the killings during the Rising were treated as battle combat casualties, and as expected, were not enough to get Tadgh executed.

In the end, because of his involvement with the Rising, combined with the traitorous act of gunrunning and an earlier charge of inciting revolution with his play, *A Call to Arms*, Tadgh was sentenced to life imprisonment, just like his ancestor Florence MacCarthaigh Reagh. He was remanded to Mountjoy Gaol.

When the verdict came down on October 8, Collins seemed quite pleased with the outcome and tried to reassure Morgan. "Patience, lass. We'll get him out. No more than two years, I can assure you."

Morgan was demoralized and devastated.

♣ ♣ ♣ ♣

Kathleen Lynn took Morgan under her wing and brought her to live with her and her best friend Madeleine ffrench-Mullen at Number Nine Belgrave Road in Rathmines, a mile south of St. Stephen's Green and the Grand Canal. The three became fast friends, although Morgan's relationship with the other couple was decidedly more platonic than their own. They organized prisoner relief and opposed conscription. Beyond all that, Kathleen became the Vice President of the Sinn Féin and sponsored Morgan in the two-year nursing program at Rotunda Hospital. In many ways, Morgan actually taught the teachers triage methods along the way, and by spring of 1919, she would have her degree, albeit under the name of Bernice Jordan.

Aidan held the fort at Creagh and started a legitimate fishing business to keep his mind off his brother's predicament. Once or twice early on, at Michael Collin's direction, Morgan returned to Creagh to check on her brother-in-law, and when necessary, talk him out of doing something stupid, like organizing a one-man raid on Mountjoy.

Any thought about seeking the O'Donnell fortune took a back seat to the ongoing and very real worry over Tadgh's well-being. No one had the heart for treasure hunting.

Whenever he could, Jack went to Dublin to console and support Morgan, the love of his life. He believed in Tadgh's Cause and in the man, yet there was a part of him hoping Tadgh would never be released. He chastised himself every time that notion crossed his mind.

Michael Collins turned his focus to planning a new guerrilla war, while the war still raged on the continent, killing thousands by the day in the horrible trenches.

Chapter Eight
Escape

Saturday, April 5, 1919
Cell 3-94, Wing A, Mountjoy Prison, Dublin

*T*adgh had been incarcerated for almost two years, much longer than most of the surviving Easter Rising patriots. He suffered under no delusion that he would be released like the other military prisoners. He had killed policemen, albeit in self-defense, in peacetime. Yet he remained convinced that Michael would get him out of prison one way or another. In a continuing effort to stay strong, he maintained a physical and mental fitness program when in the exercise yard and in his cell. He had recovered from his wounds and steered clear of causing trouble, unlike the newly arrived Robert Barton. As a result, he was treated fairly and never once had been exiled to solitary bread-and-water confinement.

Yet Tadgh worked covertly to find ways to communicate with the outside world and to plan an escape. One of the conduits of information was Kathleen Lynn, who was allowed to visit him once a month, given her reputation as healer of the sick and infirm. She became a channel between Morgan and her poor husband, which was better than nothing. Kathleen brought Tadgh news of Morgan, who was living with her and studying to be accepted as a nurse, as well as news about Aidan and Michael. He longed to see his beloved wife but understood that Morgan would be arrested if identified with him. Michael had thought at one point to bring her in, disguised, when she insisted on being allowed to see him. But when he heard about this plan, Tadgh vetoed it. Too risky.

Early on in his captivity, Kathleen was allowed to bring him paper and pencil. In order to maintain his sanity, Tadgh spent his evenings working on a new play titled *Martyrdom for Freedom*, which he hid under a loose floorboard in his six-by-eleven-foot cell.

Tadgh was forever in debt to Kathleen for her support to Morgan. He found out from her that Aidan had become a bona-fide fisherman, while his brother waited impatiently for revolution orders and a plan to help him escape. Tadgh remembered the interminable waiting before the Rising and how frustrating it had been. Kathleen had even given him information that the O'Donnells in Toronto had gone on with their lives now that they had a boy, and a girl named Claire. Tadgh had smiled when he heard that name.

Despite all this, one obsession plagued him day after day. Tadgh blamed himself for the debacle at the warehouse. He should have been able to protect the weapons. He went over his actions constantly in his mind, agonizing over his failure to deliver the arms to the Cause. What would his ancestor Florence think of him now if he were alive after all the careful planning to hide the McCarthy 'gold'? What Michael must think of him for letting a single longshoreman get the better of him with such dire consequences. He finally realized that it would eat him alive if he didn't stop beating himself up with guilt. After all, it was a fluke that the bullet struck the kerosene lamp and started the fire, wasn't it? It couldn't have been Divine intervention, surely. Despite these thoughts, Tadgh decided that his faith was being tested, and as a result, remained intact, perhaps even stronger. It had to be.

He found out that fortunately his locket and Clan ring were locked away in Jack's safe and Morgan had enough money to live on.

Now that she finally had her nursing degree, Morgan decided she could wait no longer for Collins to act. Two years of waiting was more than enough time to get Tadgh out of the Joy. She had worn out her welcome with her entreaties to him to fulfill his promise.

Morgan realized that her husband was just a small cog in Michael's war of independence and a useless one at that now that he was behind bars. But Mick had committed to getting him out and he was a man of integrity. Aidan, down in Cork West, was biding his time as a fisherman, but he kept pestering her by letter to get Collins to act on his pledge to them.

"Can't you get Michael to do something, Kathleen? If he doesn't, then I will," Morgan pleaded, as they sat around their kitchen table in the flat that the two women still shared on the evening of April 5.

"We've been over this many times, Morgan. Mick will act when the time is right and not before. You would have no chance by yourself. I know it is hard to take, but at least Tadgh is alive and keeping in good health and spirits."

Morgan admired Kathleen, a marvelous Irish humanitarian and social revolutionary. After knocking her head against the stone barrier of male doctor exclusivity in Dublin, the doctor, Madeleine, and other women activists were amassing the funding to start a children's hospital for the poor to be run entirely by women. But it rankled Morgan that Kathleen could visit Tadgh, and that she herself, now named Bernice Jordan, couldn't. Morgan realized that she was doing Tadgh more good on the outside of prison than being caught and jailed herself, but it wasn't fair that he was still incarcerated.

Through the paper-thin walls of the flat, Morgan heard a familiar rumble in the alley. "It's Tadgh's Kerry!" For a moment she imagined it was her husband knocking at the door. But it was Aidan, bringing her back to their painful reality.

"I am so glad to see you, brother!" Morgan exclaimed, as she hugged him and brought him in to the kitchen. "Why are you here? Are you injured?"

"I'm fine, Morgan. Never better!"

Morgan thought that is what Tadgh would say. She took his coat and ushered him to a chair at the table. "Doctor Lynn, and Miss ffrench-Mullen, this is my brother-in-law, Aidan McCarthy."

Aidan doffed his cap, bowing his head slightly. "Glad to make your acquaintance, Ma'ams."

Kathleen took the lad's coat, "Nice to meet you, Aidan. You're the spitting image of your brother."

It seemed odd that Aidan had left their home and come all this way in the cold, so Morgan asked again," Why are you here, brother? I haven't seen you in over a year."

"I got a telegram from Michael Collins to come to Dublin right away."

Morgan turned to Kathleen, her heart pumping. "Could it be? Do you know anything?"

"Nothing, Morgan. I would have told you."

"Do you think he has a plan to spring Tadgh from the Joy at last, Sis?" Aidan asked, wide-eyed.

"I don't know, but I'm going with you to see Mick tomorrow, Aidan."

"You look the worse for wear, lad," Madeleine said. "It couldn't have been comfortable to ride all this way on such a steed in this weather. No sense in speculating what Mick wants until you see him. We've some soup if you've a mind."

"Yes, ma'am, please. At least it wasn't snowing."

After consuming two cups of Madeleine's vegetable soup and a bottle of B & C stout, the blue tinge in Aidan's cheeks turned a ruddy hue.

Aidan had many questions. "I am kind of isolated back home as a poor fisherman without any news except what I read in the *Skibbereen Eagle* and that's a Unionist newspaper. I'd like to understand the overall situation."

Morgan was surprised that her brother-in-law was taking such an interest. He had come a long way since she first met him back in Deirdre's pub, after having been shot and trying to elude the police.

"I've a little Jameson and we've time to talk," Kathleen said, as the four revolutionaries moved to the tiny parlor, closer to the warming fireplace. It wasn't much, but Morgan marveled how the other women had furnished such a cozy space in such austere times. They had lost so much for the Cause and there was still so much discrimination against a woman doctor in the country. Now, they spent their energy helping others who had suffered.

From the red chintz chair, Kathleen asked, "What do you want to know, Aidan?"

"Is Michael Collins in charge of this war?"

"Michael is the military head of our organization and Director of Intelligence since May 1918, Aidan, but Éamon de Valera is the political President of our Sinn Féin organization. You might not know that despite being a commandant in the Rising, he wasn't executed. Instead, he was jailed in Lewes Prison until he was freed in June of 1917, while your brother was being tried for murder."

"I know we are fighting for the freedom of all Irish people, but I hear traitorous talk that it may not be possible."

Kathleen wondered how far back to go in her explanation. "In the aftermath of the Easter Rising, the British government, led by Prime Minister David Lloyd George, attempted to reach a Home Rule decision with the Irish leader John Redmond in a protracted negotiation called the Irish Convention. George clearly would only consider a segregated Ireland with 26 southern separated counties and 6 northern Ulster British ones, a position our Mick knows may be inevitable given the industrialization in the Belfast area and the majority of Protestants there."

Standing by the brick fireplace, Aidan clutched his glass of Jameson, spilling a little of the liquid on the Indian carpet. "That bastard Brit prime minister. We need to free all of our country. There are Catholics up there."

Morgan remembered Lady Charlotte's words back at Temple House. "Even some of the educated people up North think the way Mick does, Aidan. He will lead the fight to free all of our island nation, but it may not be possible in the end."

"Well, Sis, Tadgh and I will not accept that, and I'll tell Mr. Collins to his face."

"Shall I continue?" Kathleen asked.

Aidan got a rag from the kitchen counter and returned to wipe up his spill before responding. "I'm sorry, yes, please."

"This extensive effort towards some form of Home Rule culminated in late March 1918 when the British government tried to link this ongoing activity with a law that they had just passed to force Irish conscription for the war on the continent, calling it duality. An early spring offensive by the Germans penetrating the French lines in the Great War resulted in devastating Allied casualties, necessitating more human fodder for the trenches. We, in the Sinn Féin party rejected the law, and we have remained steadfastly against a segregated approach to Irish governance."

Aidan refilled his glass. "Good."

"That March, Michael was elected Adjutant General of the Volunteers, a step in his path to control the military destiny of the upcoming revolution," Kathleen said. "He needed to manage the method of battle. However, on April 3, he was arrested. Fortunately, the IRB posted his bail and he's been on the run, in plain sight in Dublin ever since." Kathleen added with twinkle in her eye, "He's a master at it. Got the Brits running around in circles, he has."

Morgan took a sip of the tea they had brought from the kitchen and set her cup back down on the Georgian walnut end table by her rocking chair. "Tell him about your Cousin Constance Markiewicz's arrest after Michael was freed, Kathleen."

"On April 12, the Germans sent ashore a member of Casement's abortive Irish Brigade from a submarine on the coast of County Clare. Richard Dowling reported a cockamamie story that Germany was going to mount an attack on Ireland to support the Republicans and divert British resources from the war on the continent. British intelligence leader William Reginald Hall of Room 40 believed the story and convinced Lord Lieutenant Lord French the threat was real. They called it the German plot and thus gave them the excuse to arrest our Sinn Féin members."

That caught Aidan's attention. "She fought with you at the Green, Sis, right?"

"Aye, Aidan," Morgan responded. "Saved my life, so she did, by letting Tadgh take me to hospital. We were visiting her on May 17th when RIC officers broke down her door and hauled her off in a police lorry."

Kathleen added, "As it turned out, they arrested one hundred and fifty Sinn Féin leaders, and they were all incarcerated, including Éamon de Valera and Arthur Griffith."

Morgan started rocking forward. "But tell him what de Valera did."

"Michael Collins learned of the expected RIC raids the day before and slipped through their net, but Éamon chose to have his supporters get arrested for propaganda purposes, including my cousin."

"Is Mr. Collins at odds with Mr. de Valera, then?" Aidan asked.

Kathleen paused before answering. "Let's just say that they don't always see eye to eye, as you might expect between military and political leaders."

Morgan rocked back. "I stayed here, and we all tended to Kathleen's support activities while I went to nursing school."

"So, what happened next?" Aidan asked.

"After most of the Republican leadership were taken out of commission, Michael rose in the ranks and became the Director of Intelligence of the Irish Volunteers that August. He named it the Irish Republican Army (IRA). He convinced our other leaders that control of British intelligence was going to be pivotal to defeating the British in his planned upcoming hit-and-run War of Independence. This gave Michael almost free reign over day-to-day operations of the Republicans."

"What do you mean by *almost*, Ma'am?"

"Michael often clashed with the chief of staff of the IRA, Cathal Brugha, a hero who had been shot several times during the Rising at South Dublin Union under commandant Éamon Ceannt.

Brugha resented Michael's power over the army because of Collins' leadership of the clandestine brotherhood."

"But that was almost a year ago," Aidan said. "What's changed?"

Kathleen stood up, grabbed the rag, and rescrubbed the rug where the sticky liquor had stained before continuing. "As you must know, the war ended with Germany and its Central Power allies surrendering on November 11, 1918. The American entry into the war had finally turned the tide and brought the Kaiser's forces to their knees. Zimmermann's gamble failed and the world, except for us, has started to restructure. Even Russia, where the Bolsheviks overthrew their Tsar two years ago, is stabilizing under the new Communist rule of Lenin. As of the end of 1918, the Irish fight for freedom has become a center of attention internationally."

She continued, "On the political side, Britain went to the polls in a general election in December 1918, and our Sinn Féin party won a majority of Irish seats in the British parliament. Cousin Constance was still in prison, yet was elected as MP for St. Patrick's, Dublin, thanks, in part, to Morgan's efforts to canvas on her behalf."

Kathleen smiled and Morgan turned away modestly. Then she continued. "These elected Irish members of parliament decided collectively that they would not go to London but rather would set up their own independent government for the Irish people in Dublin. Unfortunately, Éamon de Valera, still incarcerated, had missed the first meeting of the Irish Republic parliament, called the Dáil Éireann, held on this past January 21 at the Dublin Lord Mayor's residence of Mansion House. In his stead, Cathal Brugha officiated on that auspicious occasion. A declaration of independence had been formulated and was signed by the Sinn Féin government in defiance of British rule."

"Weren't the Sinn Féin members all considered traitors for refusing to go to the London parliament?"

"Theoretically yes, but practically no. The British didn't want to immediately start a war, kind of how they acted before the Rising.

"Not very bright, are they?" Aidan said, taking a slug of his Jameson.

"Aye, lad. With the new Irish Republic government established, albeit illegally according to the British, it became immediately crucial to liberate our president of Sinn Féin from captivity. Michael, with his lieutenant Harry Boland, successfully extricated Éamon de Valera from Lincoln Prison on February 3 this year, using a female disguise."

"I don't understand how he could get the American freed and not Tadgh," Morgan exclaimed, rocking back and forth.

"Well, maybe now he will," Aidan announced, finishing off his glass of liquor. Let's see what he has to say tomorrow."

They all agreed to sleep on it as Morgan fixed up covers for Aidan to sleep on the chesterfield. Kathleen and Madeleine went off to their room to prepare the speech that Katheen would give to the potential backers for the children's hospital the next day. They remained true to the principles of the Larkinist movement as they worked to save the destitute youth of the city.

Since jumping bail back in April 1918, Michael Collins had never stayed in one place more than a couple of days at a time. One of his favorite hideouts was the front, second-floor room at the Wicklow Hotel, in the shadow of Trinity College, right under the noses of the Dublin Metropolitan Police and the Castle military.

Sunday morning, April 6, Michael was happy that finally he was able to implement a plausible plan to break Tadgh out of Mountjoy prison, as he had promised Morgan and Aidan.

At ten o'clock Michael Collins had just started to explain his Mountjoy prison break plan to his men, Paddy Daly, and O'Reilly, when Aidan and Morgan entered his room at the Wicklow Hotel.

Paddy stood up and pointed. "Why is she here?"

Michael was taken aback, but not surprised. He closed the door and said, "Sit down, Daly. She's McCarthy's wife and an important soldier of freedom."

Morgan didn't like the attribution but let it pass. She spoke directly at the leader. "Are you planning on getting Tadgh out of jail, Michael?"

Aidan stepped between Morgan and the Director of Intelligence. "What's the plan, sir?"

Michael clapped Aidan on the back and shook his hand. Then he offered Morgan a chair. "I know you've both been waiting a long time for this day, but now's your chance to get Tadgh out."

Morgan's green eyes flashed.

Aidan shook hands with the other men and sat down on Michael's bed.

"As I was telling my men, there are three others needing to be freed as well as Tadgh. One is the Gaelic scholar Piaras Béaslai, and added to that, two Sinn Féin members of Parliament, Robert Barton, and J.J. Walsh. Barton was transferred in from Portloise Prison in January, and since then, he has led a campaign of resistance in C and D wings of Mountjoy—breaking of furniture, refusal of the prisoners to return to their cells from the exercise yard, and so on. Now that there are four, the plan becomes reality. I have been coordinating with the prisoners through intermediaries."

Aidan wanted to know if Doctor Lynn had lied.

"Kathleen Lynn? No, Aiden. She is too important to our Cause to risk her exposure with this planning at the Joy. You will need to take Tadgh to her flat after we get him out of the gaol unless the police are on your tail. Know where that is, lad?"

"Yes, sir. I stayed there last evening. The plan?"

Michael described his plan that he'd coordinated with Tadgh. After finishing, he said, "O'Reilly, you will have four bicycles outside the wall by the canal for Tadgh and the other three escapees. All right, boys. Make sure you spring McCarthy, Béaslai, Barton, and Walsh by name. Get them out and report back to me at *an Stad* when the job is done."

Tadgh had kept a calendar by crossing off scratches on his cell wall. As part of the escape plan, he had managed to get laundry assignments for himself and the other three escaping detainees on the early shift where they had been working for the last month. The path between the laundry and the cellblock took them along the north wall of the prison compound, and through the north exercise yard. With information Michael's agent had given him, he realized that the only point along that route where supporters from outside the walls could operate in broad daylight with minimal exposure was in the middle of the exercise yard. It couldn't be helped.

Now, he was finally going to break free of this hellhole to be reunited with his beloved Morgan. He was heartened to have heard that Mick had conducted a successful escape for Éamon de Valera a month earlier.

As usual, at precisely two-thirty Monday afternoon after their shift, seven laundry workers were being walked through the north outside exercise yard on their way back to the spoked cell blocks by an armed warder bringing up the rear. Tadgh had positioned himself at the front of the line with Barton, Walsh, and Béaslai behind him in order. Tadgh had seen the twenty-foot-high rough stone outer wall that encircled the complex hundreds of times before, and it always seemed unscalable, until now. He knew their escape plan was critically dependent on the element of surprise and his speed of execution.

The exercise yard at the northeast side of the prison was about a hundred feet square with a circular eight-foot-high fenced area of about 50 feet in diameter. The cage, as they called it, was located in the yard's center, and inside it the prisoners marched. Tadgh took note that today there were about thirty of them controlled by a warder guarding the open iron gate to the cage, and two other warders inside the enclosure. It was nearing the time for the marching men within the gated area to head back to their cells. More warders would soon appear.

Each warder carried a Lee-Enfield rifle at the ready with a six-shot magazine. Tadgh wondered how many additional replaceable clips they kept under their tunics. He had seen them shoot and kill when other prisoners had tried to escape. As a result, the prisoners were generally well behaved. Yet Tadgh knew that every prisoner would make a break for it if he thought he had a good chance of getting out. This could complicate matters.

At the agreed upon location mid-yard, as they walked by against the outer wall, Beaslai, the fourth prisoner in line, abruptly stopped and bent over to retie his shoelace, causing the trailing warder and other inmates to bump into him. In that instant, Tadgh casually tossed a bar of soap that he had taken from the laundry over the wall. He then walked briskly back as if to help Béaslai up.

Instead, Tadgh put his right hand in his pocket, thrusting the handle of a spoon out against the material of his prison pants, mimicking a gun for the jailer's benefit.

"Hands up," Tadgh said quietly.

A rope ladder came cascading down the inside of the outer wall where Tadgh had thrown the soap, its end two feet off the ground.

Tadgh saw that the warder was not fooled as he went for his gun.

Tadgh disarmed him with one swipe of his right arm, breaking the strap slung around his neck, causing the guard to gag.

Clicking off the safety, Tadgh butted the warder in the stomach. The officer slumped down on the ground with a thud, gasping. Tadgh thought of shooting him but did not want to attract any more attention than necessary. There were forty warders in the prison.

Tadgh ordered his compatriots quietly, "To the wall, men."

Barton moved quickly, followed by Walsh and Béaslai. The other three laundry prisoners, seeing the ladder, followed suit.

The men in the exercise cage noticed the commotion before the gatekeeping warder who was facing away from the wall realized what was happening. They rushed and overpowered the guards inside the cage before their jailers could react, grabbing their guns. The gatekeeper tried to jam the cage gate closed and pivoted in time to see Barton reaching the top of the wall on the ladder. He raised his rifle and Tadgh had to act, shooting him in the shoulder to incapacitate his shooting arm. So much for surprise.

The two-armed prisoners dispatched the cage guards.

The gatekeeping warder, shoulder bleeding, turned back to the stampeding prisoners, took out his whistle with his left hand, and blew it with all his breath. The shrill alarm was silenced as one of the now-armed prisoners in the cage shot him between the eyes.

Barton yelled out from the top of the wall, "Come on boys. The coast is clear."

That did it. Inmates pushed through the unlocked gate trampling the already dead gatekeeper warden. They dashed for the ladder, pushing Tadgh, who was standing guard, out of the way, clawing at each other for a turn to climb. They looked like rats scrambling up out of a burning building.

Tadgh held his ground looking for more warders while the melee fought their way up to freedom behind him. His three accomplices had fled.

"Drop your weapons!" Chief Warder Adams yelled from the corner tower nearest them. "You, on the ladder. Stop! We have all of you covered. When Tadgh turned to start up the rope with over twenty men already having ascended before him, Adams yelled, "You're not going to get away with this, McCarthy. This will not end well."

Tadgh knew that shooting to kill on his part would end in certain death.

The inmate nearest the top of the wall lunged upwards toward freedom. A shot rang out, and he fell back screaming into the exercise yard, mortally wounded.

The two prisoners with guns shot back at the corner tower from their position partway up the ladder. An unseen sniper silenced both of them.

That did the trick. Now the remaining rats on the ladder scrambled back down and were quickly subdued by the warders who had now rushed into the exercise yard. Tadgh dropped the rifle and was forced down onto the ground, sadly realizing that he was not going to be one of the escapees, not today.

Adams emerged into the exercise yard from the tower with another five warders flanking him, his rifle pointed at Tadgh's heart. "Well, McCarthy. This is a fine escape you've masterminded. You have failed."

Tadgh thought, at least he wasn't dead like the three unfortunates who had been the closest to freedom at the moment the warders acted. These inmates had escaped after all, and they were on their way to heaven, or hell.

One of the warders tried to pull the rope ladder down into the yard, but it was snagged on the glass embedded in the top of the wall.

Outside the wall, Paddy was at a loss what to do. They were prepared for only four escapees, and now they had twenty to deal with. They were scrambling in every direction away from the prison.

"I don't see Tadgh," Aidan yelled, having checked the faces of the men who had descended off the ladder. We're supposed to get him."

"He's still back in there," Barton said, shaking his head. "He should have made a dash for it like the rest of us."

Béaslaí stopped and lashed out, "How could he, since you invited all of them to join you before he had a chance. His job was to keep the warders at bay until we could climb to freedom. You just condemned the man who organized your escape and put his life on the line for you to an even harsher prison existence."

Aidan scampered up the ladder and peered over. The warders were corralling and then tying the remaining prisoners' hands behind their backs. Tadgh was kneeling in front of the chief warder, facing the outer wall. Aidan thought of trying to shoot the warders from his high vantage point, but he realized that the odds were heavily stacked against him.

Tadgh looked up. Aidan saw a flicker of recognition before his brother shook his head.

Below him, outside the wall, O'Reilly was calling. "More warders coming out of the prison. We've got to skedaddle." Then he dashed off.

Aidan realized that it wouldn't help to shoot warders. He would not survive, and it would make things worse for Tadgh. He hated to do it, but he had to leave him be. He turned and a warder fired, grazing his right arm.

From inside the enclosure a warder yelled, "Get him, on top of the wall!"

Aidan ducked as bullets zinged off the wall around him. He painfully shinnied down the ladder on the outside of the rough stone wall, blood trickling down to his wrist from a left arm flesh wound. It was like the Boyle chase all over again. The bicycles were gone. He started running for his life, west along the Royal Canal. At Royal Canal Bank, he sprinted south with two warders in hot pursuit two hundred yards back. After crossing the North Circular Road, he picked up the southbound Royal Canal Bank Road once again. He reached Geraldine Street and saw his salvation. Ahead on his left beyond the row houses was Blessington Street Basin, a freshwater reservoir for the Phibsborough District, with its wooded island near one end.

He darted left down the side street and cut between the houses. Then he dove into the frigid water and swam for the island. Aidan had fallen into the Irish Sea many times. He knew what to expect. The shock of the cold combined with his starving lungs from sprinting almost did him in.

He clawed his way to the island, then dragged himself into the bushes, lying face down in mud, shivering and bleeding. The warders ran by the reservoir and kept going. By the time they realized they had lost sight of Aidan and doubled back, the ripples on the lake had subsided, with any residual surface motion masked by the mallard ducks paddling in the lake.

A short while later, Aidan sat up and gazed around. When he didn't see his pursuers, he swam one-armed back to shore and made his way south-east on back streets to Rotunda Hospital a half mile away. There he saw Morgan in the triage area, tending to maternal patients.

She hummed as she worked, happier than she'd been in years. Tadgh would already have escaped from dreaded Mountjoy prison today.

Then she saw her brother-in-law in his devastated state. "My God! Aidan, is that you?"

He nodded. "Help me? Please?" He held onto whatever composure he had left in him while Morgan took him to an isolated cubicle. Then, finally alone with her, he broke down. Between sobs, he told her, "I . . . failed him, Morgan. Tadgh's—not—free."

Morgan's heart stopped. "What happened?"

"Tadgh held the jailers off . . . but too many other inmates tried to escape before he could climb the ladder. I saw him from the top of the wall . . . tried to save him, but there were just too many warders." He broke off. "I . . . am *so* sorry, Morgan."

Morgan collapsed inside, but she still had a patient to attend to. "Hush now. I'm Bernice, remember? Here, let me help you."

She got him out of his wet clothes and wrapped him in blankets. Then, while he seemed oblivious to her actions, Morgan started suturing his upper arm.

Morgan had waited almost two years for this day without even seeing her husband. Now she had no idea in the world what would happen. She fought back as tears welled up, dabbing her eyes with a cotton swab from the bedside table.

"Was he all right, Aidan? I mean, not hurt?"

"I—I think so, Sis. I saw three dead prisoners on the ground, but Tadgh was unharmed. I'm not sure after that, because they were after me."

Morgan tried to imagine what had happened to her man. She agonized over what they might be doing to him, especially if they realized that he was the instigator of the escape attempt. She had to stop herself in her stitching as her hand started shaking. Then she took a deep breath. What would Tadgh want her to do? Not panic, that's for sure. He'd already be planning the next escape.

Morgan steadied herself and resumed the repair of her brother-in-law's arm. "You did your best, Aidan. I'm sure of that. You and Tadgh are both still alive. I am sure that Michael will try again, soon."

"But Tadgh was counting on me."

"And still is. You'll see. You'll get another chance to free him. I know you will. Now you wait here while I get you a bowl of soup. I'll borrow some clothes for you. Don't leave this room."

Half an hour later, Morgan knew Aidan was feeling better, having been fed, and now clothed in a dry orderly uniform. She stepped into the outer corridor when she heard a commotion at the intake area. An RIC officer was grilling the nurse about any escaped prisoners that might have sought shelter in the hospital. Fortunately, Aidan had come in the nurses' entrance, undetected except for a few maternity patients in the ward.

"I want to talk to your patients," the head RIC constable demanded. "They may have seen something."

The now-adamant nurse snapped, "Not on your life, constable."

"That can be arranged, woman."

Morgan stepped up to the desk. "What's the meaning of this, Head Constable?"

"Prisoners escaped from Mountjoy Prison this afternoon not a mile from here. We know that some were shot. They may have come here."

Morgan asked, "Why would they come here to a women's facility when Mater Hospital is a lot closer?"

Uninterested in reasoning, the constable tried to get past her. "Out of my way, woman."

Now Morgan was incensed. "No! You cannot treat women as second-class citizens, especially those bearing children for you men. There have been no escapees in our hospital today." Morgan crossed her arms defiantly and blocked his way.

Just as the constable was raising his arm to slap Morgan, a doctor stormed out of the ward and demanded to know who was causing the ruckus. The officer explained in a more civil voice than the one he had used with the nurses.

The doctor said, "There are no escapees at Rotunda. Do not disturb our patients and nurses any further than you already have."

The head constable responded curtly, his hand on the flap of his Webley's holster. "I need to do my duty, sir."

"Well, do it elsewhere then, where your escapees might be. Now go along."

The grumbling constable looked into the ward through the rotating door and evidently decided he didn't want to anger pregnant ladies.

"All right, then," the officer reluctantly conceded. Even so, he wouldn't leave without one last display of authority. "Call the barracks if you do come across a prisoner. We know the warders shot some of the perpetrators."

With that, he was gone. The doctor returned to the ward.

Down the hall, Aidan had heard the tense exchange. He took his hand off his revolver in the pocket of his orderly uniform. He'd have tried to use the gun had it become necessary, but he had no idea if it would still fire given his watery ordeal.

When Morgan returned, Aidan threw his arms around her. "You were pretty brave out there, Sis."

"Shush, Brother. It helped that I am so upset at the moment."

Later that evening after Morgan's shift at the hospital ended, she and Aidan made their way to *an Stad* where they found an unhappy Collins in his room.

Collins ushered them in, closed the door, and introduced them to his right-hand man, Harry Boland. "Sit down, you two. I *was* pleased that twenty men escaped, until O'Reilly told me that Tadgh was not one of them. Tell me what happened."

Aidan explained. Collins pounded his fists on the table. "Damnation! I know how hard it must have been to have to leave your brother there. I'll deal with Barton, so help me. Don't you worry, lass, we'll free Tadgh, that I can assure you. As for you, Aidan, you'll have another chance. So don't do anything rash. Now, I'll arrange for rooms here at *an Stad* tonight for the both of you. Morgan, you can return to Kathleen's flat tomorrow."

Tadgh did not have a soft feather bed to sleep in that night. After being brought up before an incensed Head Warder, he was deemed untrustworthy and had to be made an example of. The prison commandant sent Tadgh to solitary confinement, "The Hole."

Chapter Nine
Hunger Strike

Thursday, August 12, 1920
Lord Mayor's Office, Cork City

*T*erence MacSwiney, sensitive poet-intellectual, was contemplating his mission in life now that he had become Lord Mayor of Cork. His good friend, and Republican mayoral predecessor, Tomas MacCurtain, had been senselessly murdered on March 20 in front of his wife and son in retribution for the killing of an officer by the IRA. Terence remembered their time together as the number one and two ranked leaders of the Cork Irish Volunteers Brigade during the Easter Rising. That aborted effort due to the MacNeill countermand had resulted in eighteen months in internment camp before his release.

The mayor had been educated as an accountant, and he was also a playwright, poet, and writer of pamphlets of Irish history. His fifth play, *The Revolutionist*, which he published before the Rising, took the political stand made by a single man as its theme. He had even prepared the booklet on the life of O'Donovan Rossa that had become such useful propaganda at the time of his funeral.

Now, he had a decision to make as he pondered the events leading up to this critical moment. The British government had just that Monday passed the Restoration of Order in Ireland Act, which put the whole country under martial law. The Auxiliary Division, the Black and Tans, and career RIC had immediately started to crack down on the citizenry. Winston Churchill, the Secretary of State for War, had created the Black and Tans as a Special Reserve for the flagging RIC, who were being targeted by the IRA. These were mostly ex-World War veterans who had started pouring into Ireland the previous March and had become infamous for their attacks on civilians and their property.

Cork was mainly a Protestant city, loyal to the English, and the police and most of the government officials were still solidly pro-Britain. He needed to serve the citizens of the city. Yet he still held the rank of President of the Cork branch of Sinn Féin. As such, he supported the ongoing fight for freedom by the oppressed Catholics. This fomenting confrontation had commenced in earnest the previous January as a result of the November ruling of dividing his beloved island north and south by the British parliament. The damned British had already outlawed the Dáil Éireann the previous September, an act that Terence considered illegal.

De Valera was soliciting political and financial support for the cause in America. He'd left soon after the government leaders at the World War Versailles Peace conference had rejected the Irish claim of sovereignty back over a year ago. In his absence, Michael Collins assumed control and had been named President of the Irish Republican Brotherhood (IRB).

After Michael Collins formed his "squad" of assassins to defeat the British intelligence community in mid-1919, the Irish war had become a tit-for-tat, hit-and-run battle. This strategy had emerged after Mick was smuggled into the Dublin Metropolitan Police G Division archives in Brunswick Street and saw the extent of the underground network of British informers and enforcers.

Terence was using his cypher key to decode some Republican documents when an RIC contingent from the barracks on South Terrace Street burst into his office, Webleys drawn. He quickly stuffed the translator in a hidden slot under his desk, but the correspondence remained exposed.

Head Constable Ferguson scooped it up. "What's this gibberish you are reading, Mayor? Seditious material, I'd wager."

MacSwiney tried to take the offensive. "What's the meaning of this? Get out of my office!"

"We are relieving you of your duty, sir. You will come with us." The constable rounded up the evidence while the office staff cowered out of sight.

Terence was at least pleased the cypher had not been discovered. His decision had been made for him.

After he was arrested, Terence immediately went on a hunger strike along with eleven Republican prisoners in Cork Gaol, claiming their military trials were being conducted unfairly. To avoid mutiny by the military and civil police, the British government refused to release MacSwiney. Within two weeks, protests came in from the United States, France, Germany, and a member of the Australian parliament to treat these prisoners more fairly. South American countries pleaded with the Pope to intervene.

By the end of August, MacSwiney was found guilty by court martial and remanded to Brixton Prison for a two-year sentence. The British bullies weren't going to have any more traitorous Lord Mayors of Cork.

Near the end of September, sage Arthur Griffiths, the originator and founding leader of the Sinn Féin movement, was currently out of jail and acting on behalf of de Valera who was still in America. The IRA had just killed three soldiers in Dublin, the first such deaths in that city since the battles in the Easter Rising. As a result, Churchill authorized the Black and Tans to begin burning towns and killing civilians. This reminded Griffiths of the slash and burn tactics employed by Cromwell's monsters during the Confederate wars of the sixteen hundreds.

Something drastic had to be done. Griffiths saw the political benefit of these hunger strikes and requested other prisoners follow suit.

Michael Collins hated the necessity of asking his men to follow this order, so he handed off the responsibility for informing the Republican prisoners in the Joy to Kathleen since she had access to some of them. Morgan, who was still sharing a flat with the doctor and Madeleine, was incensed at the thought of her Tadgh being forced to endure yet another depravation. Hadn't he suffered enough?

"I'm going to go to Michael and Griffiths and get this stopped," she insisted to her flat mate.

"That won't help," Kathleen said, gripping Morgan's hand and looking sympathetically into her burning eyes. "This tactic is having an effect on international support for our Cause. Tadgh will be all right in the end."

Morgan pushed away her friend's hand and snorted, "Nonsense, Kathleen. This will have no effect on the damned British, and I know Tadgh. He will obey orders and could die from this. Michael has done nothing in the last year to get Tadgh out. I won't have it."

Kathleen was firm. "This is war, Morgan. Soldiers die every day, as you painfully know. Michael will not change his mind. You have to accept it."

In the end, Morgan did go to see Collins. He would not change the order but once again committed to getting Tadgh out at the earliest possible opportunity. Morgan knew that was just talk. She hated Collins and his bloody war.

Tadgh had been incarcerated an additional five hundred and fifty-two days after the escape of his compatriots when Kathleen visited him on October 10. For much of the elapsed time since April 1919, Tadgh had been kept in solitary confinement, with no outside contact. But two months earlier, he had been returned to the cell block A and was now finally allowed visitors.

They sat together at a table in the corner of the large stone meeting room with other prisoners and their visitors present. A warder oversaw the visits, and he had his rifle in hand. At least he was out of earshot, given the other discussions in the room.

Kathleen hated to pass along Griffiths' hunger-strike orders to her compatriot, especially after she saw his haggard condition. After checking on the security of their conversation, she spoke in subdued tones. "You don't look at all well, Tadgh."

"I'll be right as rain now that I'm back from solitary. How is Morgan?"

"Fine. She is a nursing supervisor at Rotunda now. She could deliver her own baby."

"She always could since I've known her. But first you've got to . . ."

"I know, Tadgh. In due course, my boy."

"If only."

Tadgh slouched against the cold wall, his teeth chattering. Kathleen called for a blanket, but the guard did not respond.

She took out a comb and tried to untangle his hair. It was impossible. "I see you have a fine beard now, Tadgh."

"They don't give me any sharp objects, Doc."

Kathleen wished that Morgan had been there. She could have seen for herself. He had lost a couple of teeth. His eyes were sunken, his cheeks pasty and pockmarked.

"You've heard about MacSwiney?"

"Yes, of course, Kathleen. There's talk of it here."

"There's international support, Tadgh."

"I suppose there would be, for all that."

She hated what she was about to say, but she spit it out. "Griffiths has requested hunger strikes for all prisoners starting this week."

Tadgh nodded. "I heard a rumor inside."

"It was a request from Arthur, nothing more, Tadgh. You're in no shape for it."

"I'm a soldier. It's a command, lass, and I must obey."

"Now that you're out of solitary, we can organize getting you out, Tadgh. Please believe that."

"I appreciate the thought, lass, but I'll believe it when I see it. I wouldn't wait too long."

Kathleen remembered Morgan's pleas. Remorse ate at her. "Don't do it Tadgh. It's not worth dying over."

"It's my duty. You should know that better than I do. Tell Morgan that my love for her will keep me going until we're together again."

A bell rang. The warder called the visitors to the doorway, and ushered Kathleen, along with the others, out into the rain.

As pre-arranged, the doctor joined Michael and Morgan in her flat after the meeting with Tadgh, careful that no one followed her. She conveyed the sad news.

"Tadgh looks like he's lost fifty pounds and is weak as a kitten. But he insisted he's going on the hunger strike. His spirit still shone through his physical deterioration."

Morgan rose. "I'm going to see him, and I won't take no for an answer. He needs me." She started for the door.

Michael grabbed her from behind by the arms. "He needs you to stay safe, Morgan!"

She twisted and struggled, oblivious to his words.

"Now you listen to me, lass! I won't be able to get you both out."

"All right, then." She calmed down a bit, and pleaded, "But can't we get him out now, Michael? My God, he's been in there almost three and a half years."

"It's better than a lifetime, isn't it, girl? Now that they let him out of solitary, we will see what we can do."

"He'll die before too long. We need to hurry, Michael."

"Aye, lass. But he's a brawler, is our Tadgh."

Morgan contacted Aidan by telephone using their agreed upon code and then went to see him at Creagh by train on Saturday, October 16th. He picked her up at the Skibbereen station with the Kerry.

She was discouraged. Their home lacked the feminine touches

she had previously given it. Yet it looked like Aidan could cook judging from the dirty dishes in the sink. They sat for tea at the kitchen table.

"Who does your laundry, Aidan?"

"I have a girlfriend now. She's trustworthy."

"Not that trollop waitress, Aileen?"

"Hell no. Fine, upstanding lass. Teaches school and takes in other folks' laundry while school's out."

"Where is this saint?"

"She's no saint. Her name is Marjorie, so it is, and she lives with her mother in Skibbereen."

"Is there romance or just laundry?"

"Well, we don't have children on the way if that's what you mean."

"She sounds like somebody I'd love to meet someday. But listen, Aidan, I've given up on Collins. He's too busy to help. And Tadgh's gone on a hunger—"

"Strike? Oh *no*, Sis!" Aidan saw that his sister-in-law was uncharacteristically rattled. Something had to be done.

Morgan went on. "Kathleen met with Tadgh. He told her it's his duty."

Aidan jumped up. He started pacing and shaking his head in agonized thought. Finally, he said, "Well, there's nothing else for it, I'm afraid. I must go get him myself, Morgan."

"We can do it together. When can you come to Dublin?"

"Immediately."

"This Marjorie won't mind?"

"School has just started, so she'll be busy with that."

"Good. I know the doctor means well, and she's been grand with me, but I can't stand it that she can go see him and I can't. So, I need to act if only for my own sake. I have to do something."

"Now who's being rash, Sis?"

"I know, but I just can't wait around any longer and watch him die."

Aidan got up and went for the Jameson in the cupboard, pouring a measure for each of them before saying, "I can't disobey orders."

"Whose orders?"

"Michael Collins, for one. But I'm also part of a new flying column here, part of 3rd West Cork battalion. We have a new leader, Tom Barry, who joined in July. He's got a lot of wartime experience from the Great War."

Morgan swallowed hard. Until now, Aidan had been safe at Creagh as a fisherman. Or so she thought. Now he was another body to be mangled and killed. The images of the blasted German and Belgian soldiers that she'd had to try to piece back together flooded her mind. She fought to clear her mind. She needed Aidan's help in Dublin.

Morgan downed the rest of the liquor. "If you don't come right away, your brother will die. Tell Barry there's a family emergency, and that it's me, not Tadgh. Your superiors must not know what we are going to do."

The next day, Aidan drove Morgan back to Dublin on the Kerry. Still a wanted man, he wore a mustachioed disguise. With an alternate identity, and dressed in her nurse's uniform, Morgan had long since avoided attention from the police.

She found lodging for Aidan at the Gresham Hotel, one of Collins' and his deputy Boland's haunts, to be close to the action. That night the McCarthys took supper up to Aidan's room to plan Tadgh's escape.

Morgan poked listlessly at her meal. "Kathleen described Tadgh as emaciated when she saw him. Knowing him, he's probably been on hunger strike for a week already."

"How long could he last if they don't force feed him?"

Morgan thought for several long moments, lowering her head in her hands. Finally, she looked up and muttered, "I'd say four weeks at most."

"My God, Morgan. We don't have much time. I'll have to break in somehow." Aidan got up and stared out the window at the pelting rain illuminated by the corner streetlight.

"You're not thinking at all sensibly! They'd shoot you dead before you even had a chance to free Tadgh."

"We can't just sit here and wait. All right, then, what do you suggest?"

"Obviously, we have to get them to remove him from the prison."

"They wouldn't do that. He could just rot there, and they'd put him in quicklime."

Morgan cringed. "Don't talk like that."

She picked at her stew and then stuck the fork in and forced down a bite of lamb with a swig of stout. That meager nourishment seemed to give her inspiration. "I've got it! You know how the British hate the black influenza."

"So? We all feared it after it was brought back by the soldiers from the World War. It came from Spain initially, didn't it? But it's dying out now, isn't it, Morgan?"

"It didn't start in Spain, Aidan. They got labeled for it because they were a neutral country during the war and their newspaper reports were not censured like the belligerent countries' were. Governments, preoccupied with war were fatally slow to impose restrictions to isolate the sick and people ignored the warnings until it was too late. I understand that it has killed fifty million people around the world, three times as many as died in the Great War.

"I had no idea, Sis."

"To answer your question, this terrible flu has mostly died out but keeps coming back in susceptible areas like prisons and workhouses for the elderly. We see it every day at the hospital where I work, so we still all wear masks and are constantly washing our hands."

"Marjorie says that the children are wearing masks in her school. They lost twenty percent of them to it in the last two years."

"Proof in point. This flu kills healthy people in a day, Aidan. I've seen it happen, over and over at Rotunda. If you don't quarantine them quickly, it spreads like wildfire." The thought of the warehouse fire in Queenstown came flooding back to her as she spoke.

Aidan shook his head. "But Tadgh doesn't have the black flu, does he?"

"Oh, but he could. We could make it happen."

"Now you're talking crazy, Morgan. That would kill him in his state."

"Exactly. Now you've got it."

"Got what? Tadgh's death?"

"No, Brother, the means to get Tadgh out of the Joy." Brightened by this new prospect, Morgan was suddenly hungry. She shoveled in a forkful of stew and skewered a potato. "Sit down and eat before your dinner gets cold."

Aidan sat and swigged at his stout, then glowered at his sister-in-law.

Morgan explained. "Don't you see? We have to make it look like Tadgh has a bad case of the flu and have him start to turn black."

"Wouldn't they just throw him back into solitary until he died?"

"No, Aidan it's too contagious. At the Adult Fever Hospital down on Cork Street, they have two wings, one for those infected, and the other for those who are recuperating. So I think they would want to get him temporarily out of the prison for fear of infecting the warders. Where better to send him?"

"How do you propose we make him look like he has the black flu?"

"I don't know. Let's sleep on it tonight and we'll talk again tomorrow. Now, eat up. I can't have two emaciated McCarthys."

As she left him for the night to head back to her place with Kathleen and Madeleine, she said, "Don't let Michael see you if he's here."

On her walk to the flat in a rain squall, Morgan debated whether to bring her flat mates into their plan. But they might tell Michael.

He would put a stop to it. *Or would he?* She batted that one back and forth in her mind before deciding that he just might well do that.

The moment she arrived home, looking like a drowned rat, Kathleen pounced on her. "Wherever have you been? We've been looking all over for you. Thought you might have been arrested."

Morgan threw off her shawl and shook her body like a dog. "I must look a mess, Kathleen. I am sorry to have worried you."

"But where—"

"Just around. I needed time to get my balance."

Kathleen reached for a towel and started to dry her friend off. "And do you have it? Your equilibrium, I mean?"

Morgan smiled. "I think so, for the first time in a long while."

The doctor frowned. "I know that look. You're up to something, aren't you."

Morgan had to lie. "No, but I pray that Michael will come up with a plan to get Tadgh out before he dies."

Kathleen took her at her word. "Let's get you into a bath and then bed before you catch your death. That flu is still out there you know."

Morgan complied, hoping her friend wasn't reading her mind.

As she lay in bed, her brain was churning. Kathleen and Madeleine could be a big help. Their all-women, fledgling children's hospital at St. Ultan's at 37 Charlemont Street had been set up the year before and occupied much of their time these days with the support of Mary Plunkett, Joseph's widow. It had tended to the influenza plagued children after the Great War and was providing an overflow facility for the Adult Fever Hospital on Cork Street. These women healers, affiliated with the Cumann na mBan, would protect rebels. They would harbor Tadgh from the authorities and tend to his condition if she and Aidan could get him there undetected.

The next day before going to work at Rotunda, Morgan hurried down to St. Ultan's dressed in her nurse's whites to check its current operations. There she witnessed a spectacle. RIC Head Constable

Brady complained loudly that that staff was neglecting one of his men who had contracted influenza. One hospital gauze-masked orderly muttered something about good riddance to bad rubbish, and the officer whipped up his holster-flap, displaying his Webley.

Morgan realized she had to get the police out of the facility if she were to have any success with her evolving plan, so she stepped in to help. "What is the problem, Constable?"

The agitated officer spun around and spat out, "Head Constable if you please. I've been kept from seeing my man, Constable Hewitt. He's got the black flu."

Morgan intervened. "Best let him be if you do not want to contract it yourself. Not a pleasant way to die."

"I'm not servicing this policeman," the orderly stated, arms crossed and blocking the entrance to the ward.

Morgan saw that this would quickly get out of hand. "I suggest you take your man to see the head sergeant at Cork Street Adult's Fever Hospital. They are more British-orientated there, and you may be allowed to attend to him directly."

Brady looked at Morgan with raised eyebrows. "Who are you to tell me what to do, nurse?"

This was the third time that Morgan had stood face-to-face with the police, including that vile Boyle. When the head constable didn't appear to recognize her, she mentally breathed a sigh of relief. Maybe they didn't have an accurate description of her. "I am just giving you my recommendation."

Finally, at a standoff, the head constable said, "The blokes at that hospital sent him here in the first place.

Think fast! Morgan offered, "Maybe they will have an opening now. This hospital is primarily for children." Turning to the orderly, she asked, "Can you arrange transportation for this head constable's man?"

The recalcitrant orderly lowered her arms. "We can do that *if* our administrator agrees and *if* they have space. We're usually the overflow." She looked daggers at the head constable and added,

"They've been quite a bother, the both o' them, I say."

Brady seemed satisfied and fastened the holster-flap back down over his weapon. "See to it, then."

Morgan nodded and said, "Fine, that's settled." Turning again to the orderly, "Where is your hospital administrator?"

"Third office on the right, miss."

After the horror of the field hospitals in Belgium, Morgan couldn't understand the petty behavior of these hospital staff. She told the administrator what had occurred, then said, "I recommend you contact Cork Street and order your drivers to get those RIC constables over there before you have an even worse situation on your hands."

"Who are you?"

"Bernice Jordan, Nursing supervisor at Rotunda and flat mate of your benefactor, Doctor Kathleen Lynn."

"All right, then." The woman stuck her head out into the corridor and saw the officer standing guard, arms crossed. Acting quickly, within half an hour, she'd found an opening at the Adult Fever Hospital and the head constable and his man were on their way.

The administrator looked curiously at Morgan and asked, "Why did you come down here today?"

Morgan chuckled, wondering whether the woman thought she was romantically linked to the good doctor. She would have to involve Kathleen in her scheme to get Tadgh out of the Joy and to harbor Tadgh at St. Ultan's, but she had to determine the loyalties of the staff who would have to implement her plan. "I like to check out all the hospitals in the area."

"Your orderly seemed to be anti-British . . ." Morgan trailed off, trying to suss out where the administrator's loyalties lay.

The administrator asked, "And you?"

Morgan had no choice but to take a chance. Tadgh's life depended on it. "I support Irish freedom, Madam." She stared hard at the hospital official, her green eyes burning while she waited for a response.

The matron hesitated and then said, "We all do, Bernice. We help where we can."

"Well, I need a favor."

"Name it. You helped us avoid a nasty outcome today."

"I have a Republican falsely jailed at Mountjoy and who I plan to free. Here is what I have in mind." Morgan explained her idea, still not without trepidation. "Will you help me?"

"Yes, if I can. But it sounds like a very risky business. We had one prisoner from the Joy a while back during the height of the pandemic. The warders dumped him here, but they kept him under strict guard until he died."

"Do you have any of Dr. Klein's treatments on hand?"

"Do you mean quinine bisulphate and sodium salicylate?"

"Yes, I believe that it has been effective in treating this plague for some patients if taken in the right dosages and at the right time in the progression of the disease."

"We've had some success with that concoction, Bernice. That is what we were giving to the constable who has been sent to Adult Hospital. But it's not a guaranteed antidote, you know."

Morgan was undeterred. She knew the risks. "Could you hold some of these medicines for me, please?"

"Yes, of course, dear. But they are perishable, even on ice."

Morgan knew they would keep until Sunday.

Later, after her twelve-hour shift at Rotunda, Morgan sought out Aidan. She found him nursing a stout in his room.

"Have you eaten at all today?" she reproached him.

"Stout is a meal unto itself, is it not?"

Morgan could see from his unkempt appearance and behavior that Aidan was regressing toward his condition when she first met him. *It's all that time by himself in Creagh, agonizing about how to help his brother.* Without Tadgh's support, and with Pearse and MacDonagh gone, he was adrift on a lonely sea.

"I have a plan, Brother. I need your help."

Aidan's eyes lit up. "Does it involve . . .?"

"Hush now. Let's have supper, and I'll tell you what I've learned." She went down to the pub and ordered haddock and chips for both of them. Then she treated herself to a Guinness for the first time in ages without bringing Aidan any more alcohol. He'd had enough.

Morgan told him about her trip to St. Ultan's Hospital and their offer of support.

"But how will we get him out of the Joy, Sis?"

"I've been thinking of having the good doctor deliver something to Tadgh. She has had access to him in the past."

"A weapon? The bastards won't let that through their security."

"A small vile of the flu."

Aidan threw up his hands, scowling. "Are you mad, Morgan?"

"No, I have a real plan. I'll explain later after I get more information."

Aidan calmed down. "Won't your flat mate tell Collins?"

Morgan got up from the bed and paced the room before answering. "I don't know. We'll just have to take that risk."

"What's your alternative?"

"I go and see Tadgh myself."

"*That* sounds risky to me. *And* dangerous. If they link you with him . . ."

"Yes, that's another risk," Morgan conceded. "But an RIC sergeant today at the hospital did not recognize me. Neither of us can be caught or Tadgh's life is over, Brother."

Aidan stood up, rubbing his left leg where it had been fractured. "I could go with my disguise."

Morgan was concerned about Aidan's hot head. "No! That's not wise. I'll sound out Kathleen this evening without giving away my plan."

"I overheard something today, Morgan, that I wasn't supposed to hear."

"Does it affect what we have to do with Tadgh?"

"I don't know, it could."

"What?"

"I was in the back-snug downstairs for an early breakfast, just after opening, wearing my disguise." Aidan paused before continuing. "Three men came in and sat in the next booth within earshot. It was still dark, and I don't think they saw me. I think they were Michael's men, named Cullen, Saurin, and Thornton."

Morgan crossed herself. "I've heard Michael mention their names to Kathleen."

"Yes, well they talked about spying at a place called Kidd's Buffett. I gathered that British secret service agents frequent the place; it's down on Grafton Street. At any rate, they mentioned they'd become friends with Major Bennett, Adam Ames, and other British officers. They thought that quite humorous since it meant that they had fooled all those damned Brits."

"How does that affect our plan?"

"Thornton said that a time of reckoning was coming very soon for all those government intelligence spies in G division of the DMP, who they called G-men. So that's where Michael's focus must be right now, trying to smash the English secret service and recruiting Republican spies in their organization. He's not going to help us with Tadgh."

"I suspect you are right, Aidan. There are quite a few assassinations happening on both sides of this war right now. Hard to keep up with it all. Keep out of sight and your ear to the ground, Brother."

That evening Kathleen came home late from a Cumann na mBan meeting.

"We missed you tonight, Morgan." She let down her guard when they were alone and used her real name.

"I was held late at the hospital. Could we talk, please?"

"How about tomorrow. I'm exhausted."

"But I have been stewing about Tadgh. You said he was in bad shape, and now the hunger strike. We have to do something."

Kathleen hung up her coat before answering. "I'm sure Michael is looking into it. He always does."

"I'm sure he cares, but he is so busy, and I fear Tadgh has so little time left, Kathleen. Can you go and see Tadgh again to get him off the strike?"

"He's a soldier, Morgan. Tadgh told me he would obey. I don't think the warders would let me see him again. But if Arthur Griffiths calls off the hunger strike . . ."

"Can you talk to Arthur, then? I don't know him."

"Yes, when he meets with Michael tomorrow, I should be able to ask him."

"Would you?" Tears rolled down Morgan's face. She was trying to cling to any hope after so long.

"Certainly, girl. It's the least I can do." Kathleen took a handkerchief from her military tunic and handed it to her flat mate.

"It sounds more like the most you can do."

"Yes, I'm afraid so." The doctor knew Morgan had a strong constitution, but recent signs of stress were creeping into her behavior. No matter how she tried to hold herself together during the day, Morgan was becoming more distraught as Tadgh's life ebbed away. Kathleen wished she could do more to help. Should she advise Mick of her flat mate's deteriorating condition? Not yet, she decided.

The following evening, she brought sad news: Griffith was unwilling to call off the strike. International support was mounting. Because of this gruesome way to die, hunger strikes were becoming a strategic weapon. Even though some soldiers would have to pay the price for the Cause, it might sway the British to negotiate and thereby save many more lives in the end.

"I'm truly sorry, Morgan."

Morgan knew she and Aidan would have to act on their own soon, or Tadgh would surely die.

Aidan had expected Kathleen's news about Griffith. It was Morgan's plan that scared him when he met with his sister-in-law in his hotel room on Tuesday the 19th.

She had decided her course of action. *Where you go, I go, my love If you die, we die together.* "I'm going to go to the Joy," she told Aidan. "Maybe they'll let me see Tadgh, depending on what shape he is in. I'll go as a nurse, taking the chance they won't connect me with the warehouse disaster three years ago."

"What good will that do?"

"I'll bring him a sealed vial of the flu. The administrator can give one to me at St. Ultan's. All Tadgh has to do is break the top and drink the few drops of liquid. It's highly contagious."

"*What?* No! That'll kill him, Sis. I'm not going along with it."

"He's dead anyway if we don't try."

Aidan grabbed his sister-in-law by the shoulders to shake some sense into her. "I still say no. There *has* to be a better way!"

Morgan gently pried his hands away. "There's a treatment, Aidan, formulated by a Doctor Klein from the United States. I heard of it from Kathleen last year when this disease was killing so many of our countrymen. They saved quite a few lives by using it, Aidan." Morgan hoped that her own uncertainty didn't show up in her voice or facial expression.

Aidan rubbed his forehead side to side, "Are you sure it will work, this treatment?"

Morgan looked Aidan in the eyes and stretched the truth. "Yes, I believe so."

"So, how do we get it?"

"Already done. It will be at St. Ultan's when we arrive."

Aidan was puzzled. "Why there?"

"They support the revolution and mostly take care of children. Less likelihood of being apprehended."

"What if the warders don't decide to transfer him out of the Joy in time?"

"I'll be there to make sure they do." When Morgan saw Aidan shaking his head, she added, "I won't let him die on hunger strike."

"I can't let you sacrifice yourself, Sis."

"Nonsense. Now you're after talking like Michael. I'll need your help to overpower whoever they send to guard Tadgh when they send him to the Adult Fever Hospital. Then we'll need to get him to the children's hospital immediately. I'll give him the treatment and we will need to take some, ourselves."

"I am so worried you're going to be caught, Morgan."

"We have to face that possibility."

Morgan got up and walked to the window, moving the black drape aside. It was pouring rain again on the night street below. She knew how crazy it all sounded. Taking the risk of being recognized in an open environment like Ultan's was one thing. Venturing into the devil's lair of the Joy where they were trained to spot and apprehend felons was another. If she and Aidan were to get caught, Tadgh would die. If she administered the flu to him and then was not allowed to transport him out of the prison, he would die. As ghastly as this outcome was, if he had to die, it was better to die quickly than experience the horror of starving himself to death. But she would then be his killer after he would have entrusted his life to her. But she was at her wit's end. She turned back to Aidan, "So we have a plan, then?"

Aidan would have preferred an all-out assault on the exercise yard to this hare-brained scheme his sister-in-law had conceived. "I still don't like it . . ." He sighed and shook his head before finally conceding, "But I can't think of anything better."

"Right then, all we have to do is decide when to set the plan in motion. The sooner the better. I have to make the request ahead of time. It took Kathleen three days get approval to see Tadgh the last time. I'll let you know the day."

Aidan got up from the chair and walked to the window. Morgan sounded strong, but she was shaking. He put his arms around her from behind and she sank backwards into them.

"I won't let you and Tadgh down, Morgan. You can count on me. But be careful, Sis."

"Yes, I know, Brother." She forced a smile. "Never doubted that for a minute." She turned and held him to her chest. In reality, she had no idea if this ploy would work. There would be no sleeping until this job was done, that was certain.

Morgan strode into the inmate visitation office of Mountjoy prison two days later. The concrete block building was poorly lit, the air felt cold and clammy. Other poor souls were waiting on peripheral wooden benches, waiting to see prisoners. Finally, her number came up and she went to the one window.

"I need to make an appointment to see one of your inmates."

"Which one, nurse?"

"Tadgh McCarthy."

The woman checked in her book. "He's on hunger strike."

"I have heard. That's why I'm here."

"Wait here." The woman went back through a door, leaving Morgan at the window. A minute later, a uniformed warder came out and took Morgan to his adjacent office.

"You want to see McCarthy, nurse?" He looked Morgan up and down.

She leaned forward and planted her fists onto his rough wood table. "You want him off of his hunger strike, don't you?"

The warder sat bold upright. "Well, yes. It's bad for the government, you know."

Morgan pressed her point home. "International concern and all, right?"

"The inmates are causing all the problems, not the warders. It's awful, it is."

The warder knew the score. A great deal of pressure had been put on Liberal Prime Minister Lloyd George and the cabinet to make concessions in order to get MacSwiney to call off his fast. The British ruling class understood that Empire was as much a matter of psychology as it was of soldiers and guns. If MacSwiney were to call off his hunger strike, it would be a severe a blow to Irish morale. If he died, it would be a lesson to the Irish of how ruthless the government was prepared to be, a view reinforced by Lloyd George himself in a controversial speech he had just given at Caernavon in which he spoke of the "very strong measures" that needed to be taken in order to defeat "the real murder gang." The warder agreed with his Prime Minister.

"I work at Rotunda Hospital for women. We've had cases of the elderly where they just stop eating. They lose the will to live. We've developed some ways to deal with that."

"Forced feeding? It hasn't worked for us."

"No. Motivational methods. I'd like to try an experiment with McCarthy. If it works for him, then maybe we could try it with any other inmates that are causing these, ah, problems."

"What's your name?"

"Bernice Jordan. My brother is the Manager at Cunard Steamship Lines in Queenstown."

That didn't impress the warder who was continuing to stare at this intruder, eyes narrowing.

"Why are you doing this, young woman?"

"To reduce international pressure like we discussed, and to save lives. I swore the Hippocratic oath, so I did." She knew full well that only doctors were required to do so, but it sounded good, and the warder wouldn't likely know the difference.

"That one isn't worth saving. A cutthroat killer who'll die here one way or t'other."

Morgan had to resist the urge to slap the bastard's face. Her insides churned and she hoped her anger didn't show as she said, politely, "That's why I chose him, sir. A real test for my process."

The warder scratched his head, his beady eyes searching Morgan's face as he paused for a moment before saying, "I'll ask my superior. He's not here at present. Where can we reach you?"

"I work in women's ward B at Rotunda Hospital."

"I'll get back to you."

With that, the warder terminated the meeting and Morgan was ushered out of the building. Undoubtedly, they would check her credentials. If they gave her request any thought at all.

Morgan and Aidan spent an anxious weekend waiting. Michael Fitzgerald had starved himself to death a few days earlier in Cork Gaol. Tadgh would undoubtedly follow him to the grave.

Come Monday, October 25th, *The Irish Times* reported that Terence MacSwiney had died at Brixton Prison, seventy-four days after he started his hunger strike. His last words to the priest who attended him were, "I want you to bear witness that I die as a soldier of the Irish Republic."

The British barred MacSwiney's sister Annie from having his body land in Dublin on its way to Cork from England. His sacrifice had stirred up more Gaelic Irish ire than all the bullets flying in this annoying War of Independence.

The news of his death spread quickly around the world. MacSwiney's words rang true. "It's not those who inflict the most, but those who endure the most that shall prevail."

Chapter Ten
The Joy

Thursday, October 28, 1920
Rotunda Hospital, Dublin

A message arrived for Morgan while she was working at the hospital. The warders wanted to get McCarthy off of his hunger strike. Come in on Saturday morning at ten o'clock.

Morgan spent the following evening with Aidan in his room. They laid out the route from Mountjoy to the Fever Hospital and on to St. Ultan's and decided how to free Tadgh.

"We're set on doing this on Sunday after I give Tadgh the flu vial tomorrow."

"If you get to him and he agrees to do it."

"I will and he will, Aidan. He has to."

"Then I'll do my part, to be sure."

Morgan reached into her purse and drew out her handkerchief. "Here's the vial that I got from the administrator at the hospital today." She carefully unfolded the cloth and lifted the tiny, sealed glass tube up to the light. "It's hard to say how quickly the disease will take hold, but in Tadgh's condition, it should be overnight. This saliva came from one of the less seriously ill flu patients today. Maybe it will give us more time."

Aidan took the vial and rolled it around in his fingers. "If I broke the glass seal in my hand, would I get infected?"

Morgan held out her hand. "They don't know if the germs can be transmitted airborne, but Dr. Klein thinks so. Give it back to me before you break it."

"It's not much bigger than a bullet. Hard to imagine its contents could be lethal," Aidan said, examining the sickly yellow sputum inside the glass seal.

"You can count on it, Brother," Morgan said, wrapping the vial carefully back up in her handkerchief and putting it in an inside pocket of her handbag. "I have told the nurses at the Ultan's to be ready Sunday morning. What have I forgotten?"

"You've forgotten to care for yourself, Sis."

"There'll be time enough for that later. We've got a deadly job to do, you and I, to save the man we love and need."

"I mean, if you are going to give Tadgh the flu and then attend to him with it, you are at risk."

"We'll be wearing masks and gloves, Aidan."

Aidan crossed himself. "Heaven and Saint Brigid help us all."

Morgan showed up at the Mountjoy visitation office dressed in her nurse's uniform precisely at ten o'clock. She hoped her inside turmoil wasn't showing as her stomach was tied in knots. She felt like throwing up. After an hour of waiting, the attendant called to the window and explained that a warder would come and collect her. McCarthy's condition required Morgan to see him in his cell. She was thrilled yet apprehensive. Three and a half years of never laying eyes on him, waiting for his release. What would be his condition? Morgan steeled herself. She'd never seen emaciated prisoners before, but she remembered having saved men with limbs blown off during the Great War. *I can and must do this!*

The armed warder came with a prison matron and took her to a small examining room. Morgan introduced herself.

"It's a formality, but we have to search you before you can enter the prison proper, Miss."

The warder left the room while the matron did her duty, feeling every inch of Morgan's body and dumping her medical bag and handbag out onto a table to examine the contents. Fortunately, the handkerchief with its deadly vial remained hidden in the inside pocket of her purse.

When she was cleared, the warder returned. "I understand that you will be trying to get our notorious prisoner McCarthy to come off his strike, nurse. We'd like to avoid the publicity, don't ya know."

"Yes, sir. We've had some success with getting elderly patients to take nourishment. If I have any progress today, I will want to come back tomorrow to continue my treatment, all right?"

"I understand, lass. I'll talk to my supervisor. But I don't give your methods much chance. He's a hard one, he is."

The warder led Morgan past two locked gates then out into the prison atrium of cell wing A. It was a towering and cavernous three-story structure with a large spiral staircase near one end. Looking up, Morgan saw skylight windows in the ceiling covered over with silt and leaves. The effect was a macabre, sterile, block wall setting that would deflate the morale of anyone who dwelt within. She shivered. A buzzer sounded. Morgan jumped, her eyes darting all round.

"It's the warning that marching hour for the inmates in the exercise yard is starting," the warder said, and then snapped, "Come with me, quickly now."

They moved out of way as the gaunt prisoners dragged themselves out of their confines and lumbered along the corridors to the spiral staircase, and then down, prodded by warders with rifles at the ready. It was a gruesome sight; one Morgan would remember with revulsion for the rest of her life. *Poor Tadgh.*

After the sad procession had departed, Morgan climbed up the spiral stairs to the top level, following the warder. They headed down the caged side corridor to a cell near the end. With the prisoners in the exercise yard, the cell doors were swung open. Morgan shuddered at the claustrophobic confines of the tiny and smelly living spaces, the stench of sweat and urine permeating each hellhole. A single bed, a small table and chair, a single cold-water sink, and a covered hole on the corner of the floor that she could only imagine was a crude latrine. All this in a white block-walled cubicle. Inhumane. As if this wasn't painful enough, it was likely luxurious accommodations compared to the solitary confinement

195

that had been Tadgh's environment for much of the last year. How could she have left him here for so long without attempting to free him? She cursed herself for waiting on Collins to act.

"He's in here," the warder said, as he unlocked a cell numbered A-94. He stood at the entrance, his rifle at the ready. "Go on."

After a moment's hesitation, Morgan ducked through the door and into Tadgh's world. He lay on his bed motionless under a sheet with only his head showing. He'd been on hunger strike for twenty days now. Bread and water were set on a small table at his bedside, untouched by the look of them. The water was a dingy yellow.

She gagged at the sight of her mavourneen, his cheeks sunken in, his eyes empty sockets, and his scraggly beard long and knotted. But it was also wonderful to be with him after three and a half years of tortured separation. She wanted to go to him and hug him to her, make him know that it would be all right.

But she couldn't. Not yet. She knelt by his bed with her face near his and took out the Bible she had borrowed from Kathleen. She opened it to Psalm Twenty-Three and read it to him.

Tadgh licked his swollen and cracked lips at the sound of her voice, but he didn't open his eyes. It was just as well. Morgan couldn't have the guard learn that they were married.

"Mr. McCarthy, I am a nurse. Bernice Jordan from Rotunda Hospital. I'm here to help you."

"Morgan, is that you?" Tadgh whispered. His eyes fluttered open.

"I think he's delusional, warder," Morgan said, still looking at Tadgh and shaking her head side to side. She saw that the guard was paying attention to her words, and to see if she could get him to eat and drink.

Morgan realized she had to be very careful about what she said. Leaning back down close to Tadgh's face, she said, "I know that you think you are doing your duty, but you also have a duty to family and child. They are your future and without you they will not survive."

Tadgh murmured, "Child?"

"Yes," she lied, reaching under the covers to find his cold hand.

Tadgh slowly turned his head toward hers and she saw the sore where his face had been on the bedclothes.

"Let me fix that." She opened her nurse's kit that had been inspected at the entrance and took out gauze and salve cream.

The warder took a step forward. "What are you doing?"

"Just covering a sore. It helps the patients understand that they are being cared for."

When she finished tending to the wound, Tadgh mumbled softly, "Thank you, aroon."

"What did he say?"

"He thanked me for the kindness, warder. It's critical in these cases that the patient know he is loved and that there are compelling reasons to live." Morgan breathed a sigh of relief. Tadgh was not delusional. He knew she was there and likely wouldn't give their relationship away.

"Hard to do for this bloke. He's in for the duration, ma'am, if you know what I mean, and it won't be long now."

Morgan looked around the room and noticed the pages on the small low table. "What's this we have, here?" She got up and picked up the top sheet. *Martyrdom for Freedom* by Tadgh McCarthy, Revolutionary. "Now there's something to live for. You've got a playwright in your midst, warder."

"We found that under a floorboard, ma'am. Just another charge against this prisoner. A lot of good it'll do 'im."

Morgan saw her opening and turned to address the warder, and covertly, Tadgh. "Look at it a different way. If you want a prisoner off the strike, you've got to give him something to live for that is more important than what he's dying for. This man, for example. The play could be his salvation, for all to see his literary brilliance. Even in confinement, he has to believe there is a future for him that meets God's divine plan for him and his loved ones. That his soul, if not his body, can take flight if he will just do what is asked of

197

him now. He can start now or at least tomorrow morning to take nourishment and his life will change for the better. He has to believe that this is what his masters want him to do. Do you understand?"

The warder grunted. Tadgh moved his head almost imperceptibly up and down and blinked his eyes open. Morgan saw that there was still a spark in those amber pools to his soul. She needed a moment alone with her man. Should she feed him the flu toxin in the glass of water, or was he capable of doing it himself later? What if the warder caught her breaking the vial and dropping the sputum into the water? Shouldn't Tadgh be making his own decision about his fate? Her mind raced as she assessed this critical situation in real time.

"Could you get me some clean water for McCarthy, please?"

The warder stepped forward and grabbed the grimy glass on the table. "What is wrong with this?"

Morgan pointed at the dirty liquid. "That'll make him sicker. I need clean water."

The guard grumbled. "Oh, all right. There's a fountain in the hall a few cells down, nurse." He picked up the glass and dumped the putrid water on the floor. You stay in here with him until I come back."

Morgan looked furtively after the warder until he was out of sight and then whispered, "Tadgh, it's me. Don't acknowledge. Break this vial and drink what's in it." She took it out from inside her handbag and thrust it under the blanket into his quivering hand. "It will make you sicker. But they will send you to an outside hospital. Aidan and I will save you. Understand?"

"Understand what, nurse?" the warder asked poking his head back into the cell, handing Morgan a half-full glass of clearer water, and then looming over her.

Morgan noticed with satisfaction that Tadgh nodded perceptively, so she let him close his hand around the vial instead of pulling it back.

"Understand that I'm going to have him drink water to begin his recovery."

She put the glass to his cracked lips. At first, he clenched his jaw, but with Morgan stroking his brow with her other hand, he finally relaxed and allowed some of the liquid to trickle down his throat.

"See. That wasn't so bad, was it?"

The warder seemed amazed. How could an unknown nurse get this bloke to do what they had been unable to do for three weeks now?

Morgan broke off a small morsel of bread, thinking, *this is so stale that even I wouldn't eat it.* At least it wasn't moldy. She put the food to Tadgh's lips, but he wouldn't open his teeth.

She addressed the warder. "I guess he isn't ready for solid food yet. Can I come back tomorrow, sir? I am hopeful of this progress."

"If you can get him to eat, I think my supervisor will welcome you back, nurse."

Morgan put the glass to his mouth again, and he sipped the water. "Tomorrow, then, if he'll take more of what's given him."

Tadgh nodded, and Morgan squeezed his hand under the blanket. Tadgh's face seemed less pasty, his eyes brighter. God, how she wanted to cradle him in her arms. Morgan had to fight back tears.

The warder motioned toward the door with his rifle. "Best go now, lass."

Morgan hated to leave him. Could she overpower the guard, take his rifle? She realized it would be futile. Too many warders, too many locked gates. And Tadgh was too weak. She felt helpless. Was this plan doomed to failure? Was she just accelerating Tadgh's death? What if they wouldn't let her back in to administer to him? She realized the die was cast.

When Morgan went to take the glass away, Tadgh bit the rim to signal that he wanted more. While she was giving him more water, he brought his other arm slowly from under the covers and found her hand on the glass. He squeezed ever so slightly before he dropped his own to the bed with a plop.

Reluctantly, Morgan stood, bent down, and kissed Tadgh's forehead. "May God go with you, McCarthy." It was terrible to turn away and leave her man in such a state, having asked him to blindly take poison. She shuddered when the warder closed the door and locked it.

On the way back to the entrance, he said, "You've a way with these men, so you do. There are others."

"One at a time, sir, one at a time. I find that motivation is helpful. They are human after all."

"I see your point, ma'am."

They reached the last gate and Morgan said, "Thank you, sir. I'll see you tomorrow and we'll see if he'll eat something, all right?"

"We'll see, nurse. I'll contact my supervisor. On the morrow then, at ten."

Sunday dawned sunny but cold. It was All Hallows Eve, the last day in the Celtic calendar, called Samhain, a time to honor the dead including saints and martyrs. The papers were filled with memories of the Easter Rising leaders. Morgan prayed St. Columba would look out for the McCarthys today. *If only I had an Cathach with me now.*

Morgan arrived at the Joy at ten o'clock, praying it wasn't already too late. She hadn't slept a wink. Had the dose been too severe for Tadgh's condition? At least she had washed and pressed her white nurse's uniform. Today, she didn't have to wait in line. The warder was waiting for her at the visitation desk. This time he introduced himself as Vincent.

"I know you were hoping to feed McCarthy today as part of your treatment, but I'm afraid you will not be able to see him, nurse. He's taken a turn for the worse."

Morgan's heart skipped a beat.

"We've had to move him for the safety of the others."

"What happened?"

"He developed a high fever and cough, and in his weakened

state, we thought he might expire. His breathing is very shallow."

"Has your doctor seen him?"

"No. He's away for All Saints today."

Morgan was encouraged. "It could be the black influenza."

"How can that be? No one else near him has it now. Not for a couple of weeks at least."

"The incubation period can be that long. Let me see him. I can tell."

"That's against regulations. You're not certified to practice medicine in this prison."

"I am a nurse, with a sworn duty to help those who are ill. My worry concerns how it could spread. I can recognize symptoms we have seen at our hospitals."

The warder was fidgeting with his hands, while his rifle leaned against the table beside him. "He is starting to look like the others."

Morgan knew they were running out of time. Tadgh needed her. She spoke quietly, but quickly, letting her fear show through. "Vincent. Do you want to infect the whole prison?"

"No, of course not. We can keep him isolated."

"Did that work in the past?"

"No. We had to send them to the Fever Hospital."

"That's because you have very little fresh air in here. With your doctor gone, you'd better let me see him, before it's too late for him and the rest of you at the prison. You know that this Spanish influenza spreads like wildfire."

The warder hesitated. Morgan was petrified that he would say no.

A woman at the counter overhearing their conversation pulled him aside and talked to him in an agitated voice, pointing at Morgan.

Morgan saw Vincent shrink away from the matron's tongue lashing, thinking, *My God, help me in my hour of need!*

The warder returned and said, "All right. Show me what's in your bag."

Morgan opened her medical satchel, and the warder rummaged through it, before saying, "Very well, follow me."

Morgan breathed a sigh of relief as they started up the circular staircase. She pulled two white cloth masks from her bag and gave Vincent one, donning the other.

When he wrapped it around his wrist, she said, "Wear it. This mask could save your life."

The walk to Tadgh's cell seemed to take forever. Morgan dreaded what she might find. Had she killed him already? When she reached his bedside, he mumbled in delirium.

Morgan examined her patient, thankful that he was still alive. "Look. See, on his arms. Cyanosis. The oxygen starvation is turning his veins purple already. It's black flu all right."

Well, that was progress. Morgan was relieved that the flu had not completely taken hold. Tadgh wasn't wheezing and coughing up frothy blood yet.

Morgan didn't need to force the sound of urgency in her voice. "Do any of the other inmates in cells nearby have symptoms yet?"

Vincent stepped back from the bed and secured his mask more firmly in place. "Ah, not that I know of."

Morgan rammed home her plan. "Well, it won't be long now. We need to get McCarthy out of here . . . to the Cork Street Fever Hospital. Do you have an ambulance?"

"At the back door usually. It may not have petrol."

Damn, that is what I forgot!

"Get a stretcher and two orderlies if you have them." She took three more masks out and gave two to the Warder. She put the third on Tadgh. He was too far gone to recognize her. How brave it must have been for him to drink the contents of the vial knowing it would render him helpless.

He knew I was going to save him, she thought.

The warder was hesitating, saying he had to clear all of this with his superior first.

Morgan thought, *Who is his superior, that woman at the front desk? Not bloody likely.* Since he had been manipulated by her, Morgan decided to take charge. "Damn it, man! Move! There's no time to waste!"

That got him going and ten minutes later, he showed up with two men and a gurney. "My superior said to get rid of McCarthy but guard him."

"'Get rid?'"

"To the same damn hospital where we sent the other cases. The Adult Fever Hospital on Cork Street. He authorized use of the ambulance."

"Good. Let's get going."

Morgan assisted the men in moving Tadgh from the bed onto the gurney while Vincent held back, standing guard with his rifle at the ready. For what purpose, Morgan didn't know.

She barked, "Now, burn the bedclothes and scrub down this room and his cell. Then wash your hands in vinegar and lye soap, for heaven's sake."

The warders looked at each other and to Vincent for direction. He said, "The doctor's not here, so do as this nurse says."

The bell rang for inmate exercise so more warders held the cells closed until they carried Tadgh out toward the spiral staircase. Morgan held back for a moment as they left the cell to scoop up the pages of Tadgh's *Martyrdom for Freedom*, folding and stuffing them down into her bag.

As she exited the cell, Vincent yelled from down the corridor, "Dammit, nurse, this is your show. Come along with ya, now."

Morgan hustled after them, but they were part way down the spiral staircase before she reached it. She scrambled after them, but halfway down one of the warders coming up stopped and stared at Morgan. She thought she recognized him as the policeman Tadgh had accosted in the alleyway just before Rossa's funeral. Her heart was beating out of her chest.

"Don't I know you from somewhere?" he said, turning her head for a better view in the poor light and taking hold of her arm, the one from which her bag hung.

Morgan took a deep breath. How she hoped the mask concealed her face enough. "No, I don't think so, unless your wife was a patient of mine at Rotunda, sir."

The warder paused and scratched his head. "I pride myself in remembering a face, and your eyes are unmistakable."

Vincent called up from below. "Let her be, Angus. We've a deathly sick inmate here who could infect the lot of us."

Angus shook his head and reached to pull Morgan's mask down.

Morgan went on the offensive. She swatted his hand before he could get to her mask and cried, "I'll not have it. Don't you dare hold me back, sir. I have my duty."

The warder thought for a moment and then said, "My wife gave birth last year at Rotunda."

Morgan said, "That's it then, sir. I must be off." She broke her arm free with a swift jerk and trotted down the staircase, without waiting for further examination. Angus was left scratching his head on the stairs above her.

Morgan caught up with the two warders loading Tadgh into the ambulance at the tradesman's entrance to the prison while Vincent looked on. One of the orderlies hopped into the driver's seat followed by Vincent with his rifle across his knee, stock facing outward. The other warder sat in back with the prisoner.

After Morgan checked on Tadgh's condition in the bed of the ambulance and found him no worse, she tried to climb in beside Vincent in the front seat. She motioned and asked him to move to the middle of the cab. It was critical that she be visible so that Aidan would know Tadgh was aboard.

Vincent waved his hand dismissively while she stood on the running board. "That's not necessary, nurse. We can take him from here."

Morgan realized she shouldn't have let them get so far ahead of her. "Nonsense. I need to see this case through." She started to push Vincent over.

Vincent pushed back and stared at Morgan, while he gripped the butt of his rifle. "Why are you taking such a personal interest in this man who is about to die?"

Morgan thought, *It can't end like this.* The warders would take Tadgh to the Fever Hospital all right, but then they would guard him until he could be returned to the Joy or was dead. She had to think fast. Vincent was in no mood to dally with the black flu on board.

"With the death of MacSwiney, the papers ran articles on McCarthy, here, and how you were treating him. That's why I came to the Joy. I am a nurse who took an oath to save ill patients. I took it as a challenge to help you and save him. That work is not done. So move over, please."

Vincent hesitated. "You can ride in back with McCarthy, if you must come."

"I prefer not to get the flu, being in that confined compartment. I won't be much help if I do, now, will I?"

He still dithered.

Morgan pleaded, "I got him to drink yesterday, didn't I? You need him alive. What will the papers print about the prison if he dies of the black flu after being on hunger strike?"

Knowing he was still suspicious, she added, "I know the administrator at Fever. They may still have an experimental treatment that they keep for special cases. She would give it to me."

That did it. "Oh . . . all right, but don't get in my way, nurse." The warder shifted his hefty frame, squeezing into the driver.

Morgan jumped up and slammed the door shut. "C'mon. There's no time to lose. Get this ambulance going."

With little traffic on Sunday morning, the two-mile trip south on Phibsborough Road across the Liffey to the hospital took only ten minutes. The ambulance turned west off The Coombe onto Cork Street, then slowed to navigate the right-hand curve to the hospital on their left. Morgan saw Aidan standing in the road on the right. They had chosen this point in the route where there would likely be no other traffic. He raised his Webley and fired almost point-blank as the ambulance approached him. The bullet pierced the windshield and struck Vincent in the chest. He slumped forward. The driver looked wildly around. The warder in back yelled out, wanting to know what was happening. Morgan grabbed Vincent's rifle by the stock, yanking it out from under the wounded warder and pointed it at the driver.

"Stop the vehicle!" Morgan yelled as she reached forward with her other hand and felt Vincent's carotid artery. No pulse.

The driver slowed down but kept going. "I'm not giving up this prisoner. You'll have to shoot me, too."

Morgan squeezed the trigger. The bullet just skinned the driver's nose and shattered the side window. "Stop! I mean it."

Shaken, he momentarily took his foot off the accelerator but still didn't stop.

Morgan jerked the rifle's bolt back and forward again, ejecting the spent cartridge and chambering a fresh one. Just as she was willing herself to shoot him, Aidan ran around the back of the ambulance. The warder in back took a shot out the back door and missed him. Aidan realized that his first priority was stopping the vehicle and saving Morgan.

The shot caused the distracted driver to look backward, allowing Aidan time to race up to the driver's side of the cab, and scramble up on the running board. He didn't hesitate and put a bullet in the warder's head. Morgan tried to veer away, but it was too late. Blood and brains sprayed onto the front of her clothing and onto the inside of the windshield.

The ambulance swerved to the right while Aidan fumbled with the door. With two dead men in her way, Morgan couldn't reach the controls.

Just before the vehicle hit the curb, Aidan wrenched the door open and grabbed the steering wheel. He spun it counterclockwise. The vehicle lurched left.

Hanging onto the steering wheel with his left hand, Aidan

grabbed hold of the driver's collar with his right, yanked him out of the cab, and let him fall onto the road. Aidan jumped in behind the wheel and brought the ambulance to a stop.

The remaining warder jumped out of the back of the ambulance and appeared at the driver's smashed window with rifle drawn. Before Aidan could react, a shot rang out. The warder slumped to the pavement. The bullet from Vincent's rifle had missed Aidan's head and found its mark.

Morgan was shaking as she dropped the rifle.

Aidan was already out of the ambulance. He quickly collected the two bodies and dragged them into the back of the ambulance, stacking them like cordwood beside his poor brother. There was no time to check Tadgh's condition. Aidan hurried back to the driver's seat.

Morgan was in shock. Vincent's blood had seeped into her clothing. The stark reality of hypocrisy flooded over her. This time, to save the life of her mavourneen, she had killed without a second's hesitation. How could she fault Tadgh and Aidan for doing the same when they had seen their parents brutally murdered by the British? Or any of the other Republicans whose lives had been shattered by this vicious enemy? She had not hesitated to take a life, a violation of her sacred oath as a nurse.

Aidan banged the vehicle into gear and accelerated west on Cork Street. "We're all right now. You were magnificent, Sis."

When he saw that Morgan was incapable of responding, he added, "We were damned lucky that it is Sunday morning, All-Hallows. I guess people are in church or sheltered. The street is deserted."

The entire attack was over in less than two minutes. As the ambulance receded into the distance, orderlies from the Fever Hospital ran out into Cork Street.

"Were those gunshots I heard, or the ambulance down there backfiring?"

"I dunno. It's a crazy war we're in. We all tend to shy away from such noises, at least until they're over."

"Aye, Ian. There's no point in being caught in the crossfire."

They missed the streaks of blood on the pavement where Aidan dragged the bodies, and headed back into the hospital, returning to the fever patients.

"My God, Morgan. You really pulled it off. Does Tadgh have the flu? Did you have to expose your identity?"

Seeing that they had successfully left the scene of the murders, Morgan recovered. Her mind focused on Tadgh's condition. "Yes and no. Hurry, Aidan. We all need that treatment for Tadgh."

They headed southeast on the South Circular Road. It took nearly ten minutes to reach 37 Charlemont Street. Aidan backed the ambulance up to the patients' entrance of St. Ultan's. Morgan threw a cape over herself from her bag, covering her bloodied blouse, and then she rushed inside for assistance.

Not fifteen minutes later, Tadgh was in a sealed private room, with the first course of the treatment having been administered to him, as well as to Morgan and Aidan.

After wiping the ambulance and eliminating evidence, Aidan drove it out of the city and ran it into the Liffey at a prearranged spot where the water ran deep. The dead warders were entombed in the back of the submerged vehicle. Then he rode the Kerry that had been hidden there back to the hospital. Aidan was appalled at Tadgh's condition. *But at least Tadgh is alive and out of that miserable prison.*

Morgan mother-henned the other nurses as they tended to her husband.

"Give him liquid slowly. He's been on hunger strike."

The purple marks had not worsened. Only time would tell whether he would pull through. Morgan was not going to leave his bedside until he did.

Later that day, when the warders didn't check in to the Cork Street Fever Hospital, the police started investigating. A warrant was issued for Bernice Jordan. Officers questioned Jack Jordan. He acted astonished and said he hadn't seen his sister in quite some time, which was indeed true.

The word was out to Collins' intelligence community. At dinner that All Saint's Eve night, he, Kathleen, and Madeleine marveled at Morgan's ingenuity and courage. Michael chuckled, "I'll bet my reputation that Tadgh's brother Aidan was part of that prison break."

"I wonder where they took him," Kathleen said, as she served herself another piece of meat pie.

Michael knew they would turn up. Meanwhile, Tadgh was in good hands.

That evening the police came to the St. Ultan's Children's Hospital looking for their convict. They did not find him. Everyone swore that they had seen neither Tadgh McCarthy nor Bernice Jordan.

On Monday, November 1, the start of a new Celtic year, Arthur Griffith decided the hunger strike had accomplished its purpose. He agonized over Terence's ordeal and called off the sacrifice.

Chapter Eleven
Bloody Sunday

Monday, November 1, 1920
Ultan's Children's Hospital, Dublin

*M*organ could not return to work. The newspapers blared the headline: *Nurse Springs Lifer with Black Flu from the Joy. Three Warders Missing.* The ambulance containing the dead warders had not been found. Foul play was suspected, and Bernice Jordan was labeled the culprit, although no one could understand how she overpowered the warders.

Aidan had stayed overnight at the hospital with Morgan and Tadgh until he assured himself that his brother would recover. Then in the morning, at Morgan's insistence, he raced back to Creagh on the Kerry to get away from the turmoil that they had caused.

Morgan summoned Kathleen to come to St. Ultan's that Monday morning. They met in Tadgh's private room. Because of the newspaper reports, the good doctor had been worried sick about her roommate when she failed to show up at their flat the night before.

After Morgan gave her a rundown of the escape events, Kathleen said, "My God, girl! Such a bold plan. It must have taken immense fortitude—not just to go there and see Tadgh in such a state, but to give him that deadly poison. What if they hadn't let you see him the next day?"

"They almost didn't. The alternative to my plan was certain death for Tadgh. Michael was too busy, so I took charge." Sitting on the edge of the bed, Morgan rewet her towel in the basin of water on the table and wrung it out before applying it to Tadgh's brow. He stirred and murmured something unintelligible before nodding off again.

Kathleen took Tadgh's pulse. "He's still quite ill, Bernice."

Morgan glanced up at her friend with wide eyes, forehead furrowed.

Kathleen laid Tadgh's arm gently back on the bed. "Ninety-eight."

Morgan sighed. "That's better than an hour ago. Fortunately, the treatment seems to be working, although his fever is still raging, and his veins are still discolored. As you can see, though, he's still very weak from his hunger ordeal. Liquids only, for a while."

Talking with Kathleen, Morgan was suddenly struck with the craziness of her scheme to free Tadgh. What if he had died from the flu in captivity? She would have killed him. She wouldn't have been able to live with herself. She stood up and turned away, toward the window, so that her flat-mate couldn't see the tears welling up.

"Well, lass, Michael certainly thinks you walk on water now." Her voice faltered. "Did you kill the guards?"

Morgan turned to face her friend with streaming eyes. "What do you think?"

"A woman would have done it to save her man, I'd venture." Kathleen stepped forward and put her arm around Morgan's shoulders, then handed her a handkerchief. "Just blow."

"I helped Aidan with the dirty work. Not proud of it, and against my principles, but it had to be done."

"Aye, Bernice. Your secret stops with me, that's certain. Your ordeal's over now, but Arthur just called off the hunger strike today, you know."

Morgan sniffed. "I heard. Bad timing, I guess, but it forced me to get Tadgh out, so I'm grateful. He would have died anyway. He was almost gone."

Morgan cleared her nose and handed the handkerchief back. "I'm staying here at the hospital until Tadgh recovers. Safest place for Tadgh and me for now."

"Michael will stop by when Tadgh is able to talk." Kathleen

gave Morgan another hug, this time more fiercely. "Let me know through the nurses here if you need anything."

"Could you explain to the administrator at Rotunda that I am sorry to leave them in the lurch? It couldn't be helped."

"That would imply that I know where you are. No, I think it best for all concerned if you just drop out of sight. They have backup."

With that, the good doctor was gone, leaving Morgan to tend to her man.

Morgan stayed with Tadgh until the crisis passed, sleeping on a cot the orderlies brought her. On the third day, his fever broke and the purple stain of the veins in his arms and legs receded. She had to feed him fluids slowly since his body was completely dehydrated. By Friday, he recognized who she was and could take a little porridge.

"You're my savior, aroon," he croaked.

"As you were mine, mavourneen. You believed in me."

"You were an angel, appearing in the fog. I thought all was lost until that moment."

"I would not let that happen, Tadgh," Morgan said, caressing his sunken cheek.

"I trusted an angel from God, and I am free."

"You are safe with me now, my love. I will never let you go. You are all that matters in life."

Many of the Irish folk in Dublin were cheering for Bernice. Others were hoping to find her in order to get the one-thousand-pound reward the police put up.

District Inspector Maloney questioned Jack again in Cork. The Cunard manager stated that he hadn't seen his sister in the last two years, which was true since she had died on the *Lusitania*. Inwardly, he feared for Morgan's life once again. *What had happened to her?* he wondered.

Having taken backstreets like a ghost, Michael Collins arrived unannounced the following Monday on his Raleigh bicycle, parking it out of sight behind Ultan's.

Morgan met him at Tadgh's door.

Michael shook her hand vigorously. "There you are, ah, Bernice. My favorite lass."

"You seem oblivious to the risks of being arrested or killed, Michael."

"I find that it is best to hide in plain sight and keep moving, lass. I don't carry a gun; in case I'm ever stopped. How's Tadgh faring? I've been worried."

"Come in, see for yourself. He's improving."

Morgan showed him to the private room where Tadgh was convalescing. She had shaved his beard, trimmed his moustache, and washed his hair in preparation for this meeting.

"Hello, Mick," Tadgh said weakly from his chair by the window. He raised his arm limply to indicate another seat, then shook his school chum's outstretched hand. "Come sit down, sir."

Collins pulled the other chair over to be face to face with his friend. "You've served our revolution with distinction, lad. The hunger strikes have proved to be a grand weapon in our fight. You look almost battle fit again."

Morgan remembered how Antoine Depage would use the same tactic to motivate the wounded men to get better and return to the Belgian Front. She had not told Tadgh that the strike had been called off and hoped Michael didn't bring it up.

Collins turned to Morgan. "When Tadgh first introduced you, I confess I was skeptical. But you've proven yourself worthy of our Cause and your husband. And you, Tadgh, you've been away for quite a while. We're in the midst of a different kind of war now."

"I heard rumors in the Joy. You've made progress in three years, Mick."

"The Rising taught us we have no hope of mobilizing an army

214

large or well-equipped enough to defeat the British. Their army is too strong, especially now after the World War. We fight on as guerrillas. But we've got to make the world, especially America, see the justice of our Cause and make it impossible for the bastards to continue to tyrannize us. Your sacrifice, and Terence's, has helped to do just that."

"McGarrity said as much back at the beginning of 'seventeen when I was purchasing the guns."

"I'm now Director of Intelligence. That may not sound important, Tadgh, but it is the most crucial aspect of our fight. We need to completely neutralize the subversive British secret service. They knew our every move until recently. I have been planting agents in their midst to determine their plans before they execute them. I've set up my own assassination squad to eliminate their intelligence agents. And we had our own dirty laundry. I've had to weed out the Irish spies in our midst. A painful ongoing task, to be sure."

Morgan saw Tadgh's perspiring brow and was worried. She brought him a dry towel and dabbed his forehead.

Tadgh thanked her and turned back to his boss. "How do you fight, Mick?"

"Hit and run. We have a major purge mission coming up shortly. We commandeer arms by raiding RIC barracks, destroying over six hundred of them so far. Got them on the retreat finally, I think."

"The whole world has changed while I've been away." Tadgh reached out and grasped Morgan's hand.

"Aye, lad, it has. We disrupt the railroads by refusing to transport British military personnel. We play havoc with the postal service by intercepting the mail, and our jurors refuse to serve in the court system. We bomb roads to interrupt passage. Anything to bring down their infrastructure."

"They must be mad as hornets."

"That's why they brought in the Black and Tans."

"I heard about those bastards, inside. Ex-World War army. Slash and burn."

"We're up to it, Tadgh."

"That goes without saying, Mick. How can I help?"

Michael took the cloth from Morgan and wiped Tadgh's forehead to remove beads of sweat. "You've been a grand crusader for our Cause, and you will lead the charge again. Be patient. Right now, you need to get well and stay out of sight with Morgan here. I operate right under the enemy's nose down at Number Three Crow Street, between the Castle and Trinity. I want you two to stay there when you're able. Then we'll see."

After Collins left as unobtrusively as he had arrived, Tadgh collapsed on the bed, exhausted. Morgan could tell from his rapid breathing and elevated temperature that he had overdone it, trying to appear fit with his boss. It took a day before he was back on the road to recovery.

That Tuesday evening, November 9, Tadgh took his first solid food, Irish stew.

Morgan fed it into him, bit by bit. "C'mon, mavourneen, this is good for you."

He gagged at first, but then swallowed each spoonful.

"Some bread too, Tadgh." Morgan had cut off the crusts. He nibbled the edge. All the while, she forced him to drink water.

"Where is Aidan, Morgan?"

"Back at Creagh. I felt it best for him to get out of Dublin, and someone has to mind our home."

Tadgh put his hand to his neck. "My locket and our rings?"

"Jack took them before the police could arrest you."

"Contact him and get them back."

"Speaking of Jack, they've given him leave of absence."

"Why?"

Morgan looked down at the bedclothes and straightened them before answering. "I'm afraid that I am the cause."

"How so?"

Looking away to avoid his gaze, she answered in a low voice, "I only escaped capture with you by pretending to be his sister."

Tadgh started to sit up, then grabbed his head, and propped himself on one arm to stop shaking.

Morgan grabbed him by the shoulders and gently laid him back down. "Lie still now, mavourneen."

She tried to tuck him under the covers, but he reached out and grasped her arm to stop her. "What? Jack has a sister?"

"Had a sister." Morgan explained how she had been impersonating the dead Bernice Jordan.

"Died on the *Lusitania*, you say. Close resemblance to you." Tadgh's eyes clouded. "Is that why he dotes on you?"

Morgan flared. "He does no such thing. Honestly, Tadgh! Is that why you look so green at the gills?"

"So why is he on furlough?"

Morgan sat on the edge of the bed beside him. "You're not thinking straight yet, are you, my love. The police think that his sister was the one who disposed of three prison guards to get you out of prison. As a result, his company management now correctly thinks that he had something to do with moving your guns to that warehouse. His Cunard man was killed in the fire. Because of us, Jack remains under suspicion, but not fired, not yet. He's a good friend, Tadgh, that's all. You may not have realized it at the time, but he pulled you from the warehouse fire and saved your life, and with him being in a wheelchair just a year earlier, that was a brave feat."

Tadgh understood that Jack had helped him, yet the thought of Morgan being close to the man, while she pretended to be his sister, stuck in his craw. He crossed his arms and scowled. "I'll have to remember to thank him when he brings back our jewelry."

"You do that." Morgan turned her back on Tadgh for a moment, her patience strained.

"You heard what Mick said, lass," Tadgh muttered, his eyes cast down. "They have to scrounge guns from the RIC. I let our guns get destroyed."

Morgan put her hand out and lifted his chin, then locked eyes with him. "Hardly. You gave up your fortune to go and buy them in America and risked your life to get them back home. Then, when threatened, you tried to save them and almost lost your life in the process."

Tadgh softened to her touch as her fingers lingered, but his mind would not let go of the mission ahead. He focused on her green eyes, the lovely orbs that he fell in love with, and she did not pull away. "The most important thing we can do for the revolution now is find the O'Donnell treasure. Red Hugh O'Donnell and our revolution are counting on us to do so." He placed his hand over hers, holding it close. "Can you please have Jack come up to Dublin? We need my locket. Until Mick assigns me, we need to focus on that task." Then he remembered. "Where are Collin and Peader?"

Morgan knew he was right about her O'Donnell ancestor's riches. At least Tadgh's mind wasn't that cloudy when it came to the treasure, a good sign for his recovery. Anything that diverted his attention from the killing of war and away from the horrors of his last three years was a step in the right direction, in her opinion. But his thought process made her think of her brother Collin's obsession with finding her. She would have to be careful that this search for O'Donnell valuables didn't become a dangerous compulsion that would damage their marriage.

"Collin is in Toronto, where he should be, with Kathy, Liam, and Claire."

"Claire? It was a girl?"

"She has curly black hair like me. Collin sent pictures. She's three now, and Liam is four. Here, look, I have them with me." Morgan rummaged through her purse and found two dog-eared black and white photographs of the children. "See?"

"Christ, Jesus, I *have* been gone a long time." The scratchings on the cell wall to mark time had been mind-numbing minutiae, Tadgh thought. He had never given up on the hope of escape until going on the hunger strike. The fact that Collin had a daughter, now three, struck home. All that time wasted in isolation while the World War ended and the revolution started, with his missing it. He wondered how Morgan felt but dared not ask. Not with her brother, and Kathy with two fine children, and herself, with a little one lost in pregnancy. And himself away in America. Yet she had accomplished a miracle, getting him out of that hellhole. He swore to himself that he would make it up to her. At the same time, he vowed he would never again let himself be captured by the bloody British, not alive anyway.

Morgan's voice jolted Tadgh back to the present. "I don't know anything about Peader's whereabouts. I overheard Michael talking about forming flying columns of guerrilla raiders all over the country. He knew Peader was from Donegal. He said he met him at the GPO when he was helping you."

"While you were recovering from your gunshot wound at Rotunda." The remembrance of her life-threatening wound because of the Cause made his heart sink. For the first time since his escape, Tadgh reached out and drew Morgan in, kissing her long and lovingly on her lips.

He wanted her to know that everything was going to be all right.

It took another week and a half before Tadgh had the strength to walk any distance. Jack came up from Queenstown and helped Tadgh and Morgan move quietly into Mick's hideout on narrow Crow Street. That one-block alley, running north off Dame Street, lay between Trinity College and the Castle and only a block southeast from the Temple Bar Pub. That put Collins and the Squad in the middle of British Dublin, within eyesight of the enemy.

When they were settled in their rooms on the second floor, Jack went to his coat hanging on the back of his door and took a handkerchief from the breast pocket. He handed it to Tadgh unopened. "I've been keeping these safe for you. I hope you don't mind."

219

Morgan looked at Tadgh to respond.

Tadgh spread the folds and revealed his locket and their rings. He put the locket's chain that Jack had repaired around his neck, slipped the signet ring on, and put Morgan's wedding ring on her left-third finger before answering. "Morgan told me that you were quick-witted at the time to remove and hide these precious treasures when the police came. We and our ancestors of the Clans Pact thank you, Jack. You are a true friend."

Morgan was happy that Tadgh didn't make a scene about her previous involvement with the former Cunard manager, and she was relieved when her husband thanked him for saving her life.

That night, Thursday, November 18, the trio headed to the Temple Bar Pub just up the street and around the corner. After checking to be sure there were no British police present, Jack led them inside.

The pub owner and sometimes bartender, Deirdre yelled across the pub when they walked in, "Morgan, is that you? My God, it's Tadgh and Jack, too." She rushed out from behind the bar and hugged them all.

Tadgh whispered, "Best keep our voices down, lass."

"I read the papers, Tadgh. I've been so worried."

Tadgh twirled the end of his bushy moustache between his right thumb and index finger in swashbuckling flair. "Have you now, Deirdre? I can assure you that I am alive and well."

"You'll be needing some fattening up, I warrant. Come, sit and eat."

Morgan wasn't sure she liked the repartee between the two. With the exception of the one passionate kiss, Tadgh's demeanor had been reserved since his escape. This was the first jovial spark she had noticed, and it wasn't for her.

Once they were all seated in a cozy snug away from most of the patrons, Deirdre came back with B & C stout for all.

Tadgh held up his hand, declining the drink. "We'll need to

make mine milk for now, lass. My stomach wouldn't take well to any brew at the present."

Deirdre's laid her hand gently on Tadgh's shoulder. "Oh, yes. I see."

She went away and returned with a glass of milk. "I haven't seen you all since your wedding. What is it now? Four years and four months, if I'm counting right. I thought you'd have wee lads and lassies by now."

Morgan glanced away. Tadgh reached out and grasped his wife's hand, before answering Deirdre. "Not with a war for our freedom still going on. I've been, uh, away you see."

"Oh yes. How stupid of me." Deirdre turned toward Jordan. "What brings you to Dublin, Jack?"

"I've thrown my lot in with these ruffians, so I have. I'm resident here, now."

"Well, you are welcome here at my Pub any time. I'll bring you all the house stew."

Later, when they were leaving, Deirdre said, "Please come again. I'm glad that you have survived and are fit as a fiddle."

"A fiddle that needs to be tuned up, lass."

Morgan thought that Tadgh must be feeling better to be bantering with her bridesmaid, Deirdre. But she still didn't like it.

The building at Number Three Crow Street housed J.F. Fowler Printers on the ground floor, an apt front for the clandestine IRA operation in the basement with its intelligence center, and on the second floor, with its living and meeting rooms. When the trio arrived back from the pub, they discussed their course of action in the McCarthys' room. Although the striped wallpaper was faded and splotched from years of mildew, the furnishings were clean and functional. Michael's quartermaster brought them a table and four chairs to turn the bedroom into a meeting place for their convenience. An east-facing casement window looked out onto Crow Street when the heavy old drapes were opened. Overall, the atmosphere added to the mystery of their conversation, with a flickering electric bulb dimly lighting the chamber through its hooded shade.

Circling the room and stroking his moustache, Tadgh started talking, "I've had the time to think on our puzzle for these past years. Remember that the MacCarthaigh Reagh *Book of Lismore* showed the way to the McCarthy treasure on the Rock of Cashel."

Morgan admonished, "Sit down, for heaven's sake, Tadgh. You're as bad as Aidan with your nervous bouts and you'll make yourself ill again." He had changed in his demeanor. She imagined him pacing the small cell ad-nauseum and had to drive that thought out of her head.

Tadgh perched on the corner of the bed. "I think that we will find clues to the O'Donnell treasure in the O'Donnell-acquired *Book of Ballymote*[4]. The old man in Ballymote said so. And why, otherwise, would Red Hugh's grandfather have acquired the document?"

"And then there's the ghostly vision I saw of Sir Owain riding in the Temple Castle ruins."

"Morgan. I don't think he is involved."

"I'm not so sure, my love. So what should we do?"

"Someone needs to see Professor Lawlor at the Royal Irish Academy and set up a meeting to examine your ancestor's book, Morgan. Besides, I need the notes he gave me on the Ballymote book that are at Creagh."

They agreed Tadgh would telegraph a coded message to Aidan, and Jack offered to contact Lawlor the next day since the furloughed Cunard manager was not wanted by the police.

Morgan went to the window and closed the drapes against the cold. "What about Collin?"

"I don't see how he could help us from Canada, but we should keep him informed by coded telegram."

The next afternoon, Jack reappeared with news for the McCarthys. "Professor Lawlor is teaching at present, so he doesn't come to the RIA very often. The attractive woman at the desk couldn't help me with the *Book of Ballymote* but said we might contact him at this Sunday's Gaelic football match at Croke Park. The professor is an avid fan of the Dublin Gaelic team, and he has his own two box seats. She was invited there once with him, so she gave me his seat numbers."

Morgan thanked Jack for the information, and then exclaimed, "Why don't we go, mavourneen. The outing will do us good. If Michael can hide in plain sight right under the snooty British noses, then we can, too."

Tadgh considered their options. "We need to find Lawlor, that's for certain, and we'll be less conspicuous in a large crowd than trying to talk to him in Trinity College. I think I'm up for it."

"That's sorted then," Jack said. "I can get three tickets somewhere near the professor."

Saturday evening, Michael Collins held an attack meeting at one of his headquarters in Devlin's Public House on Parnell Street.

One of his operatives, Dick McKee, had been put in charge of planning the operation to execute over fifty British intelligence officers and informers, but Cathal Brugha, the Minister for Defense, forced them to reduce the targets to thirty-five. Unfortunately, Dick had been arrested a few days earlier. Michael's deputies, Liam Torbin, Tom Cullen, and Frank Thornton now coordinated the offensive. The British agents' addresses had been discovered from sympathetic housemaids, careless talk from some of the British, and an IRA informant in the RIC Donnybrook barracks named Sergeant Mannix.

Torbin led the meeting. "We need a coordinated attack on twenty traitors at precisely eight o'clock in eight places in the city. The assassinations must be simultaneous."

Collins was upset with Brugha, but excited that they were going to strike a long-overdue blow for freedom. "This must go off with precision and without hesitation, lads. We've talked of this before. When you pull the trigger, think of your targets as the masterminds of our demise who have caused the killings of our Volunteers."

Each member of the Squad read out his assignment until they were all clear on their tasks.

Michael gave the final trumpet call. "I know that I am asking you to go beyond duty in this assignment to kill potentially unarmed men in cold blood. There is no crime for detecting and destroying in wartime the spy and informer. They have destroyed without trial. We will pay them back in their own coin."

November 21, 1920, dawned as Bloody Sunday in Dublin. Collins reflected afterward about the fourteen key members of British intelligence, many known as the Cairo Gang by their IRA counterparts that had been executed and another who was mortally wounded. Only one Squad member had been arrested. He smiled, knowing that this intelligence coup would wipe out the British secret service for some months to come. Those who remained alive would fear for their lives, as would any residual British sympathizers in the IRA ranks.

The one and a half mile walk north to Croke Park stadium from Crow Street took Morgan, Tadgh, and Jack right past Mountjoy Square. Morgan called ahead and Sean O'Casey was waiting for them with lunch at Number Thirty-Five.

Sean grabbed his protégé by the shoulders, holding him at arm's length. "Tadgh, my boy! You look a little worse for wear, lad."

"Better now, Sean, since my lovely wife got me out."

"I heard about it. Escaping the Joy, now there's the feat. Morgan's a wonder, that's certain."

Morgan gave Sean a daughterly hug.

O'Casey mock-scolded her. "Now you and Tadgh are both on

the run, just like before."

Tadgh laughed. "Ever the same until we banish the buggers, teacher."

"Would that be true, lad."

Tadgh motioned to their companion. "Let me introduce you to Jack Jordan. He's one of us. He saved my life four years back, didn't you, Jack."

Morgan added, "And mine, five years ago now."

Jack stuck out his hand. "Tadgh and Morgan exaggerate. Pleased to meet you, sir. I read your book on the Story of the Irish Citizens Army. I understand why you abhor violence."

"First, I've never known the McCarthys to exaggerate, and second, it's not often I get a visitor who has read my drivel. Come in and let us talk some more."

When they were all settled into the playwright's parlor, Morgan said, "We're on our way to Croke for the football match, Sean."

"Are you now, lass? I'd be careful there today after what happened this morning."

"What was it that happened, Sean?" Tadgh asked, looking his benefactor in the eyes. "We've been in our rooms until this walk."

"Collins and his Squad attacked the G-men after months of warning them. Got fourteen of them, I understand. The Castle's in an uproar and out for blood."

"Well, that's grand news, to be sure."

"Waking a sleeping giant is good news? We don't need a repeat of the Rising, lad."

"That won't happen. A hit and run offensive is what is in store, Sean."

"It will catch up to you all, you know."

"Not this time. Just grist for your fertile playwright's mind, teacher."

"We'll see." O'Casey took a pen from his pocket and flourished it in the air as if were a sword. "Meanwhile, be careful on the streets today."

After a lunch of chicken pie and green beans, the Republicans headed out to the game.

"We'll see you soon, Sean," Morgan said, giving him a wink.

"If you survive. Take care."

Despite the morning's violence, the stadium was packed to the rafters with five thousand war-weary football fans waiting for the game to start. The ticket-takers were still hawking their wares for the few empty seats as the trio arrived.

"Where do you think A 334 section is?" Morgan asked after they had entered through the south canal entrance at two thirty. It had taken longer than expected in Tadgh's condition to walk the three-quarters of a mile from Sean's home. Jack was trailing the McCarthys, checking the tickets. They walked along the track that separated the pitch from the stands, looking up to spot the section numbers.

Tadgh remembered having been to this pitch many times. "Those seats must be on our left to the west, in the pavilion. Let's see if we can find the professor."

Morgan noticed that the stands formed a horseshoe with the open ends to the north fronting on Clonliffe Road beyond a hill and railway embankment.

Tadgh said, "It's odd that the neither the Dublin home team nor Tipperary's visiting team are practicing on the pitch for the game." Tension hung in the air, and it was palpable.

The home team in their traditional double blue uniforms, the Dublin Gaelic, burst through the western entrance onto the pitch. The crowd erupted. The visitors in their white jerseys with a green diagonal sash ran into the stadium fielding boos from the partisan crowd. Morgan was almost bowled over by a lad with the name of Hogan on his football jersey as he rushed by. She could smell his sweat lingering in the wake of that team's arrival.

"Up there." Tadgh pointed above into the pavilion. Since neither Morgan nor Jack had met Lawlor, they took Tadgh at his word. Around ten minutes later, they arrived in the section where the professor and a saintly-appearing lady sat conversing in the midst of the most vocal Dublin supporters. Before Tadgh could reach them, the head referee blew his whistle to start the game. It was three-fifteen already. The game was starting a half hour late.

"Shouldn't we be trying to get to our seats?" Jack asked, pulling on Morgan's sleeve. "I think we are nearer the south end on this side."

"Just a minute, Jack. Tadgh needs to talk to Professor Lawlor first," Morgan said, gripping her husband's hand before he darted away. They waited at the end of the K row while Tadgh slid in front of the patrons.

"Professor," he cried out above the din as the home team took its first kick on goal.

Lawlor looked up from the action on the field and saw Tadgh advancing four seats across to his left. He looked at him quizzically, then waved him over.

An aircraft flew over the pitch and shot out a red flare. Suddenly, Tadgh heard gunshots coming from the south canal entrance to his right. RIC and Black and Tan police burst into the stadium firing up to the left into the stands. Wild confusion reigned. Immediately, spectators made a rush for the far side of Croke Park. Shots were fired over their heads and into the crowd.

Tadgh yelled at Morgan and Jack to get down. Patrons were streaming past him when Tadgh dove to his right and intercepted Lawlor and his wife.

"Get down, sir, and ma'am. Under the seat." Then he ducked, himself. He was in no condition to run anyway. A bullet shattered the seat back where Lawlor's wife had been sitting a moment before.

From his position peering out over the back of the vacated seat in front of him, Tadgh could see the bedlam. Spectators were crushing each other in vain attempts to get away. Some on the other side of the pitch tried to scale the perimeter wall. The police shot at them, and one fell off the wall, presumably dead.

Unseen by Tadgh, as the spectators streamed out, an armored car on St. James Avenue fired its machine guns over the heads of the crowd, trying to halt them. The attack only lasted ninety seconds, yet it left fourteen dead, including seven assassinated at the scene, five more mortally wounded, and two spectators trampled to death. Later reports would list the wounded at over eighty.

The trio and the Lawlors didn't move from their hiding places until five minutes after the shooting stopped. Out on the pitch, Morgan saw the Tipperary coach attending to one of the players lying near the north end. They rolled his dead body over on his back. It was Michael Hogan from the visiting team who had almost knocked her down.

The police left the stadium, presumably chasing after those who were fleeing. Morgan assumed that the perpetrators probably wanted to get as far away as possible from the massacre. Ambulances started to arrive, and Morgan's instinct was to rush down to assist. As she started to do so, Tadgh grabbed her arm and pulled her back.

"Not this time, aroon. Too dangerous. This is retaliation for Michael's assassinations this morning."

Remembering that she was now a fugitive, Morgan stopped in her tracks before saying, "Sean was right. An eye for an eye begets blindness. Heaven help us all." The crowd had dispersed from their section of the stands, leaving them to witness the gruesome removal of the bodies below.

Professor Lawlor came over to Tadgh. "God in heaven, this is a tragic day for Ireland, McCarthy, isn't it? You certainly know how to handle an emergency, lad. My missus and I thank you for protecting us from those bullets."

"Glad to be of assistance, sir. We came to this match to ask for your help."

"Did you, now? It must be important."

"You suggested we explore the *Book of Ballymote*."

"Yes, the connection to your friend Peader O'Donnell, I believe."

"Aye, and for my wife Morgan, Peader's cousin, and a former O'Donnell. Let me introduce you."

Lawlor raised his eyebrows and shook Morgan's hand. "Well now, young lady. Pleased to meet you. We seem to have a plethora of O'Donnells interested in that old book, don't we, now."

Morgan smiled, her green eyes flashing. "Yes, sir. And I have a brother Collin in Canada who takes an interest as well."

Tadgh broke in. "We need to look at this document as soon as possible. It is a matter of life and death."

"Not as urgent as what we just witnessed, surely."

"But crucial, sir. I feel it is essential to help stop this brutality once and for all, I can assure you."

"I'm all for that, lad. In that case, I can meet you at the RIA tomorrow afternoon after my teaching, say four o'clock. I need to gain approval for you to examine the document. Would that suit?"

"Yes, of course. Now then, sir, let's get you and your wife to safety."

The next day *The Irish Times* published a statement from the Castle.

'A number of men came to Dublin on Saturday under the guise of asking to attend a football match between Tipperary and Dublin. But their real intention was to take part in the series of murderous outrages which took place in Dublin that morning. Learning on Saturday that a number of these gunmen were present in Croke Park, the Crown forces went to raid the field. It was the original intention that an officer would go to the center of the field and speaking from a megaphone, inviting the assassins to come forward. But on their approach, armed pickets gave warning. Shots were fired to warn the wanted men, who caused a stampede and escaped in the confusion.'

A condemnation of the police action followed. The commander of the British forces for the attack, Major Mills, later admitted that his men were excited and out of hand.

In reality, this was an act of tit-for-tat, fourteen for fourteen, as it turned out. Another tragic day in the war of independence, yet one that would change the tide of the fight for freedom.

Chapter Twelve
Book of Ballymote

Monday, November 22, 1920
Stag's Head Pub, Dublin

*M*ichael Collins asked to see Tadgh. They met for a meal at noon in the private back room at the Stag's Head pub just off Dame Street and ordered lamb shank. Tadgh drank his first ale since captivity.

"I see you are feeling better," Michael observed, while they were making short order of their meal.

"Never better, Mick. We attended the match at Croke Park on Sunday. You must have made them plenty mad."

"We got most of them, Tadgh. Brugha wouldn't let us get the rest. Said there wasn't enough evidence of their guilt. I hate the politics I have to endure. Tell me what you saw at Croke."

Tadgh filled him in on the horror that had transpired.

Collins set his lips in a grim line. "They murdered three more on Sunday night at the Castle after torturing them—Dick McKee and Peadar Clancy, who helped plan the assassinations of the G-men plus Conor Clune. The bastards claimed they were killed while making a getaway, but I know different. Both you and Morgan need to get home to Cork, Tadgh. One of my informants at the Castle told me they're after you both. The head warder at Mountjoy wants to make an example."

"It looks like you could use a hand here in Dublin, Mick."

"I need you to join Tom Barry. He helped me organize and now runs the 3rd West Cork flying column. There's trouble in Cork City with Tomas and Terence dead and gone. I want you to have him use your Creagh facility as his base."

"Of course, if that's your request," Tadgh agreed. "I can arrange transportation. Do you have telephone connection to Creagh?"

"That can be arranged from Number Three Crow Street. We have new codes. Memorize the ones they have there before you leave. One more thing. I've been in contact with your friend Peader O'Donnell in Donegal. I remember you were working on him to move past his socialist beliefs. Well, he's a convert now, lad. He'll be setting up a Donegal flying column shortly. We badly need the support so close to the Ulster mob."

Tadgh sipped his ale. "I won't let you down, Mick."

"I know, comrade. I expect nothing less."

With that agreed, Michael Collins disappeared like a ghost into the fog.

Having arrived back at Crow Street, Tadgh picked up Morgan and headed for the RIA down back alleys, while Jack stayed back to arrange transportation to Creagh.

Lawlor greeted them at the door precisely at four o'clock. Glad to see you're still alive and on the loose, McCarthy."

Morgan stared at their host. "You read the papers, then?"

"Yes, lass. I should turn you in, except that McCarthy here likely saved our lives two days back."

Tadgh tossed off the compliment. "Don't believe everything you read in the papers, sir. There's a lot of skullduggeries about these days."

"Indeed, son. It seems we haven't progressed since that day I met you during the wretched Rising."

Tadgh let that lie. No need to anger his host. "May we see the *Book of Ballymote*, sir?"

"Of course. Come with me. I have it prepared for you." The professor led the way back through the darkened reading room towards the rare books examination area.

As they walked, Tadgh said, "Morgan and I visited Ballymote and the Perceval family at Temple House back in sixteen." It seemed so long ago now.

"You went there? Was there talk of the book?"

Morgan said, "Lady Charlotte of Temple House knew of it being sold to the O'Donnells and an old man in the village spoke of a secret it contained."

Lawlor stopped in his tracks. "What secret?"

"That's what I asked him, sir. He said that if he knew it wouldn't be a secret, now would it."

The professor dropped his head and shuffled on. Then he asked. "Did they talk of Sir Owain?"

It was Morgan's turn to stop suddenly. "Why, yes. I saw him in the mist of the Templar Castle ruins at night."

Lawlor froze and turned around to face her. "You saw him clearly? How did you know who it was?"

"Charlotte told me and said that he only appears to those who need resolution of a great mystery, or words to that effect. She said he helps you find what you are looking for."

"Did you have a mystery and was it resolved, lass?"

"Yes, as a matter of fact. My identity was unknown due to amnesia. The next night my long-lost brother found me after searching for years and seeing him restored my memory.

Lawlor made the sign of the cross. "I knew it. Divine intervention. I'd offer that you are educating me more than you will be able to learn from me in return." They started walking again, the professor side by side with Morgan.

"You know about Sir Owain?"

"Most certainly, my dear. *Tractatus de Purga-torio Sancti Patricii* by Henricus of Sawtrey tells the tale of the knight's penitential trials at the portal to purgatory in Northern Ireland. He came from Europe by way of the western Ireland route. Did you know there was a branch of the Ballymote monastery on the very site of the Templar castle two hundred years before they built it? Sir Owain was said to have stayed there back in 1154, according to the *Chronicles of Roger of Wendover*."

"Is that book also here at the RIA?"

"Yes, child. I think so, somewhere." They arrived in the inner

233

sanctorum. "But you came for the *Book of Ballymote*, so here it is." Lawlor opened the glass door and led them into the cubicle.

Tadgh remembered it from when he and Peader examined *an Cathach* four years earlier.

The book was a handsome tome bound in leather with oak boards and carefully organized on a clean white cloth on the examining table. Beside it, three pairs of silk gloves were laid out in order.

Lawlor motioned to the gloves and put on one pair. "There are 251 vellum folios, sixteen by ten inches, written in two columns, with decorated capital letters of interwoven designs in red, black, green, vermilion and chrome. Quite magnificent, can't you see?"

Having donned her gloves, Morgan asked how they should proceed to examine the work of art. As she reached out, Lawlor stopped her. "I'll help you if you want to look at the illuminations. If you want to read the text, you can look at the copy over there on your left. No gloves necessary."

Tadgh donned his gloves anyway out of respect for the ancient relic and sat down beside Morgan. "Can you explain the history of this sacred manuscript as you know it, Professor? We're looking for information found at the beginning and end of the sections."

"Certainly, Tadgh. The *Book of Ballymote*, like others of its kind, has passed through many hands. After it was scribed in around 1390 at Ballymote Castle, it was a treasured possession of the McDonaghs of Corran. In 1522, the O'Donnells purchased it. After the defeat at Kinsale, Rory O'Donnell kept it until he fled for continental Europe with ninety followers in September 1607. Its whereabouts were unknown again until 1620 when it was acquired by the Provost of Trinity College. We know this because he commissioned a copy of part of the document at that time. We don't know which part, however. From 1620 until 1767, it was in the library of Dublin's Trinity College."

Tadgh eyed the professor. "What happened to it after that, sir?"

"It disappeared from the library and was later found in

Burgundy, France. In 1785, it was returned to Ireland and acquired by the Royal Irish Academy where it still remains as one of the Academy's most treasured possessions."

"Thankfully, there is a copy," Morgan said, sitting down and shifting her attention to the replica.

"Yes, the work was photographed by the Academy in 1887 and edited by our own Robert Atkinson. Two hundred copies of it were made, mostly kept in libraries."

Tadgh looked at the original and then the copy. "Just like before."

The professor said, "Just like your friends' review of a copy of the *Book of Lismore* almost four years ago now, as I recall. Was that helpful?"

Tadgh replied, "You mean the *Book of MacCarthaigh Reagh*, and yes, it was fruitful. Thank you."

Lawlor thought for a moment before responding. "Yes, of course, Tadgh. It came from your family, didn't it? It is odd that the O'Donnells came to see your ancestors' treasure and now here you are to review the O'Donnells' compendium. Where are your relatives, Morgan, by the way?"

"Back in Canada where they live, sir. And my cousin Peader is a teacher in Donegal. By treasure, you mean—?"

"The wonderful compendium of knowledge in your family's book, of course." Lawlor looked up over his pince-nez and smiled.

Morgan smiled to hide her concern. *Could he know what we are seeking?* No. She responded. "Of course, sir."

"What is the purpose of your review today if I might ask, Tadgh?"

"Suffice it to say, sir, that our research is of the utmost importance to the well-being of our country."

"Just like your research of *an Cathach*. You patriots were looking for beginnings and endings there also."

"Yes, that's right."

Lawlor sat in front of the original and said, "I can stay. Let's look at the actual manuscript, shall we? In case something's been lost in the poor photography." The professor opened the front cover of the original manuscript. "All right. The beginning page of this book is a drawing of Noah's Ark as you can plainly see."

The McCarthys saw a rough sketch of a single-mast boat riding on the waves with two men, three women and perhaps a child. The ship looked ancient, and the drawing seemed out of place, as if it had been added *after* the original manuscript was created.

"I don't see any animals except that bird on the bowsprit," Morgan said.

"Well, young lady, we have interpreted the drawing based on the fact that it is followed by a description of the ages of the world, then followed by a treatise on the history of the Lost Israelites and their migration from Israel into Europe with their descendants becoming the Gaels and Anglo-Saxon people. Many of the annals, including the *Annals of the Four Masters*, start with the flood, so the connection is obvious."

Tadgh examined the spine of the book. "Does it look as if the book has been tampered with?"

"Just like the *Book of Lismore*, you mean? Please understand. These books were not in a controlled environment for much of their lives. The first folio after the drawing is missing."

Tadgh was impatient. "How about the end section?"

Lawlor turned the book over and carefully opened the back cover to the last page. "The book ends with several translations from the Greek—the destruction of Troy and the wanderings of Ulysses, followed by a summary of Virgil's *Aeneid*, beginning with Nestor's speech to the Greeks."

"Really? Isn't Helen of Troy mentioned in that epic?" asked Morgan, fascinated.

"That's right, Morgan. In Book II of the *Aeneid* by Virgil, Prince Paris seduces Helen away from her husband Menelaus, the King of Sparta, to take her back to Troy in about 1250 B.C. The first Greek historian, Herodotus, wrote that Paris's ship was blown off course and ended up in Egypt. King Proteus of Egypt in Memphis forbade Paris from taking Helen from Egypt. So, Paris returned to Troy without her. The Greeks wrote that Helen stayed with Proteus for ten years during the war that destroyed Troy, after which Menelaus returned her to Sparta."

"That's all in this section of the book?"

"More or less, young lady."

Tadgh scanned the last page, but it was in ancient Gaelic, so he didn't understand. "What do these words at the end of the page say, exactly?"

Lawlor read them out, and translated, describing a long sea voyage. The story was truncated.

Tadgh shook his head and consulted the telegraphed sheet that Aidan had sent them from the page the professor had given him four years earlier. "I don't see any connection between these two ends of the book and what we are interested in."

"I see you kept my scribbles, Tadgh," Lawlor said. "Admirable. A man after my own process."

"What about the section on genealogies of the clans and kings of Ulster?" Tadgh asked, pointing at his notes.

They traced through that together, then went on to look at writing about the six invasions of Ireland by the Tuatha Dé Danann and Milesian civilizations.

"I notice a few marginal notations on the folios," Tadgh said, pointing to one jotted in the *Lebor na gCeart*, the *Book of Rights*.

"Yes, unfortunate. In 1719, it was lent by the Trinity College library to Anthony Raymond, vicar of Trim, and thence to other scholars. In 1785, the manuscript was presented by Chevalier Thomas O'Gorman to the newly formed Royal Irish Academy as its first acquisition for safekeeping. Apparently, O'Gorman acquired it from a millwright's widow in Drogheda for £20. So those notes could have been written by anybody. It's a travesty that this sacred document has been defiled like this."

The grandfather clock outside the enclosure struck ten. Tadgh, Morgan, and the professor had finally finished examining the sections on the Brehon law and the Ogham language. "These folios are the most definitive information that we have in the Irish language on these two subjects," Lawlor said, moving to close the book. "I'm afraid we are going to have to call it a night at this point. I teach early in the morning."

Morgan, who couldn't understand any of the Gaelic, was scanning through the photolithographic copy for any interesting drawings or illuminations. "There are several margin notations, but what does this one say, I wonder?"

"Where is it, lass?"

"In the section you mentioned on Jewish migration at the bottom of folio twelve. It is so small."

Lawlor came over to the photolithograph. "Oh, that one. We've always thought it was just a smudge imperfection in the vellum."

"I don't think so. It is very blurry."

"That's a problem with those copies, my dear. Photographic records back in the 1870s were very rudimentary, I'm afraid. Let's take a look at the original."

Tadgh scrutinized the scrawl on the original vellum. "It's faded. Looks like tiny sticks of that Ogham language to me. Do you have a magnifying glass, professor?"

"Yes, in my office. Don't touch anything. I'll be back."

"Come and look, aroon. What do you see? Your eyes are better than mine—in many ways, actually. Must be the green in them." He winked at her.

Morgan looked over from the copy. "Go on with you, Tadgh McCarthy." She pursed her lips, puzzled. "It looks like somebody wrote a note at the bottom of the page, but I can't make it out."

Lawlor returned with the glass and a Moroccan graduate student he introduced to them. "Fazaar, here, is studying Knights Hospitaller history on Rhodes and Malta and he knows that Ballymote was related to that order after the demise of the

Templars. His eyes are better than mine."

Fazaar donned the professor's gloves, took the glass, and pored over the smudge on the ancient document. "It's a cryptic note, that's for sure. So small, in English. I see a word that looks like investigate or interrogate."

Tadgh took the glass from Fazaar but still couldn't make it out. More than a year in and out of the dark dank of solitary without proper food had left his vision weak.

He handed the glass to Morgan. "What can you see under magnification?"

"Somebody give me pencil and paper." Tadgh handed her a pad. Lawlor drew a pencil from his pocket. She started writing down letters and numbers, then erased some and wrote new ones.

"I think it says 'fleeing or freeing K or RT. What did they. . .' Ah, the next word is smudged. Starts with a 'k' I think. Then 'FF'?. 'Investigate' or 'Interrogate'. Then 'WT - TCP. 1610' or '1870'. I'm not sure. It is strange, though."

Tadgh squinted. "How so, Morgan?"

"Well, all the other notations in the book are quite sizable, though very faint and scrawled. But this one is so infinitesimal. It must have been extremely hard to write. It is almost as if someone was trying to hide it in plain sight for someone to find later."

Despite the lateness of the hour, the professor's ears pricked up. He grabbed the magnifying glass and scrutinized the minute characters. "That's very curious. You've illuminated a puzzle here, Mrs. McCarthy, that's certain. So many scholars have studied this document, O'Currey, Raymond, O'Gorman, and Atkinson, to name a few, and none have observed what you found."

Tadgh noted Lawlor's animated interest while Fazaar seemed oddly disinterested. "It could just be a meaningless thought by someone who read the document along the way. So it's likely nothing."

"You are right, my boy, of course. And there are several other legible notations in the book that are inconsequential. Of course, if the date is 1870, then it would be a notation made while the book was still away in Burgundy."

It seemed to Tadgh that the professor was now being overly dismissive. For what purpose, Tadgh didn't know. Maybe it was just the lateness of the hour.

Lawlor closed the book, took off his gloves and said, "It is past my bedtime, so we must leave this subject for today."

The McCarthys thanked their host and his student and returned undetected to their room at Mick's hideout on Crow Street.

The first freezing rain of the season had started, and Collin was late for dinner on Monday evening. They had inherited the Lizzie from Sam and gotten rid of the horribly unreliable Hudson, so at least he had transportation.

Kathy's hands were full, with three children in their new home on Leuty Avenue. Liam was four, Claire now three, and their three-month-old baby Shaina was named after her husband's poor dead mother. Sure, Kathy missed being with thirty-five children in her old classroom, but she was very satisfied with her own brood, three bedrooms to accommodate them, and an electric refrigerator.

Life had been on an even keel with Collin ever since his brother-in-law Tadgh had been put in jail. That effectively stopped any talk of supporting an Irish revolution. Collin had checked in with Jack that his sister was safe. Of course, Kathy felt badly for Morgan. They telegraphed and invited her to come to Toronto for a visit after the war ended. Collin was sad when she declined, but Kathy understood. Her husband Tadgh was still alive, and that is where she needed to be, nearby.

Kathy was proud that her husband had ascended the ranks within the *Tely* to become chief political correspondent, yet apprehensive that he might be sent off to some Godforsaken corner of the world.

"Liam, please get your sister from her room and get washed up for dinner. Your father will be home directly."

"Yes, Mama. Can we play with the logs that Norah and Dot gave us after supper?"

"We'll see. Perhaps, if you eat all your dinner." Kathy retreated to the kitchen to baste the chicken roasting in the oven.

The front door slammed, and Kathy dropped her baster into the pan. She heard footsteps. Collin appeared in the kitchen doorway, water dripping off his clothing. He hadn't even bothered removing his soaking-wet Burberry trench coat or his Wellingtons. He just stood there.

"Big news came over the wire at work today, darlin'."

Kathy was afraid to ask.

"The Irish War of Independence that's been festering erupted yesterday in Dublin. They're calling it the Sunday massacre. First the IRA killed G-men and then the British goons mowed down citizens at a football game."

"How bad?"

"It means the damned British are finally up against a formidable adversary, so it does."

"Well, I have news too, Collin."

His jaw dropped and he turned pale. "Kathy you're not . . ."

"No, no, not that. We agreed that we have enough little O'Donnells, and our prevention is working."

"Well!" He took a deep breath and slowly exhaled. "What is it, then?"

"A letter came addressed to you from Jack Jordan today. Looks dog-eared. Probably sent on one of his slow boats. I didn't want to open it. Check the hall table."

Collin gave his wife a peck on the cheek and headed back to the front door to hang up his coat, calling back, "That chicken smells wonderful."

At least now, two years after the November 11 Armistice, there was good food to be had for the fortunate ones in Canada. With

Collin's promotion came a raise in pay, giving the family more comfort.

When Collin didn't come back right away, Kathy poked her head into the parlor. "Everything all right?"

Her husband sat in his chair by the fireplace stroking his chin. The open letter lay on his lap with its torn envelope on the floor beside him. He didn't say a word.

Kathy's heart jumped up into her throat. "What is it?"

Collin swiveled the chair around to face her. "Come here, lass. Sit by me."

Kathy hesitated. Collin got up and drew her into the parlor.

"This letter from Jack is dated three weeks ago. He apologizes for not writing sooner."

"What does he say?" Kathy laid a hand on her husband's arm. "Is Tadgh dead? Is Morgan all right?"

"Quite the contrary. He says that Morgan and Tadgh's brother Aidan broke Tadgh out of Mountjoy Prison all by themselves. They are safe, but Morgan is now on the run, being sought after by the police. Apparently three prison guards have gone missing in the escape."

"My God, Collin! How brave of Morgan."

"Jack says Morgan doesn't know he was writing, and she wouldn't have approved of it because she doesn't want to worry me."

Kathy realized this was terrible news. She paced the room. Great for Tadgh that they were together, but not so good for her husband. Collin would worry, so much so that she expected him to want to go to Ireland to protect his sister. Count on it.

Sensing his mother's distress, Liam cried from halfway up the stairs. "Mama, what's wrong?"

Kathy didn't know how much he might have heard or understood. "Come down now, Liam, and bring your sister. Supper is ready and everything is all right."

Collin reread the letter. His heart skipped a beat. His sister would be on-the-run again with the hounds of hell after her.

Kathy saw the furrow on his brow and the crumpling of the page as he made a fist and tried to reassure him. "I'm sure Morgan will be all right, dear. She has Tadgh back now to protect her." But she knew as her heart sank, *Collin's going to go after her*. She pulled Liam to her bosom as he exited the stairs and prayed she was wrong.

The next day, Morgan became increasingly worried about Tadgh's condition. The physical effects of the deprivation throughout his long incarceration were dissipating, yet the melancholia remained. She couldn't imagine having endured such torture for so long. The spark to fight on still burned bright, but the self-assurance and can-do exuberance of youth were gone. That, combined with obsession for freedom, could prove deadly. *My job is to rebuild his spirit*, Morgan told herself. But she didn't feel so confident in that area.

"How about some supper and stout, Tadgh?"

"Aye. I suppose," he said, staring absently at the telegram Aidan had sent them with the book's contents.

"The Wicklow restaurant, then? Maybe your friend Paddy will still be serving there."

"I'd prefer the Temple Bar pub, Morgan. It's just a block away."

"Fine, Tadgh. Let's go. I'm famished."

"I'd also prefer that you didn't use that word, lass. It brings back memories."

They picked up Jack who had been trying to write to his Cunard superior and headed for the pub. Morgan was relieved that her husband didn't have to walk too far and hoped the camaraderie of the evening would cheer him up.

Jack's position at Cunard had changed as a result of his connection to the fugitive Bernice Jordan. They kept him on for logistics support, but he was no longer the manager of the

Queenstown office. That suited him fine since he had become such a staunch supporter of the McCarthy adventures and Tadgh's Cause.

They sat in the same corner snug at Temple Bar as before, where they had privacy, but could still see who entered and left the establishment. This time, Deirdre came over and greeted them instead of calling across the room. "Well, well. If it isn't the happily married Clan Chieftain, his queen, and trusted chivalrous knight. Greetings, most noble lords and lady." She curtsied.

Tadgh laughed then blustered, "Cut the bullshite and bring us some stout, wench."

Deirdre hugged Morgan who was sitting on the outside and winked at Jack. "You look mighty fine this evening, Master Jack."

Jack got up and kissed her hand. "You're beautiful as ever, love."

When Deirdre went off for their drinks, Morgan smiled broadly and said, "My, my. The sparks seem to be flying there, Jack."

Jack shrugged his shoulders. "What do you mean?"

Morgan chuckled, "I saw how you two looked at each other."

"Nonsense, Morgan. Just friendly banter."

Morgan wagged her finger at their friend. "You mark my words, Jack. She'll be after you someday soon."

"I truly doubt that, lass." Jack reached inside his coat and pulled out a battered envelope. "I almost forgot. A telegram came for you yesterday, my dear, at my Cunard office, and it's from Collin."

"Oh, just give it to me, please, Jack. I get so little news," Morgan said, her eyes wide.

Tadgh looked daggers at Jack's use of the endearment but said nothing.

Morgan ripped open the envelope and read the note. "Wonderful news, boys. Collin has been assigned as a foreign war correspondent here in Ireland. Apparently, his boss thinks the War of Independence escalated with what they are calling the Bloody Sunday battle. In any event, Collin is considered an expert on our politics after his earlier reporting on the aftermath of the Rising. He arrives in Queenstown on December 10 and wants to meet us." Her eyes shone. "And most importantly, Kathy has had a second baby girl." Morgan looked down and tears started to flow.

Sitting beside his wife, Tadgh held her tenderly. "What's the matter, aroon?"

"Nothing. I'm so happy. They call her Shaina after my Ma. Oh, it'll be grand to see him after all this time."

Tadgh offered Morgan his handkerchief. "We'll need to have him come to Creagh since I have to return and report to Tom Barry. But don't put the word Creagh in a telegram."

Having stemmed the tide of her tears, Morgan returned Tadgh's hankie. "Can't we stay here in Dublin until the tenth, Tadgh?"

He shook his head. "Sorry, lass. I must get back home."

Morgan didn't protest further. Home sounded wonderful to her. "Can you come with us, Jack? You're on furlough from Cunard, aren't you?"

Tadgh scowled. "I'm sure Jack has interests here, like Deirdre. Right, Jack?"

Deirdre arrived, tray in hand. "Here's your stout, friends. What can I get ye, Jack first?"

Morgan noted that Jack was looking up at their friend Deirdre with more than a patron's eye.

After he ordered roast chicken and potatoes for all, she saw him watching the proprietress as she walked away, her backside swaying, and then he said, "I think I will stay in Dublin for a time. I need to get back in the good graces of Cunard and their head office for Ireland is here. Don't take offense, but it's probably better for me not to be in your company for a while. But I can arrange transportation for Collin to your home after he arrives."

Tadgh smiled. "That's sorted, then."

"I wonder how Kathy is taking the news of Collin's pending absence," Morgan said, sipping the foam off her brew.

Tadgh knew from when he visited them in Toronto. She would be furious.

Chapter Thirteen
Ireland Bound

"**Are you really** all right with Collin going to Ireland on assignment?" Lil asked Kathy as they sat in the parlor by the fire. They had just been laboring over supper preparation in the kitchen and chicken was now safely cooking in the oven. Lil had invited the O'Donnells for a meal because she wanted to find out the plans for Collin in Ireland.

Remembering how agitated and immature she had acted when she threw tantrums after Collin rushed off to Ireland to search for his sister, Kathy was determined not to let her anxiety show, even to her best friend. She mustered her courage and said, "He's been a trooper ever since we found Claire, er Morgan, as if a great weight was lifted off of him and therefore off of me. He is much more self-assured now, and more attentive to me and the children." She wondered if she had fooled Lil with her new approach.

"That's remarkably mature of you," her friend said, yet Kathy wondered if her own irrepressible furrowed brow and penetrating stare would give away her real feelings. She was happy when Lil didn't question her further since her own façade was fragile indeed.

Kathy turned her attention to her children to deflect further conversation on the matter. "Liam, stop chasing your sister. Remember, she's only three."

"Don't they grow up so fast, Kathy? Heavens, Norah's eight already. It seems I was changing her nappies just yesterday."

"I know, Lil. It's hard to imagine Liam will be five in a few months."

"Could it be that with three wonderful children you are more comfortable with your own place in life, too?"

Kathy got up and grabbed her son by the arm. "I mean it, laddie." Releasing him, she then turned to her friend. "I'm sure that is part of it. Are you done with your brood now?"

"I hope so. Stephen makes a matched set of four."

"It's a delicate subject, I know, but have you thought of contraception?"

Kathy could see Lil frowning at a subject she obviously would prefer not discussing.

Lil shook her finger. "It's illegal in Canada, I believe."

"But that's old-fashioned. We women need to take control of our family size."

"I don't know. If the Lord wants us to have children, then who are we to interfere?"

"Are you serious, Lil? You should be able to choose whether or not you would like to have another child."

"By doing what?"

"By having your husband use a condom. They're rubberized now, you know. You hardly notice them."

"You don't?"

"No. Collin wears them regularly, as of a month ago. Three children are enough, in this modern age. You should try using one."

Lil gave her a funny look.

"I mean Sam should," she blushed, "if you want Stephen to be your last."

"You're a vixen, you are, Kathleen. I'm not a prude, but I wouldn't know how to talk to Sam about such a thing. And I'd die if I had to buy one. Where can you get them anyway?"

"What are you talking about, Mom?" Norah asked, as she came down the stairs.

"Adult things, not for children's ears."

Norah pouted.

"About having children. You wouldn't be wanting to know."

"I'm interested in that."

"At your age? There's plenty of time for that when you grow up."

"But I am grown up, I'm almost nine." She giggled. "And I want children someday. I know you have to have a man to have children." She stood near her mother. "Like you have Daddy. How —"

Lil was happy when Collin walked in through the Finlays' front door and distracted the conversation. "Where are my little munchkins?"

"I'm in here, Daddy. And we're not blue yet," Liam called out from the kitchen.

Lil looked quizzically at Collin, then asked, "Oz?"

"Yes, Kathy's been reading to the children from the Frank Baum book, *The Wonderful Wizard of Oz,* at night before bed. Come here, son."

Liam appeared in the parlor with cookie crumbs all over his mouth, still chewing.

"If you are munching, then you must be a munchkin."

Kathy got up and went to her son, steering him toward his father. "How many times do I have to tell you not to eat sweets so close to dinner? And your aunt Lil's to boot," she snapped.

Lil noticed the tension in her best friend's voice and grabbed her hand. Did it have to do with Collin's imminent departure for Ireland?

Liam looked hurt. He swallowed hard.

Collin sat down and took Liam on his lap. "The boy just has a sweet tooth, Mom. He'll eat his supper, just backward because he already had his dessert." He gave Liam a hug and his son brightened considerably.

Claire was playing at dressing a doll on the scatter rug by the fireplace. Collin picked her up, from his seat in the padded rocking chair and gave her a big hug. "How's my little girl tonight?"

"Fine, Daddy. See Priscilla's new dress?"

"It's, very, ah, orange."

"No, Daddy. It's pink."

"I see it now. Is she a princess?"

"No, silly. She's Dorothy from the Oz."

"Is she? Where's Toto?"

"The doggie is sleeping now, Daddy."

Collin fingered the black curls that now flowed down to his daughter's shoulders. And those green eyes. Just like Aunty Morgan's, her namesake.

"Where's Sam, Lil?"

"Painting in his study, as usual. He has an exhibition coming up at the Art Gallery of Toronto in January. He wants to make a good impression on the group of artists he associates with at the Arts and Letters Club." Lil stood up and tied her apron around her waist. "They just formed the Group of Seven this year, and Sam is learning a great deal to develop his style of light reflections, mainly from A.Y Jackson, I believe."

Kathy went to the painting of the family picnic in Silverfern Park on the Rouge River hanging on the parlor wall. "I've noticed that Sam's paintings have more intense colors these days. His use of sunlight and shadows, particularly on trees, is amazing."

"You are becoming quite the art connoisseur, Kathy," Lil said, and turned toward the kitchen. "You children go wash your hands as supper will be on the table shortly."

"I guess it rubs off after so many years travelling with him to school each day." Kathy giggled. "Maybe I could ask him about that subject we talked about earlier."

"Don't you dare," Lil hollered over her shoulder as she left the room.

"Don't you dare what, lass?" Sam asked, coming into the parlor to see what all the commotion was about.

"Talk about how to keep your family limited to four children."

Sam looked around. The kids had left the room. "You mean condoms, I presume." He cleared his throat.

Collin winked and chimed in. "We're stopping at three, and I've been trying them out. No problems."

Lil poked her head into the parlor, shaking her ladle at Kathy.

"I didn't say anything, Lil. Sam brought it up. We're all adults, here."

Lil scowled, sweeping her arms towards the children. "Really, Kathy. They'll be no further discussion on the matter."

The conversation in the parlor turned towards football. The Toronto Argonauts were scheduled to play the Toronto Varity Blues for the 8th Stanley Cup on December 4. They hoped it wouldn't be snowing.

As supper was ending, Lil said, "Upstairs now, my girls. Get undressed and I'll be up to draw your bath."

Sam selected his favorite pipe from the rack on the sideboard. "Speaking of war, tell us what you can about your assignment to Ireland, me boyo."

"I am leaving on the *Aquitaine* from Montreal on December 2. I will be posted in Dublin, and as before, will be working with *The Irish Times* staff including Maureen, Kathy's cousin. Mr. Robertson wants me to cover human interest stories as well as the events of the War of Independence."

Sam came right to the point. "Did you ask for this assignment because Tadgh is now out of jail? Are you worried about Morgan again, lad?"

Kathy fidgeted with the utensils on her empty plate and stared at her husband.

Collin reached for the Jameson bottle at the end of the table. "So, Kathy has told you of the letter from Jack Jordan, has she?"

Lil spoke up. "Collin, your sister must have taken a terrible risk to get Tadgh freed."

"A calculated risk, I am sure, Lil. And it worked out for the best, now didn't it."

Kathy got up from the table and put her arm around her husband's shoulders from behind his chair. "Collin's agreed to stay out of trouble—*haven't* you, my love?"

"Kathy is supportive of my going, Lil. That's the difference this time."

Lil looked askance at the newspaperman and then over to Kathy.

Kathy's face had stiffened. "Under certain conditions."

Sam tried to get Kathy's terms. Based on past experience, that might be important to them all. "What conditions?"

"Collin can voice his opinion but shouldn't try to order Morgan around regarding her role in the Irish war. She is capable of handling her own affairs. He should come home as soon as possible if the War of Independence is over or no longer relevant to Canada. He must avoid any situations that would put his life at risk and come home at least every two months."

Sam puffed on his Prince Albert. "How do you feel about that, Collin?"

"I agree with all of Kathy's criteria. I hope to be back home in a couple of months for good when the level of hostilities dies down."

"But you're going to miss Christmas, Daddy."

"We're going to have Christmas early, Claire, before I go."

Liam piped up. "But Santa Claus doesn't come 'til Christmas Eve."

"He will still come on Christmas Eve. If he brings me a present, will you save it for me?"

"Yes, Daddy."

"That's my lad and lassie." Collin grabbed his children and placed each on a knee, glowing with pride.

They threw their arms around him and nuzzled their heads under his chin.

Around eight o'clock, the O'Donnell family bundled up and headed out into the cold. On the way out the door, Collin slipped a packaged condom into Sam's hand and whispered, "I keep one in my wallet in case Kathy gets frisky when we are away from home, but you can have this one."

Sam chuckled. "Who gets the urge and where are the children?" Into his trouser pocket it went.

At least the forecasted snow hadn't started falling yet. Collin opened the doors on trustworthy old Lillie, the car that had safely taken him and Kathy to New York and back five years earlier. He had bought the prized center door sedan from Sam when his friend bought the Lillie II, a newer 1920 model with the Ruckstell two-speed rear axle. Collin was thinking of having this modification retrofitted, which would double the number of forward gears to four and enable higher speeds when climbing a hill.

After they got home and had put the children to bed, they went into the kitchen for a nightcap.

Kathy sat at the table twirling her hair in her fingers, sipping Orange Pekoe tea. She had noticed that Collin was spending much more time with the children than before. *He must have some reluctance to leave them-and perhaps, me.*

She looked up and said, "I want you to go and get your stories and then come home. Can you do that?"

Collin had been chugging an O'Keefe from the bottle by the icebox. He came over to the table and put his arms around his wife. "I will do my job and come home as soon as I can, darlin.' I am going to sorely miss you and the children." He calmed her nervous fingers and kissed the soft hair at the nape of her neck.

She reached around and pulled his face close to hers, looking him in the eye. "I don't want you to get mixed up with looking for treasure. We almost died last time."

"That gave us a fright, I'll grant you. However, Boyle and his henchmen are dead now. No need to worry anymore. Jack sent us the good news that Tadgh is out of jail, at least, but I have no idea what he and Morgan are up to."

Kathy had to pick her words carefully. "I'm sure that Morgan is a stabilizing influence, but you know how headstrong Tadgh can be."

Collin remembered the solemn Clans Pact that he had agreed to with his brother-in-law, a blood bond and promise that he had kept from Kathy to avoid worrying her. "I will see what's going on with those two and communicate closely with you before involving myself with their activities."

Kathy saw him ball his left fist, putting it behind his back, and said, "But no treasure hunting, right, Collin?"

Collin fingered his locket with his other hand. "Don't you want to know what Red Hugh buried for me and for you?"

"Not if it means that you get hurt."

"Well, then, I promise that nothing will harm me."

Kathy sensed he was dancing around the words without answering the question. "How can you promise that?"

Collin knelt and cupped her face in his hands. "Because I love you and the children, and I won't jeopardize our life together here in Toronto."

"Oh, Collin. That's what I was hoping you would say."

Kathy stood up, pulling him to her, and gave him a lingering kiss on the mouth. "You promise?"

"Yes, my love. I promise."

"Then let's go to bed."

"I'm all for that, darlin'," Collin said, encircling Kathy's waist, lifting her in his arms and carrying her up the stairs.

On the way up, he kissed her on the neck again. "Let's check out whether our new baby is sound asleep."

Kathy tightened her grip around his neck. "We'll have to try to be quiet, love." There would be lovemaking, yet she already felt the pain of separation, of not knowing, the loneliness.

Fazaar waited in the Moroccan restaurant El Bahia on Wicklow Street, between Trinity College and the Castle, on land reclaimed by William Temple in the early 1600s. Here he could swear he'd been transported straight into an ancient restaurant in Marrakech, with brocaded and tasseled cushions surrounding low mahogany tables and dim, fringed-shade lights. The hookah between his squatted knees gave off the sweet lemony smell of hashish in the isolated smoky enclaves of the room. Just as he was about to nod off, his brother Abbad emerged from the gloom. Although they kept up the façade of using anglicized names for their roles in the British Israeli Association, they conversed with their given names in their long-standing Janszoon family affiliation.

"Don't get up, brother. Let me join you." Abbad was a good two inches taller than his slender brother, but with the same olive-skinned leathery features and pointed hooked nose. Unlike their North African brethren, they both wore European suits and ties.

Taking a long draw on the pipe, Abbad asked, "What is so important to drag me away from a boring British Israeli Association meeting?"

Fazaar whispered, "They found something, in the sacred book."

Abbad dropped the pipe in his lap. "Who, that fossil Lawlor, or his minions?"

"No, an Irish couple they called Tadgh and Morgan McCarthy. She found it."

"Who are they, Fazaar?"

"I don't know, but I followed them to the pub. They know Deirdre."

"Do they? That bitch is our nemesis. She's in cahoots with your studious professor, you know. If she's involved, our holy mission is threatened."

"I thought our father eliminated that problem during the digging, Abbad."

Abbad looked through the smoke to confirm their isolation. "As a feigned member of the Association, he did execute Deirdre's meddling father at the excavation site on the Hill of Tara back in '99. Who knew his daughter would be strong enough to pick up his crusade? What did they find?"

"A tiny cryptic hand-written note that appears to be by Temple back in 1610. Everyone else including me had missed it."

"What is in the note?

"Lawlor asked me to examine it for him with a magnifying glass. I, uh, don't remember all the symbols or words and some of it was smeared, but it ended with WT-TCP. I know that much."

Abbad leaned forward and shook his brother's collar. "What section was it in?"

Fazaar took a draw of the hookah and leaned over toward his brother, eyes glazed, and hissed, "That's what's so exciting. It was on folio twelve, Jewish migration."

Abbad's black eyes widened. "Allah be praised!" He thought for a moment. "You must go back and resume your role as the loyal student to the good professor. Gain access to the book and record the note for me. I will eavesdrop on Deirdre when this Irish couple comes to call. What do these two look like?"

Fazaar gave a detailed description of the McCarthys.

Abbad spoke in low tones. "My job is to follow in our father's footsteps as a trusted Association member, hoping to gain information for our mission. They are completely fooled, the idiots. I think I will deal with Deirdre just like our father dealt with her father."

"Is that wise, brother?"

"It may be necessary. We must uncover what our ancestors Murat and Flooren failed to find. Contact me when you have discovered the Temple note. And lay off the hashish, now, you've had enough."

With that, Abbad stood up and disappeared into the smoke, leaving his brother puffing on the pipe.

Before dawn, on Wednesday, the morning of the twenty-fourth, Tadgh was still awake. He hadn't slept a wink all night, just like in solitary when day and night were indistinguishable. He wondered if he would ever have a solid night's sleep again.

The information that they had received about the *Book of Ballymote* was overwhelming. He saw so many possible areas that could be clues to the O'Donnell treasure, but he couldn't connect the dots. The Brehon law, the Ogham language, the history of the Kings of Ulster? Nothing popped out at him. It all swirled around and around in his head and left him frustrated and mentally exhausted.

The beginning and end of the Book seemed totally disconnected from the O'Donnells. Noah's Ark and the story of Helen of Troy. What could they possibly mean?

Then the convolutions in his brain slowed as the softness and warmth of his lover sleeping soundly beside him filled him with sensual peace. He was thankful that Morgan and God saved him from the hell of the Joy. If she hadn't taken that chance, he would be looking down upon her from heaven right now, or maybe up from hell.

He moved on his left side to gently hug her from behind, snaking his arm under her warm body and cupping her breast softly. She stirred and then resumed her sleeping, her breast moving slowly and rhythmically in sync with her breathing. Tadgh finally dropped off to sleep, his mind relaxed, his body fatigued.

Morgan awoke at seven o'clock to find her husband draped over her, sound asleep. Good. He hadn't been sleeping at all since breaking out of prison. She could only imagine how hellish it had been in captivity.

Checking his heartbeat against her shoulder blade, Morgan felt safe for the first time in more than three years. She had resisted the powerful urge for lovemaking because of his condition, but now he seemed to be regaining his physical strength.

The loss of her unborn baby still haunted her soul. She knew the only way she could put this agony behind her was to have another child. Surely Tadgh had already given his all for the Cause. The Republicans could fight their bloody war without him if he became a new father. She reveled in the possibility. She could control her family's destiny with God and Mother Nature's help. Then she awoke from her fantasy. Tadgh would never retire from the fight as long as there was breath in his body. The Rising martyrs had wives and children who were left behind.

Michael had ordered him home where killing and potential death awaited them both. What if she really had found a lead to her hidden family treasure in the *Book of Ballymote*. Wouldn't Tadgh be serving the Cause more forcefully by finding that wealth so it could be used for the revolution as her ancestral chieftain had ordained? Only if they could capitalize on it now, here in Dublin before heading out into the fray.

Morgan turned her thinking to the scrawled note she had found. What were the letters exactly and what did they mean? Was it important or just hen scratching? What would it have to do with the Jewish migration, whatever that was? The questions just kept circling in her mind, over and over with no resolution.

Morgan's brain churned until it could churn no more. She was getting nowhere. Better to focus on Tadgh body and breathing. At least that was here and now and wonderful.

As she rested, the image of Sir Owain pointing his lance at her once more on the moors of Temple House, his steed snorting and pawing the ground, suddenly jumped into her brain. It was as if he was reaching out to her from the grave. She twitched and then resisted the urge to jump up and look out the window into the night. As quickly as the medieval knight had flashed into her consciousness, he evaporated leaving her heart racing. Morgan took a deep breath and lay still. Although her mind was seething with questions, she didn't want to move another muscle and deprive Tadgh of sorely needed sleep.

Chapter Fourteen
Temple

Wednesday, November 24, 1920
Number Three Crow Street, Dublin, Ireland

*F*inally, **Tadgh stirred** and awoke. It was late morning, and his left arm was numb. A wonderful feeling of love and peace enveloped him with his wife's body molded to his own.

Morgan, sensing he was awake, turned over to face him, relinquishing his deadened arm. She kissed his scruffy beard. "So, you finally decided to return to the land of the living, eh, mavourneen."

"Ummm. Everything but my left arm, it would seem." Tadgh extended the arm, repeatedly squeezing and releasing his fist until the blood started flowing and feeling returned. He kissed her on the lips and felt himself harden.

Morgan murmured sleepily, "I felt that my love. You must be getting better."

He moved his leg slowly up between hers, nestling it where they joined, and wrapped his arms around her tightly.

Morgan whispered in his ear, "I've missed you desperately, and need you, now."

Tadgh's amber eyes brightened as Morgan's legs opened, ready for him.

Tadgh's burst of strength proven, and Morgan satisfied, they fell into a gratified slumber.

When they awoke again, Morgan asked, "Are we going to follow up on what I found in the book, love?"

"That depends."

"On what?"

"On how urgently Michael needs me to join Tom Barry's column and bring it to Creagh."

Morgan snaked her arms around Tadgh's waist, holding him fast. "Don't you think that we need to follow up on what we learned yesterday before we leave Dublin, because I don't think we will be coming back here any time soon."

"We'll see after I talk to Mick, lass."

Morgan kissed him on the forehead. "Just think what my Clan's fortune could do for the revolution, Tadgh."

"Aye, but that tiny scrawl may mean nothing at all."

"We'll see about that. Tadgh. All right. Let's get up and have breakfast. I'm starving."

"You have no idea what it is like to be starving, aroon," Tadgh said, breaking free of Morgan's grip and slipping out of bed. He shivered. "I think I am qualified to say that I know how my ancestors felt back in Skibbereen during the Great Hunger."

"Yes, you are, and now you're here with me. I promise to be more thoughtful in the future on that subject." Morgan pulled on her robe and swatted his behind on her way to the bathroom.

While consuming a late breakfast of eggs and ham at the Temple Bar Pub, Morgan fell uncharacteristically quiet. She stared into her cup of tea as if she were reading the leaves. Finally, she shook her head and said, "I saw Sir Owain again last night, Tadgh."

"What? Where?"

"In my mind. He was signaling me."

Tadgh gave a laugh and thrust his arm in the air as if he were jousting. "Was he, now?"

"Don't you mock me, Tadgh McCarthy. You'll remember what happened after the last time I saw him. It's *déjà vu.*"

Tadgh didn't believe in ghosts, but he had to admit it was spooky that Collin had found his long-lost sister the very day after she had seen the vision at Temple House.

"I've been tossing that marginal note we found over and over in my mind and can't make heads nor tails of it, Tadgh. Sir Owain came to me right after I was thinking about it last night, and Charlotte said he appears to help those in turmoil find their way."

"That you found, aroon."

Morgan smiled, her eyes glistening. "All right, I found." She took the paper she scribbled on yesterday out of her handbag and passed it to Tadgh.

He read quietly. "Fleeing or freeing K or RT. What did they k...? F P? *Investigate or Interrogate.* WT - TCP. 1610, 1670, 1810 or 1870." It looked like Greek to him as he too puzzled the meaning.

Morgan brought him back as she said, "That tiny scribble may be nothing, but it is bothering me that I can't decipher it. I wish Collin had been there with his camera. What do you make of it, Tadgh?"

"Why focus on that note?"

"The others were clearly written and, as Professor Lawlor explained them, quite straightforward references to the book's contents in those locations. This one is hardly readable and quite mysterious. Almost like what's written in your locket."

"I see. You may have something there. What section was it in?"

"An early one describing the migration of the Jewish people to Europe, I think."

"I think it holds no consequence for us, then, Morgan."

"Well, just to be sure, what do you think it means?"

Tadgh moved his head close to his wife's and whispered, "All right, for the sake of argument, let's see. If the date is when this note was written, then 1610 would be only ten years after the Clans Pact. If it's 1870 then it could have been written in Burgundy or by the millwright's widow in Drogheda whom Lawlor mentioned."

Morgan took a sip of her tea. "Speaking of Lawlor, do you think that he tried to steer us away from this note after I found it? He whisked us out of the RIA pretty quickly. And his student. An odd fellow, to be sure."

"Did I hear you mention Professor Lawlor, Morgan?" the pub owner said as she strode up with their breakfast.

"What big ears you have, Deirdre. Do you know him?"

"I've heard about him. He studies ancient Irish manuscripts, doesn't he? Down at the Royal Irish Academy, I believe."

"Yes, that's right." Tadgh's eyebrows raised as he studied Morgan's former bridesmaid carefully.

Setting down their plates, Deirdre asked, "None of my business, but how do you know him, Tadgh?"

"I just read about his examination of the *Book of Armagh* in *The Irish Times*."

"I read that, too. What did you think of it?"

Tadgh thought Deirdre's comment odd, since he had just made up the story. He put his hand over the piece of paper with the note on it, but not before her eyes glanced at it.

"Too mythical for me, I'm afraid."

Deirdre grabbed silverware from a nearby empty table and gave it to Tadgh. "I know what you mean. I saw that note on the table where it said WT - TCP. I've seen those initials before. Do they have something to do with the professor?"

Morgan looked up from her breakfast plate. "What do you mean, Deirdre?"

"It's probably a coincidence, but the man who settled the Temple Bar area was William Temple. He was the fourth provost of Trinity College. A man of means. Some say that his residence was located where this pub stands today."

"Do you know when he became the provost of the college, Deirdre?"

"Good question, Tadgh. I've heard patrons say that he became provost in 1609 and remained in that position until his untimely death in 1627."

Tadgh thought, *so WT-TCP 1610, if it is 1610, could refer to William Temple, Trinity College Provost, 1610.*

Deirdre said, "They used to abbreviate the title as TCP, I

believe."

"Interesting. How is it you know so much about that gentleman?"

"Well, Tadgh, I make it my business to know the heritage of my pub, especially since it was built on the ruins of William Temple's extensive estate. It's good for business to have that knowledge to share with customers, don't ye see. Kind of a mythical attraction, as Morgan would put it."

As she hovered over their snug, Deirdre motioned to her waitress to bring more tea and a stout for Tadgh. It was after eleven and the pub was open. The breakfast patrons were paying their bills and heading off to work oblivious of their conversation.

Tadgh poked at his breakfast with his fork.

Morgan dug into her eggs. "That makes sense, Deirdre. What do you think, Tadgh?"

"It certainly would be a coincidence we're eating breakfast near where William Temple lived, and we have a phrase that might have been written or attributed to him."

"Or Divine intervention, Tadgh."

"Could be that, I guess, Morgan. Sit down for a minute, Deirdre. You have waitresses to serve the food. Talk with us some more about this William Temple."

Tadgh pulled out a chair and he noted Deirdre's shapely derriere as she sat down.

"I can spare a minute for friends. Eat up, Tadgh. Don't you like my food?"

Tadgh took a forkful. "I do. It's that I was deprived of food for so long that I'm having some trouble eating again."

Deirdre reached over and patted his hand. "Poor boy. It must have been hell."

"Yes, in fact, it was. What can you tell us about Temple?"

"From what I've learned, he was a man of letters early in his career, a supporter of Peter Ramus who tried to discredit the logical system of Aristotle."

"You amaze me, Deirdre. You have a learned mind for a bar

wench, so you do."

Deirdre threw her head back and laughed. "G'wan off it, Tadgh McCarthy. A pretty girl can be more than that."

"So it would seem, lass," Tadgh said, patting her hand.

Morgan looked up from her eggs, pulled Tadgh's hand away and stared at the proprietress. "All right, you two. That's enough of that." She wondered if their recent lovemaking had put a spring in her husband's step. He wasn't one to have a roving eye.

Deirdre caught her meaning and changed subjects. "Do you want to hear more about the founder of this Temple Bar area, Morgan?"

Morgan was sure that Sir Owain had appeared to her for a reason, right after she was thinking about this note in the secretive O'Donnell compendium. She believed in Divine intervention. "Yes, I do."

Deirdre pushed her long tresses behind her ears and smiled. "All right then. It is general knowledge that in 1594 England, William Temple became the secretary to Robert Devereux, who was then the Earl of Essex. Have you heard of him?"

Morgan said, "I'm not a student of history, but wasn't he romantically linked to Queen Elizabeth?"

"They were very close back in the 1590s. Temple accompanied the earl to Ireland in 1599 when Essex was sent here by Queen Bess to conquer the Clans. The earl was the queen's favorite. That's why she entrusted him with that crucial task. Apparently, Temple described Essex as the noblest and worthiest lieutenant Ireland had ever seen."

Tadgh interjected. "I do know Devereux was remarkably unsuccessful in conquering the Irish Clans even though he had a much superior force of men. He eventually made a treaty with Hugh O'Neill."

Deirdre smiled and signaled her waitress to bring another bottle of stout and more tea. "That's right, Tadgh. It angered the Queen so much she recalled Essex in disgrace. The earl attempted a coup against Elizabeth, which she squashed. Devereux was beheaded in

1601 at the tower of London, I believe."

Morgan thought that the conversation was straying from her objective of deciphering the scribble, if indeed it was made by William Temple. "What does all that have to do with William Temple?"

Deirdre stopped talking when the waitress appeared, bearing an earthenware teapot on a tray and a bottle of B & C. She set the tray down on their table and left. Deirdre lifted the teapot's lid and dangled a couple of silk muslin tea bags in the hot water. "I get these from Thomas Sullivan in New York. Quite the invention, don't you think?"

Morgan peered into the pot and exclaimed, "What will they come up with next. Such a font of knowledge you are, Deirdre."

Deirdre poured herself a cup. "I am more than meets the eye, Morgan McCarthy, if that's what you mean. Shall I go on?"

"By all means, O Learned One."

Deirdre laughed. "I learned that William was suspected of aiding Devereux at the time of his coup attempt."

"Did he?"

"I really don't know for sure, Tadgh. What I do know is that William was detained in 1601 to be indicted and arraigned. Without clear evidence, he was released midyear with a stiff fine. His reputation was tarnished, so he had trouble finding meaningful employment."

"How did he land the provost job, then?" Tadgh asked, draining most of the stout into his tankard and taking a swig.

Deirdre poured Morgan a cup of tea and offered her milk. "Queen Bess died and eventually Cecil, the Chancellor of the fledgling Trinity College here in Dublin, used his influence to get William Temple the post of provost in 1609."

Morgan was astonished that Deirdre had so much knowledge about this fellow who founded Temple Bar. She decided to discuss this with Tadgh when they were alone.

Tadgh picked up on one of Deirdre's earlier comments. "You

said that he had an untimely death, lass. How so?"

"He acquired a good deal of land during his tenure at Trinity College, which made him a wealthy man by medieval standards. This first quarter of the 1600s gave ample opportunity for, let's say, skillful men to take over land relinquished by the Clans after the Flight of the Earls in 1607."

"The bastards!" Tadgh slammed his fist down on the table so hard that Deirdre's cup skipped in its saucer. Some tea spilled over its rim.

She grabbed the cup before it teetered off the table. "Easy there, Tadgh. I'm just telling you what I learned. Temple had enemies. His business methods were questionable, So, in late 1626 there was talk of Trinity officials removing him from his post. Then, in January of 1627, he died suddenly of a supposed heart attack."

"How so?"

"You seem very curious about Mr. Temple, Morgan."

Morgan glanced at Deirdre, and then over at Tadgh for support. When he didn't respond, she said, "If he is referenced in the scribble, then I am interested in him."

Deirdre looked at Morgan for a second before responding. "Apparently, his wife Martha found him in his study. It was reported in the paper that she was very upset and left Ireland to live with her relatives in England, leaving their eldest son John to manage her estate in Temple Bar."

Tadgh polished off his breakfast and slowly put down his utensils. He thought it strange that Deirdre hadn't asked where the scribble came from, but he wasn't willing to tell her. "What do you know about his estate here in Temple Bar, Deirdre?"

"When William moved back here from England in 1609, the River Liffey had two branches, the one that remains today, and another farther south nearer Dame Street between the Castle and the college. William decided to reclaim the sand bar that separated the two, filling in the southern branch, and building his estate on the land. My understanding is that his residence stood on the ground where my Temple Bar Pub is now."

"What happened to the residence, then?"

Deirdre's face clouded. "That's a tragic story, Morgan. William's son John lived in the place throughout his life even though he acquired more property in county Carlow. He became Master of the Rolls, a senior government position. John's son became Sir William Temple, a baronet who lived in England. He was born in London just after his grandfather died, and died at his home, Moor Park, in Surrey, in 1699. The baronet was the famous Temple, the English statesman and diplomat who formulated the pro-Dutch foreign policy employed intermittently during the reign of King Charles II. His thought and prose style also had a great influence on many 18th-century writers—Jonathan Swift, for one."

Tadgh took a slug of his stout. To keep up with this story he needed the alcohol. "You really have researched the Temple family, lass. Where's the tragedy in your story?"

"Sir William Temple—the baronet—became an ambassador at The Hague, in 1668. He negotiated the Triple Alliance between England, the Netherlands, and Sweden. His crowning achievement, literally, was to arrange the marriage between Charles II's niece Princess Mary and William of Orange, stadholder of Holland in 1677."

Tadgh was incensed. He remembered the story of the Battle of the Boyne where Irish Catholic forces led by King James II were destroyed by that evil Protestant conqueror in 1690. "You mean this bastard Temple enabled that dastardly Protestant devil to become King of England?"

"The very same, I'm afraid, in 1685, Tadgh."

All this talk of Temple generations was hurting Morgan's head. "Is that the tragedy?"

Deirdre looked up from her teacup to scrutinize Morgan's eyes. "Partly."

"I should think that's enough of a catastrophe," Tadgh said, his eyes glittering.

"There is more. Temple reorganized the English Privy Council during the reign of Charles II and for a time enjoyed considerable influence in the new body. Nevertheless, by 1681, he found himself out of step with Charles's policies, and he retired from politics."

"But the Temple residence is no longer here, Deirdre," Tadgh said, stroking his moustache. "What happened to it and the descendants?"

Deirdre hesitated before responding as if collecting her thoughts. "They gravitated back to England in the time of Sir William. After his death, his one heir lived for a time in the old place in the 1700s when he wasn't in England. In 1707, the Dublin Customs House, controlling all import and export business, was built on the south shore of the Liffey in Temple Bar. This stimulated businesses in the area."

"How is that tragic?"

"Let me finish. In 1791, the new Customs House was established in its current location downstream on the north shore of the river. As a result, the businesses in Temple Bar began to decline. Then, in 1802 came a terrible flood that wiped out the Ormond stone bridge just upstream of here near the Four Courts. It also destroyed buildings in Temple Bar, including the Temple residence, I was told. Citizens saw roofs of houses, a millwheel, a dead horse, and calves washed away in the deluge. The city condemned much of Temple Bar and leveled all the damaged buildings."

Morgan poured herself tea before asking, "How do you know so much about the Temple family and history of the area?"

"I was told that his pub was established on the plowed-under ruins of the residence. It was a grocery that also sold spirits and beer at first. As I said earlier, I made it my business to research all of this so that I could advertise the pub's lineage to increase patronage."

Morgan had been taking all this in while Deirdre talked. Clearly, this woman she called a friend had business and research skills that surprised her. *It must take a very smart woman with an iron will to own and operate a thriving pub in Dublin.*

"How long have you lived here, Deirdre?" Morgan hastily added, "If you don't mind my asking."

The proprietress frowned. "It seems that it has been my whole life, so it does. My father John bartended here before the turn of the century, and I took over when my mother died back in '13."

Tadgh raised his tankard. "Well now. Here's to ya, lass. You're doing a fine job of it, that's certain."

"Ta." Deirdre paused. "So where'd you get that scribbled phrase that might have been by William Temple?"

Before Tadgh could stop her, Morgan blurted out, "Have you ever heard of the *Book of Ballymote*?" He kicked her shin under the table. Morgan shot him a fierce stare.

Tadgh noticed the pub owner's eyes widen when Morgan spoke of the book.

"No, I can't say that I have," Deirdre answered.

Now why might she be lying? Tadgh wondered. She clearly knew more about Lawlor than she let on. He wished Morgan had not spilled the beans.

Before he could stop her, Morgan ignored his intervention and continued, "Well, it's a compendium of knowledge that was created for Clan Chieftain McDonagh in Ballymote back near the end of the fourteenth century. Professor Lawlor showed it to us yesterday."

"Oh. Why are you interested in that book, Morgan?"

"My O'Donnell ancestor acquired it back in 1522, and I wanted to find out why he might have done that. I love a good mystery."

"So do I, Morgan. I guess we are two birds of a feather, then. These letters and the date you had on your paper came from that book?"

Tadgh shot Morgan a cautionary look, but she shrugged it off, presumably feeling Deirdre could be trusted. After all, hadn't she hidden them when Boyle was hot on their trail? And hadn't she served as one of Morgan's bridesmaids?

"Yes," Morgan said. "This indecipherable and obliterated note was scribbled at the bottom of a page of that document."

Deirdre toyed with the bag from her cold tea, feigning disinterest, then asked, "Where was it located?"

"In a section associated with a description of migration of the Jewish tribes to Europe, my dear bridesmaid." Tadgh thought he detected a momentary twitch before Deirdre regained her composure.

"How odd," Deirdre said.

Tadgh took a swig of his Guinness. "That's what I thought. Likely meaningless drivel."

"I'm not so sure, my love. Look at the rest of the phrase." Morgan laid out her paper in front of them all. "Deirdre came up with an interesting interpretation of the back end of this drivel, as you call it. Maybe she can help us with the beginning since she loves a mystery, as she herself said."

Morgan gave her bridesmaid a hug when she moved closer to them, nudging Tadgh out of the way to examine the handwritten scribble more closely.

Deirdre scanned the words, and her eyebrows went up again. She couldn't believe it. Here in the patron ancestor of her establishment's own letters was the connection she and her father had been searching for all these years. Clearly, he had written, *Fleeing Knights Templar. What did they know? FP? Investigate.* They were still escaping to Scotland through western Ireland, and in fact, Ballymote, in the fourteenth century when the book was written. William dated the note as 1610, a full ten years before the recorded date when the book showed up in Trinity College library. He probably studied it carefully before announcing its presence at the college. He must have convinced his Knights Templar colleague, Dowcra, the former Governor of Derry, to force the traitorous Niall O'Donnell to disclose where he had hidden the sacred book after the flight of the Earls three years earlier. Since both Niall and his son Neachtain had been imprisoned for life as a result of their involvement in the 1608 revolt in Derry, Dowcra probably threatened to have the son executed.

So, the stories that her mother had told her when she was dying, long after her father's murder, were true. *Could the British Israeli Association bastards have been digging in the wrong place back in 1899 when father discovered their plan? She would have to talk to Lawlor more about this revelation. He must be shocked as well.*

Now she needed to know what religious relic was hidden, who FP was who hid it, and what these friends of hers knew. Could it be the sacred word of God that she was sworn to protect? She decided to let the McCarthys do the legwork. She would stick close.

Tadgh moved his seat between the two women, innocently brushing Deirdre further down the table. He had noticed Deirdre's reaction.

Deirdre turned to Morgan and said, "I don't know what the first few letters mean, but I would guess that Temple, if it was Temple, wrote those words, 'What did they know? FP? Investigate.'"

Tadgh spoke up before Morgan could answer, "If that were to be true then who are 'they' referred to?"

"I don't know," Deirdre admitted. "FP, whoever that is, I'd guess."

Tadgh twirled his moustache. Two could play this game. He would try to find out what Deirdre knew. "Professor Lawlor said that the book only showed up at Trinity College library in 1620. If you are right about provost William Temple writing the marginal note, then how could the date be 1610? The date couldn't be 1670 because you said he died before that, in 1627."

Deirdre looked Tadgh in the eye. His body up against her stirred her senses. "I don't have the foggiest clue about that, Tadgh, unless he had it in his possession before he turned it over to the library."

"For ten years?"

Deirdre realized that Tadgh was now doing the interrogating. There were brains behind his manly warrior bravado. She would have to be careful. "Yes, I know. It does seem strange, doesn't it? We can talk more about this later, but I have to check on the kitchen before the dinner patrons show up."

Unseen by the group, Abbad lurked behind a newspaper in the shadows of a dark nearby snug, listening. He wore dark glasses and wide-brimmed hat. When necessary, he would fold the paper so he could hold it in his left hand while he took notes with his right in a book with the letters B. I. A. etched into its cover.

Tadgh paid the bill and took Morgan back to their temporary residence a block away on Crow Street. Only after they were ensconced in their room, Tadgh opined, "I think spending time on this marginal note in the book is a wild goose chase. First of all, we don't even know if the *Book of Ballymote* holds a clue."

"I sense that it does, Tadgh. And Sir Owain. I was meant to find that smudged note. It leapt out of the book at me, and I don't know why, except that it had a few English letters I could understand. I have *déjà vu*, remember?"

"Hocus-pocus, my dear. I only believe in facts, not imaginary visions."

"So you don't believe that some of what has happened is Divine intervention, like your finding me at sea, for example?"

"Maybe in that circumstance."

"What about the ghostly Sir Owain? And then Collin showing up at Aunt Biddy's home a day later after so many years of searching for me?"

"I'll grant you that was a coincidence."

"Balderdash, Tadgh. I feel these things in my bones."

"All right, then. What do you think about the fact that Deirdre showed an interest and knows of Professor Lawlor? I am suspicious of her, Morgan. I saw her reactions."

"What? Dear Deirdre? She's interested in the history of her pub and used Lawlor to give her information. That's all."

"Maybe, aroon. We'll see soon enough."

Morgan changed the subject. "What if William Temple knew that there was a Clans Pact and that a clue to the O'Donnell treasure could have been hidden in the *Book of Ballymote*, when Red Hugh owned it? And what about the fact that Temple died mysteriously in 1627?"

Tadgh shook his head, chuckling. "Your suggestion that this William Temple could have known about our Clans Pact is very farfetched, to be sure. I don't see the connection in this mystery, aroon."

"Wait a minute, Tadgh. Your comment just now triggered my memory. Doesn't Collin's locket map start with CCtip for Cormac's Chapel, which led us to the rock of Cashel?"

"Yes, but what does that have to do with the O'Donnell treasure?"

"What saying is etched into your locket? It is likely a map for the O'Donnell treasure. Remind me how it starts."

Tadgh opened his locket, removed the cameo of his Mam, and read, "It starts with the letters PPPC."

"I thought so." Morgan stared at the scribbles on the page. "What if Deirdre is right, and the phrase is *What do they know?* and *PP*, not *FP*? The letters were faint, and I might not have seen the written line closure of the F to a P."

"Interesting idea, lass. FP or PP could be a place and not a person."

"In which case Temple could have been searching for the O'Donnell treasure. Didn't Deirdre mention that Temple was the property-and-money-grabbing kind?"

"Yes."

"Well then, Tadgh. Could Red Hugh have written this note and not William Temple? It is written in the same type of alpha numeric code as the clues in the lockets."

Tadgh got up from the table and paced the room before answering. "The words *What do they* are written in English. Red

Hugh would have used his native tongue, Gaelic. No, I think an Englishman wrote these words. I still don't see the connection between Temple and the O'Donnells, though."

Morgan stood by the window, looking out onto Crow Street below before turning back. "Deirdre said he was in Ireland in 1599 helping Devereux in his attempt to conquer the remaining Clans, which would have included Red Hugh. Maybe there was a connection there? I wonder if he was still there until October of 1600."

Tadgh stopped pacing and joined her at the window. "Deirdre said that the coup attempt was in 1601, didn't she?"

"No, Tadgh. She said that Devereux was executed in 1601. Temple still could have been in Ireland in late 1600.

Tadgh had to admit, this potential connection to Deirdre and the Temple Bar Pub was the only lead they had. "I suppose so. It's worth pursuing, Morgan, but only for a couple of days. We need to get back home to Aidan and my assignment from Mick. There's a war going on, and we're going to win it."

Morgan cringed again at the thought of Tadgh returning to the hell of battle, or worse. "Agreed. What do we do now?"

"We need to find out more about William Temple. Try to confirm if he came into wealth suddenly. Find out from his records where PP is." Tadgh resumed his pacing. "Mary, Mother of God. Now I'm beginning to sound like you."

"I know. Isn't it grand? But you pace like Aidan. Come and sit down with me."

Once they were seated across from each other with the scribbled page between them, Morgan said, "Temple ended up a rich man. We must face the fact that he could have found the treasure twenty or more years before Boyle found the Clans Pact. We have to find out if we are on a fool's errand searching for our O'Donnell's treasure, for sure."

"I agree. But if this scribble means anything, which I don't think likely, lass, where is FP or PP?"

"We've known since we found the etching in your locket that

PP was likely the start of our O'Donnell treasure search. Now, if my intuition is right, we may have a person, Temple, who knew where it was located."

"So having killed a live villainous adversary in Boyle, we would now have a dead one in Temple."

"Yes, mavourneen. Almost three hundred years dead, and unfortunately maybe having beaten us to our providence."

Map 2
Portion of the Plan of Dublin by Samuel Byron, City Surveyor,
1793 (courtesy of the Board of Trinity College, Dublin)

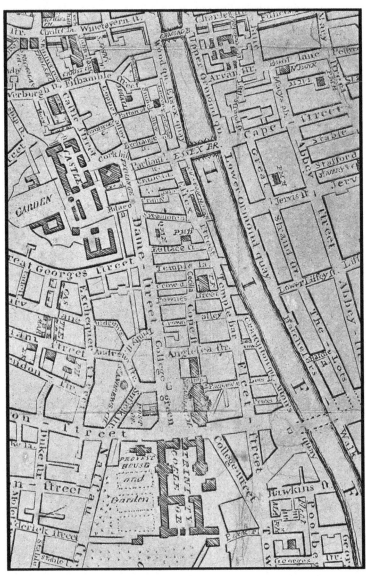

Chapter Fifteen
Arson

Wednesday, November 24, 1920
Temple Bar Pub, Dublin

*D*eirdre **had stewed** about the note in the *Book of Ballymote* all afternoon. Finally, at closing time, she got a break and slipped back into the kitchen where her cook, close friend, and sometimes bodyguard was finishing the cleanup. She brought him a Guinness.

Derek Slocum was a wiry forty-two-year-old ex-prizefighter with sandy hair and a smile a mile wide. He had started working for her father John back in '97, when she was just three years old. Being deceptively strong and skilled in self-defense, Derek still had a jovial nature and always brought her a treat. He would sit down and be any character that Deirdre wanted him to play when her father and mother were too busy with the pub/grocery. Only six when her dad was murdered, Deirdre knew Derek's involvement in trying to save him from the British Israeli Association goons' attack. Afterwards, Derek felt responsible and became the loyal companion and protector of her mother and her. Now, with her mum gone, it was just the two of them.

"I had a strange and revealing conversation with the McCarthys today." She described the scribble's contents and what it said, and their conversation about it. "I think they are after the word of God."

"What makes you think that?" Derek paused in untying his cook's apron.

"They have a strong interest in the sacred book. Morgan found the note that we all, including Lawlor, missed, and she seized on its importance. Tadgh was skeptical but that may have just been to put me off the scent."

"Did they understand that the first letters were 'fleeing Knights Templar'?"

"No. I don't think so. And I didn't offer that interpretation."

Derek raised his eyebrows. "Then why—?"

"I don't know!" Deirdre stated flatly.

"Clearly, the eldest William was leaving a trail for his descendants to find, Dee. He probably thought that the book would stay in the family's care at Trinity forever."

Deirdre took a swig of her cook's stout. "He obviously couldn't decipher the secrets of the book and none of the rest of us could do that either over the last three hundred years, until now. These McCarthys may be able to unlock the mystery, and we need to make sure they don't unearth it. We may be the last Knights Templar left in Ireland, yet the most important ones in the history of our crusade."

Derek offered, "We need to find out what *FP* means."

"Mum said there were documents in an iron chest that revealed whatever William found out, which were lost when the residence was destroyed in the flood. Now, with this threat from the McCarthys, maybe we should try to find it."

"How did she know this?"

"She said that my father told her before he died. Apparently, this story was passed down as a secret through the family generations. We were never sure because our family lived in England and didn't return to Ireland until my father took an interest in the old ways."

"Is that why he bought the grocery and distillery and turned it into the Temple Bar Pub?"

"Yes, that's right, on the site of the old residence. He dug the basement storage area himself, looking for evidence of the home and that old box, to no avail. I was only five, but I remember him being very discouraged."

Derek frowned. "That was just a year before I hired on. Wouldn't the iron chest have been swept away by the flood and be buried in the mud somewhere downstream under the city?"

"That's what my ancestors thought. Yet we've always been

mindful of the risk of someone else finding it during city renovations someday."

"But you don't know for sure that there was important information in William's chest, if it existed, that would threaten our mission."

"You are right about that, Derek. But with the McCarthys we must be vigilant. This scribble Morgan found could help unlock the puzzle, especially if it was written by William himself. Let's help them search and then on the off chance that they are successful, we will reap the rewards."

"How do you propose we do all that?"

Deirdre grabbed a clean butcher knife from a wooden block and inspected the blade. "Dull as a hoe!" After rummaging in a drawer for a whetstone, she commenced sharpening the knife with it while she talked.

"We need intelligence on what Morgan and Tadgh are doing," Deirdre said, as she sighted with one eye along the blade's edge, now razor-sharp. "I will get close to their friend Jack, if you know what I mean, and you will slow them down if they get too close."

"Don't get too close, my lass. They all may have to be dealt with if they find out about what we are looking for."

"I'm quite aware of that, Derek," Deirdre said as she stabbed the butcher block with the knife, leaving it quivering in the wood.

"Sounds like a plan, boss."

Before she left the kitchen, Deirdre added, "The Association's been sending a snooper around again. This time, it's young Abbad. I want to kill them all, but I'm not letting on. Maybe the young Moroccan will lead us to his masters when the time comes."

"That would be sweet revenge for you, Dee."

♣　♣　♣　♣

Tadgh awoke on Thursday morning with an idea. Morgan was already dressing. Before she could get her shirtwaist on, Tadgh bounded out of bed and pulled her in to him so that her breasts were crushed against his chest.

"I see that you are feeling more chipper this morning, mavourneen. Your nurse might remove the no-lovemaking restriction on you soon."

"It had better be damned soon."

"I'll ask her when I see her, then."

He crushed her mouth on his, nibbling at her lower lip.

"You best do that today, lass."

"Only if you agree to shave first."

Tadgh released her and searched for his trousers. "I had a thought."

"That's novel, my love."

"Funny. If your hunch is right about William Temple, then he might have kept documents that would help us find PP. What if we could find them, somehow?"

"I thought you were the sceptic, Sir Owain and all, no?"

"Well, lass, you found something from the 1600s that likely has PP in it, and that's the starting point in my locket."

Morgan thought, *Plant a seed and it will grow.*

"Good thinking, Tadgh. Trinity College might have archived Temple's papers, which may give us additional clues."

"Or they could have been kept by the family in the residence destroyed by the flood that Deirdre mentioned."

"I think we should ask Deirdre. Besides, she makes a great breakfast."

"All right, Morgan. But we aren't going to share with her what we are looking for, right?"

"Right." Morgan glanced out the window at the threatening sky. "Better bring that umbrella. It could rain any second."

Deirdre was as anxious to see the McCarthys as they were to see her. After a full Irish breakfast was served, she came over to their secluded snug and sat down, whispering, "We had Black and Tans in this morning, looking for Michael Collins. No trouble that I can't see to, but you both should be careful. *The Irish Times* is still reporting the search for you two."

Morgan scanned the room outside the snug with wary eyes. "Thanks, Deirdre. This hiding in plain sight might work for Michael Collins but it makes me quite nervous. I can't wait to get home again."

"Where's Jack this dreary morning?" Deirdre asked, looking around the pub.

Morgan smiled. "He'll be along shortly. Do I sense an interest there?"

"I admit that I find him intriguing, Morgan. But I'm not the marrying kind."

"You never know until you meet the right one." Morgan gave Tadgh a squeeze, which spilled his coffee.

After mopping it up with his napkin, Tadgh said, "We have a question, Deirdre. In case those scribbles in the *Book of Ballymote* are significant, we were wondering whether William Temple left any documents around that might have found their way into the pub records."

"The grocery and distillery was opened in 1819, seventeen years after the flood, I was told. By that time, the Temple residence was history, swept downstream. I don't have any documents from earlier times, I'm afraid. I have a question for you. What are you looking for in the *Book of Ballymote*?"

Morgan stirred her coffee and added some cream before responding.

"I have been fascinated with O'Donnell history. When we stayed in Ballymote at Temple House last year on our way to visit Peader in Donegal, we heard about the book, and an old man in the village said there was a secret in it. So I am simply curious. It helps me take my mind off the troubles of the war."

"What secret?"

"Funny, that's what Professor Lawlor asked. And what I asked the old man."

"What did he say?"

"He responded to me, saying, 'If I knew then it wouldn't be a secret, would it.'"

The pub owner thought for a moment before speaking. "There was an old story in the neighborhood that the Temples kept their records in an iron chest in the residence. I understand that it was never found after the building collapsed during the flood and was plowed under."

Jack strode in with his cane and plopped down at the bench opposite the McCarthys, hemming Deirdre in. "Hello, my buxom beauty. What's your special breakfast today?"

"For you, Jack, you silver-tongued devil, I'll fix you steak and eggs." She winked and smiled.

Jack's eyes wandered from her face. "That would be first-rate, lass." Jack stood and let the proprietress out.

"Getting the royal treatment, I see, Jack," Morgan commented. "Watch out there, lad."

"She's a looker, that's certain. And so are you, I might add, Morgan."

Tadgh scowled and moved closer to her on the bench. "As my wife says, watch out there, Jack."

Deirdre came back momentarily with a cup of coffee for Jack. The ex-bosun's eyes followed her every move.

Tadgh cleared his throat. "Jack, if I can get your attention, I have a task for you this morning."

Jack took a slug of his coffee and wiped his mouth. "All right, Tadgh. What do you have in mind?"

"Morgan and I are not free to wander very far, but you can. We need you to go to Trinity College library and ask whether they have any records about the fourth provost, William Temple, in their archives, including his obituary. If so, make a list of them for us. Also, please ask them for a city map from the seventeenth or eighteenth century, and if possible, one showing where the Temple residence was in Temple Bar. Can you do that, Jack?"

"Sounds intriguing. Sure, I'll do it."

Deirdre returned with Jack's breakfast. The steak was hanging off both ends of the plate. "Why don't you all come back for supper tonight, say, around seven? I can get the waitresses to cover. I'll have Derek make us a meal upstairs in my residence."

Morgan's green eyes lit up. "That sounds grand, Deirdre. I accept, for me and the boys."

At noon at the El Bahir, Fazaar met with Abbad, who had just come from spying at the Temple Bar pub.

"Do you have the note, Brother?"

"I snuck into the RIA stacks last night with a magnifying glass and retrieved the sacred book." Fazaar spread his thin lips in a crooked smile, revealing teeth yellowed and broken from chewing on the hookah pipe. "Such a sacrilege if the professor ever found out. Anyway, I copied down the note but there were parts too faint to read." Fazaar gave Abbad the paper that bore his jottings.

"We'll discuss this later, Fazaar. We've got more important issues. I've decided that it's time to get rid of Deirdre. Her family has been a thorn in the side of the Association, and more importantly, she is a threat to our sacred family quest. We need only one adversary. Then it will be easier to deal with the Irish couple and what they know."

"But won't this risk our holy mission, Brother?"

"In fact, it will save it, Fazaar. I think that the pub itself is a part of the solution. We need to get her out of there. Here's the plan."

Abbad outlined his intentions in subdued tones and his brother's smile grew.

"Kill two birds with one stone, then."

"Precisely. I will implement my plan tonight."

Jack came back to the Crow Street digs just before six and reported in. "It's certainly getting windy out there," he said, flinging off his coat and hat. "I heard that we're in for several days of torrential rain in the next few days. Quite unusual for this time of year."

"So, what did you find out, Jack?" Morgan asked, offering him hot tea.

"The records that they had for William Temple were only personnel-related. Date of arrival, salary over time, that sort of thing. Nothing personal to him. He worked there a long time, right up to his death. Almost eighteen years. There were some complaints lodged against him in the latter years. Apparently, the college directors didn't like his outside business methods and deals. There was one internal letter suggesting he be removed from his post."

"When was that written?"

"Just before Christmas, 1626, only a month or so before his heart attack. He was probably under a lot of stress."

"Was there an obituary in the paper when he died?"

"Not that the college had noted, but there was a police report that said he died of a heart attack in his study, as confirmed by his wife Martha who was with him at the time. The report strangely stated that they found bruise marks on his body. His wife said that happened when he hit his head falling during the seizure. They held a board of inquiry but ruled that his death was a simple heart attack."

"Nothing with the letters PP in the records, or a place with two words starting with 'p' that might have been one of his possessions, then?" Morgan asked, drumming her fingers on the meeting table in their room.

"Nothing I could see like that. But I did get a map. I copied a portion of it that you might be interested in." Jack spread his tracing on the table. "This is the Plan of Dublin drawn by Samuel Byron, the city surveyor in 1793. I found it in the *Gentleman's and Citizens Almanack* dated 1778 to 1793." Pointing, Jack asked, "Do you see Temple Bar there?"

284

Tadgh nodded. "Yes, I see the Temple Bar Street and Temple Lane intersection where the pub stands on its northwest corner."

"What's that building that's shown blacked-in, kitty-corner to the southeast of that intersection on the next street south?" Morgan squinted at the map. "It looks like Cecilia Street just here at the north end of Crow Street."

"That's right. The annotation on the map for the building is either TR or TX. What do you think it is, Jack? You copied it."

Jack squeezed his eyes shut, then opened them. "T.R., I would say."

Morgan looked closer. Her green eyes sparkled as she whispered, "Temple residence."

"That must be it, aroon," Tadgh said. "The residence was just slightly southeast of where the pub stands today, still on the grounds of what was certainly the Temple estate."

"I think we should show Deirdre this map this evening, boys. Good work, Jack."

Jack was pleased that the love of his life would praise his efforts on behalf of the Clans. He thought, *Heaven help me, no matter how tempting Deirdre's obvious charms are, Morgan truly still holds my heart.* Then he blushed and hoped the McCarthys didn't notice.

Tadgh did. He raised an eyebrow but said nothing.

Deirdre's flat above the pub was more well-appointed than Morgan remembered from when she had put the McCarthy boys and herself up after Aidan was shot and chased by Boyle. That seemed so long ago now. Business must have been good between the end of the war and the current Irish altercations. This hunter green room was connected through an archway to the parlor, both with Tudor-era dark-beamed ceilings. The proprietress pointed out old, framed photographs of her mum and father on the wall over the fireplace. They were oddly unnamed.

"Do you miss them, Deirdre?" Jack asked as he recognized the facial similarities between the mother and her daughter.

"Every day, Jack. Are your parents alive?"

Morgan looked over at Jack.

"I'm afraid not, lass. My father died in the Boer War in '99. I was a wee lad of ten. My mother died in childbirth three years later, after a stranger raped her in one of the alleys of Portsmouth."

Deirdre squeezed Jack's hand, leaning forward as if to examine her father's picture and affording him a direct view of the top of her ample breasts. "That must have been awful for you. My father died in '99 too. We have a lot in common."

Jack nodded and Deirdre put her free arm around him. "Can you smell the dinner, my lad? We should go in to eat now."

Jack sniffed the air. "Mutton, I think. Such a sweet meat."

Derek served grilled lamb chops with mint sauce, baked potatoes, and green beans with slivered almonds on Deirdre's oak dining room table.

This was such a drastic change from what Tadgh was subjected to for the last three years, that he had to be coaxed to eat heartily, afraid that his stomach would not tolerate the rich food. He had decided to play along with his hostess to see what developed. He noticed that Derek was more than a cook to Deirdre, likely a bodyguard. At almost six feet, he certainly had the muscles for it, even at his age. Tadgh guessed former military, highly disciplined. There didn't seem to be any romantic attachment between them.

Deirdre asked Tadgh to say grace. "Thank you, Lord, for this thy bounty and for these true friends. Bless this grand food to thy use. And most importantly, thank you for giving my wife the strength to free me from my bondage by the infidels. You must have higher purpose for us here on earth. Amen." His eyes teared up.

Morgan got up and gave her husband a big kiss.

After dessert of apple pie and cheese, the group retired to the parlor. Deirdre made a point of sitting beside Jack on the sofa. Derek appeared with a tray of tea for the ladies, and Jameson whiskey for the men before retiring to the kitchen in the pub below.

Deirdre said, "I've got some news. This pub started as a grocery and distillery store, and I've always wanted to own one. There's a need for a good produce store in this part of downtown."

"Are you thinking of adding back groceries to the Temple Bar Pub?" Morgan asked, adding sugar to her tea, and stirring.

"No, of course not. There's a store that has been struggling just directly opposite my pub on the next street over to the east. It's on the corner of Temple Bar Street and Fownes. Perhaps you've seen it, Gilroy's Groceries. We both back onto the same delivery alleyway. I've been in negotiation to buy it as Mr. Gilroy wants out of Ireland because of the war. The deal closed last week, and I took occupancy today. The produce will spoil if I don't start operating it immediately. How would you like to run it for me, Jack? Yes?"

Deirdre put her hand on Jack's inner thigh as she turned towards him for an answer. "There's a grand apartment above the store where you could live."

He could only stammer, "I—I guess I do need a full-time job at the moment, and of course I want to stay here in Dublin. Oh, but lass, I've never—"

"I'd show you the ropes, Jack. We could do it together. It should be easy, compared to running the Cunard Steamship Lines."

"I didn't run the whole company, Deirdre."

"Well, you think about it, please. At least help me out to get started since I still have the Pub to run."

"That much, I can do, my dear."

"Good. That's settled. We'll need a grand opening." Deirdre waved her arms, imagining the banner for the storefront.

Morgan could see that Jack was star-struck and would do anything Deirdre asked of him at this point. "Jack's got something to show you, Deirdre," Morgan said, shifting her eyes from one to the other and smiling.

"Yes, I do," he affirmed. "I looked up where the Temple residence was compared to where the pub is today." He took the copy of the old surveyor's map out of his breast coat pocket and laid it the oak parlor table in front of them. "See the building here labeled TR. We think that was the Temple residence."

"Really?" Deirdre leaned over and stared at the tracing. "We aren't exactly on top of where it was located?"

"It doesn't look like it. Maybe two hundred feet northwest of it."

Morgan chimed in, pointing. "If the residence was over there, then perhaps William's box could be buried there, do you think?"

Deirdre didn't want to squash their enthusiasm, but she understood from her mum that her father had found that old map and determined that TR stood for the Theatre Royal that was at the end of Crow Street back in 1793 and not the Temple residence. It was after that discovery that he had excavated under the pub looking for the iron chest. She wanted to consult with Derek before sharing this bad news. And she wanted to praise Jack.

She gave Jack a peck on the cheek and put her arm around his back, letting her left breast push against his shoulder. "Thank you, Jack. This is a valuable addition to the Temple history of our area."

"I'm glad it helps you, lass. I aim to please."

"I'm sure you do, big boy." Deirdre purposely put her hand on Jack's seated thigh in order to stand and flaunt her breasts in his face on the way up.

Morgan thought that she was starting to act like the loony Aileen, Aidan's old girlfriend.

Deirdre looked at her clock. "Oh my. It's getting on. I almost forgot that I have an appointment."

"What, at this hour?" Jack asked, going to the dark window, and peering out. Dry lightning flashed in the west. "There's a wicked wind out tonight. A storm is coming."

"It can't be helped, dear boy. I got a note from Edward Walsh, the owner of the Pelican's Nest Bar further down on Temple Bar Street. He wants me to meet with him because of some threat to the pubs in the area by the police tomorrow. It can't wait. We stick together during these tough times, so we do."

Jack consulted his watch. This didn't sound like a good idea after dark. Something was amiss. "It's closing time for the pubs because of the war-time curfew soon, isn't it? Can't it wait until tomorrow?"

"Apparently not."

"I'll go with you then," Jack said, getting up and grabbing his walking stick.

"You'll do nothing of the kind. It's only three blocks away. This won't take long. You folks relax and enjoy your evening here. I'll be right back." With that, Deirdre picked up her coat and went downstairs, where she told Derek to close up the pub in half an hour.

When she didn't return after fifteen minutes, Jack said, "I'm going after her."

Morgan said, "You rest your back. I'll go and fetch her."

With his strength improving day by day, especially with Derek's cooking, Tadgh jumped up and spoke, "Sit tight, the both of you. I'll go see what's keeping her."

Donning his coat downstairs, he then got directions to the Pelican's Nest from Aileen. With her you could never be sure if she knew her right from her left.

Morgan cautioned him to be careful.

When he stepped out onto Temple Bar Street, it was obvious which direction to go. To the right, per Aileen's instructions, Tadgh could see smoke billowing up from an establishment three blocks down. He broke into a run. By the time he reached the Pelican's Nest Pub, the building was spewing flames, whipped up by the wind.

Tadgh broke down the door and rushed into the bar area, thinking about the conflagration in Cashel Cathedral ruins. Dreading the worst, he cupped his hands around his mouth and yelled at the top his lungs. *"Deirdre!"* No answer. He yelled again. *"Deirdre!"*

He gauged the danger. The long bar was fully engulfed in flames. One of the bottles exploded in the heat. Then more. The flames were spreading to the inflammable booths. The entire area would be impassable within a minute.

Tadgh took the chance of being impaled by flying glass or burning to a crisp by darting behind the bar. Deirdre wasn't there.

Maybe she never arrived. Maybe she left already. Tadgh decided to check the office where she would likely have met the owner. Its door was already lit by flames.

Tadgh kicked it in and rushed into a room filled floor to ceiling with documents on one side and liquor bottles stored on the other. His eyes watered and stung from the smoke. There, sprawled on the floor was Deirdre, unconscious. Had she succumbed already? The owner of the pub was nowhere to be seen.

Suddenly the wall between the bar and the office burst into flames. Bottles on the office wall detonated, sending glass shrapnel flying in the confined space of the room.

There was no way out by the front. Tadgh frantically looked around the burning office to determine a way out. Then he saw the tradesman's back door from the office through the dense smoke. He dove down to floor level beside Deirdre and dragged her to the exit.

He had to stand to open the door. Fire licked at the door frame, warped from the searing heat. He dared not touch the doorknob. Tadgh knew that the backdraft would cause the flames to shoot outward when the door opened.

He took a step back into the inferno and drove his shoulder into the door. The frame splintered and the door collapsed outward. In the same motion, he dove to the floor and pulled Deirdre's inert body out into the alleyway, barely escaping the blowtorch above them.

Tadgh's coat was on fire. Doffing it, he scooped Deirdre in his arms and fled down the alley with her.

Only moments later, the roof of the Pelican fell in with a great crash.

Tadgh wished to hell that Morgan was there. He could see a gash on the back of Deirdre's head. It didn't bleed profusely, thank goodness. But she wasn't breathing.

Tadgh laid Deirdre down in the alley and began working on her the way Morgan had taught him after she'd resuscitated him on the *Republican* so long ago. Tadgh alternatively pumped on her chest and breathed into her mouth. One awful moment, he thought he had lost her. Finally, Deirdre coughed and retched. She had inhaled a lot of smoke.

Tadgh looked around for a safer spot to move her. Soon, the police would arrive. He carried her out of the alley and back towards the Temple Bar Pub along the back streets near the River Liffey. Some late-night strollers looked askance at the two in the distance but decided it was just lovers heading to another tryst.

At the other end of the alley, behind some stacked garbage cans, Abbad wrung his hands. *Damn! The plan was so simple. Why in the name of Allah did that meddling Irishman have to show up when he did?*

Chapter Sixteen
Blackmail

Thursday, November 25, 1920
Temple Bar, Dublin

*T*adgh carried Deirdre back to the Temple Bar pub. She was breathing in spasms. Coughing seemed to wrack her chest. He could hear the sirens of the fire pumper and police descending on what was left of the Pelican's Nest behind him. As he crossed Temple Bar just opposite Deirdre's pub, he could see a crowd milling about to his left down the street, despite the curfew.

He set Deirdre down, one arm around her waist while she leaned heavily against him. He tried the pub door—locked! He pounded on it and yelled for someone to open up, until Aileen finally did. *Took her own sweet time about it,* Tadgh cursed.

Aileen's eyes widened when she saw the condition of her boss. She bounded upstairs. "Morgan! Morgan!"

Tadgh carried Deirdre up the stairs. He almost collided with Morgan and Jack halfway.

Jack cried out, "My God, Tadgh! What happened?"

Morgan took charge. "Bring her into the parlor and set her on the chesterfield."

Tadgh complied. Morgan examined her patient. The pub owner's breathing was erratic but strong. Burns to her shoulders and arms were minor and at least her golden locks were not singed. It was the gash on the back of her head that needed the most attention. Derek rushed in with an aid kit, which Morgan quickly inventoried. To her surprise, Derek had included a packet of needles and a spool of catgut thread. *Thank God!* Morgan went to work. Deirdre required five stitches.

Jack moved to open the parlor window, letting in fresh air. It was smoky. Tadgh stopped him and bolted the window shut. "Better not to breathe the city air now."

Deirdre moaned and stirred listlessly on the chesterfield.

Derek demanded to know what had happened of Tadgh who had miraculously avoided burns except for the loss of his coat.

Tadgh relayed, "The Pelican's Nest was on fire and Deirdre was unconscious on the office floor when I got there. Couple minutes later and . . ."

"Someone hit her over the head. Look at that gash. Who would have done something like this?" Jack demanded, incensed.

Tadgh didn't have an answer.

Morgan found salve, cotton, and bandages, with which she treated Deirdre's burns and other wounds. "I'm going to stay here with her tonight, Tadgh. She's taken in a lot of smoke. I think she will be all right with rest."

Jack, who was holding Deirdre's hand, said he would also stay. Tadgh decided to go back to the scene of the crime. Borrowing Derek's coat and a broad-brimmed hat, he headed up Temple Bar.

With the hat pulled down over his ears, Tadgh crouched, hiding in the shadows of the alleyway until the crowd dispersed. He didn't see any Black and Tans, or RIC police, and thought that perhaps they stayed away on purpose to avoid being labeled as the arsonists.

The fire had pretty much burned the pub to the ground. Fortunately, the firemen confined the blaze, thereby saving the businesses on either side. Any remaining embers were finally extinguished. Inching closer, Tadgh could see a man standing in what had been the bar, gesturing frantically to a fireman who was holding up a scorched and dented can of some sort. If there had been police present, they had already left the scene.

Tadgh hugged the side of the intact building next to the pub's burned-out ruins. He heard the fireman say, "It looks like arson to me, sir. Where were you an hour ago?"

294

"If you are insinuating that I would have burned down—"

"Not at all, sir. I just wondered when you closed for the night."

"I wasn't gone ten minutes after ten before I saw the smoke."

"Do you know anyone who would have wanted to harm you or your establishment, sir?"

"No, but I am Unionist, and I don't keep that a secret. These days everyone has enemies."

"Right you are, sir. Well, I'm wrapped up here for the night. I expect the police will want to talk to you tomorrow."

Tadgh blended back into the shadows. *Arson, eh? And the owner wasn't there to meet with Deirdre.*

Deirdre slept through the night with Morgan by her side in the parlor. Tadgh returned and briefed Derek and Jack on what he had learned. They stayed in Derek's quarters behind the kitchen.

About four in the morning, Abbad picked the lock on the front door of Deirdre's pub and snuck inside. Stepping quietly behind the bar he deposited a paper in the utensil drawer before tiptoeing into the pantry where he positioned two kerosene cans behind boxes of tinned goods. With a Brownie camera, he snapped several pictures of these items. Then he was gone the way he had come, silently in the night.

He went straight to his darkroom to develop the pictures before dawn.

At seven in the morning, Abbad knocked on the street door of Mr. Walsh's house. The pub owner opened the door but barred entry as the Moroccan spoke. "I'm sorry for your troubles. I'm a photographer and I can shed some light on who torched your pub last night." He gave the pub owner a phony business card he had produced overnight.

Walsh stood in the doorway, arms crossed. "And who might that be?"

"Here, look at these pictures." Abbad handed him an envelope. "I followed the owner of the Temple Bar Pub last night from her establishment until she picked her way into your pub after the patrons had left. The street was empty at the time. She was carrying a can. She's a revolutionist, you know. Have you ever had a run-in with her before?"

"That Deirdre's a looker but we've never seen eye-to-eye. She's a tough one, she is."

"Well, I think she was out to get you because of your beliefs, sir. See this picture of her in your bar last night, the clock on the wall. She left the door open, and I snapped it without her knowledge."

"Yes, it is her, and this was just after I had left for the night."

"And this photograph of an unsigned message with patched-together newsprint letters to you from her, threatening all Unionists. I suppose she is planning to deliver it to you anonymously today."

"Where did you find this?"

"In the utensil drawer behind her bar. I was drinking there last evening, and I noticed her pasting the last of it on the ledge where patrons couldn't read it, swearing, and then putting it there. So, I photographed it when she was serving a customer in the snugs. I followed her out, intending to warn you, but you had left the Pelican's Nest before I got there."

Walsh scanned the photo. "She is a vicious cow. I would never have guessed that she hated me this much."

"Maybe she was just trying to get rid of competition here in Temple Bar."

"Maybe. What's this third picture?"

"Kerosene cans in her pantry. When I read that note and before she left, I went snooping around and saw this."

"Those look like the can the fireman showed me last night. Even though the outside was burnt, its shape and size are the same as the ones in this photograph."

"Yes, and you can see her kerosene can in the first picture. It's clearly the work of this mad woman."

Walsh looked at Abbad suspiciously. "Why are you being such a good Samaritan?"

"I am a Unionist myself. There have been entirely too many reprisals from the rebels on our good citizenry, sir. I seek justice for the good folks of Dublin. It's my calling!"

"I see." Walsh took his coat off the peg by the door. "We'd better go to the police with this information."

"Hold on, sir. If we do that then this woman will be brought to justice, but it won't bring your pub back."

"Did you see it afterwards? Nothing will bring my drinking establishment back. There was no insurance." He shook the envelope in the air. "Let's make her pay!"

"I think there is a way, sir."

Walsh threw up his hands. "How, without the police?"

"You could meet her and threaten to go to the police if she doesn't transfer her pub to you. You know she is harboring rebels wanted for murder, don't you?"

Walsh's eyes widened. "What?"

"A man and woman named McCarthy." Abbad described them based on having seen them in the pub and his examination of recent newspaper articles. "They killed several policemen and the woman broke McCarthy out of the Joy recently. So you see that Deirdre is a rebel herself."

Walsh's eyes hardened and his nostrils flared. "The bitch. I never liked her."

"I hear you, Mr. Walsh."

"Why would she give up her pub? It's been in her family for a long time."

"If she is exposed, she will go to jail for a long time if it is proven that she was sheltering known Republican murderers. The Black and Tans would likely torch her pub in reprisal. If she refuses, you get justice, but likely neither of you end up with a pub."

Walsh thought for a moment and shouldered his way into his coat. "Let's do it now, then, before the police get further involved."

"It's best if you go alone, sir. You are the one affected."

"But these are your photographs."

"It won't matter as long as you have them. Go to the right-hand drawer behind the bar, and to the cases of dry goods in the pantry, then expose her."

"I'll bring my five strapping sons in as witnesses. They serve as my bartenders and bouncers. I'll just get them now."

The Saturday morning papers were full of the story of the arson at the Pelican's Nest. The owner felt he was being targeted because he was a Unionist, and the police were looking for the perpetrator.

Deirdre and Morgan took their breakfast in Deirdre's residence. She was decidedly better, although swearing a blue streak because of her sore head. Tadgh and Jack joined them and asked her what happened the night before.

"I went to see Mr. Walsh. His front door was open, but the bar was closed for the night," she explained. "I called out to him and received no answer. Then I checked the bar and went back to his office. That's all I know. Someone gave me a big whack on the back of my head and the next thing I know a man was reviving me."

Morgan didn't like the thought of that, but she was glad that her husband had been there in time. "It was Tadgh, you know, Deirdre. He saved your life."

"I know. I am so grateful." Deirdre weakly stood and put her arms around Tadgh, giving him a kiss on the mouth. "Like this?"

Tadgh blushed. "Not exactly, lass."

Jack looked peeved and Morgan stepped between. "That will do. You'll survive."

"They found a kerosene can, Deirdre. Did you see one?"

"No. It all happened so fast."

Aileen came up from the bar. "There is an angry man downstairs to see you, Deirdre."

298

"What? Tell him we are not open yet."

"I'm afraid he's too mad for that. He's got five others for company."

Morgan helped the pub owner down the stairs with Tadgh trailing behind. Jack was asked to stay in the residence.

"Mr. Walsh, how are you, sir?" Deirdre said, extending her hand in friendship. "We heard about what happened to your pub last night. Terrible business. How can I help you?"

"You can deed me your pub here, you viper." Walsh hissed, standing ramrod straight.

"What? You must have lost your mind. I know it's a shock, but—"

A red-faced Walsh shook the envelope containing the pictures in her face. "But nothing woman. I know that you burned my place down last night. I have proof."

"That's absurd. I didn't do it. Why would I? I came in response to your note and got a smack on the back of my head for my trouble. I almost died in the fire."

Walsh hissed, "I didn't write you a note. You're lying."

John, a burly six-feet-three, the kind who would take no guff from God, stood guard at the door while his other brothers circled inside the pub. "Go get it, Da," he said, and Walsh moved to the back of the bar.

Tadgh watched closely as he opened the right-hand drawer and pulled out a paper.

"Aha, as I was told." Walsh brandished the sheet. "I'll just keep this as evidence."

Deirdre glared. "Show it to me."

Walsh gave her the sheet. "Read it aloud."

Deirdre went pale, staring slack-jawed and pop-eyed at the paper. "This is not mine."

"You were going to deliver this to me today anonymously, weren't you, witch. Read it!"

Deirdre saw the crudely cut and pasted letters.

"Walsh, you unionist pig. You are a disgrace to the Republic of Ireland and should be burned out of Dublin. Your Pelican is charred and gone so get out."

Deirdre's eyes burned into her accuser. "It's not from me. Someone planted this there. Who lied to you about this?"

Walsh snatched the sheet out of Deirdre's hand. "Never you mind, some honest citizen, that's who. I'll just keep this as evidence. My sons are my witnesses."

"That doesn't prove anything," Tadgh said, eyeing one of the sons walking toward the kitchen.

Moments later Tadgh heard a yell. "I found them, Da. Come in here. More proof."

They all followed the son into the pantry where young Walsh was pointing to something behind the cases of dry goods. Derek saw the commotion from the kitchen, picked up a butcher knife and started toward the others, but Deirdre shook her head to stop him.

"See, over here. The same kind of kerosene cans that they found in our Pelican's last night after the fire," young Walsh sneered.

Sure enough, Tadgh looked and could confirm that the two containers looked the same as the scorched one the fireman had shown to Walsh the night before.

"Those are not mine!" Deirdre yelled, her voice cracking.

Walsh pushed his arm into her shoulder before Tadgh could stop him. She stood rock steady against his attack. McCarthy went to the defense of his host and young Walsh stepped in to aid his da.

Morgan broke up the altercation. "Calm down, now. Surely there's been some mistake here."

Walsh stood his ground, staring down Deirdre. "I know that you came to my pub after closing last night. It was you. I have proof. See here?" He pulled out the photograph of Deirdre standing in the Pelican's Nest bar. It was a dark image, but the name was plainly visible above the bar as was the clock reading 10:10, just after closing. And there, on the floor to her left under a stool, was the container of kerosene.

He held the photograph for all to see but wouldn't let it out of his grasp.

"So I know it was you, you bitch."

"I was there, but I didn't set the fire. I was a victim," Deirdre sputtered. "And I am not a rebel."

"Is that why you are harboring these Republican fugitives, then?" Walsh said glaring at Tadgh and Morgan. "I've a mind to turn you all in. I'm sure that these murderers influenced you to commit this dastardly deed. They may in fact have been your accomplices."

Tadgh saw that Walsh's boys had closed in on the group. They would be hard to take down, even with Derek's help from the kitchen. He wasn't about to bolt with Morgan and leave Deirdre in the lurch.

Walsh was talking. "You've got two choices, Deirdre. Deed me your pub and leave Dublin forever, or me and my boys will turn you and your accomplices in to the police. We noticed patrols outside not a block from here before we came in. Shall we summon them?"

The five boys produced billy clubs from their waistbands and shook them at the three suspects.

Tadgh realized that whoever had set Deirdre up had given Walsh the phony evidence. Who would be targeting her and why? But all that didn't matter. Things did look bad for her and his own presence in her company didn't help her case. It would be his and Deirdre's word against the real culprit who would undoubtedly have an alibi. What a mess.

"Give us a minute in private here in the pantry," Tadgh said. "You can block the exit."

Walsh stared at him and then ordered his sons to withdraw. He locked the pantry door and shouted, "Knock when you've decided."

Derek knew his boss and she wanted him to remain detached at that moment, so he busied himself with the soup for lunch, staying with his back to the Walshs. But the butcher knife was only a foot away from where he was working.

Deirdre was furious. "How dare he—?"

Tadgh grabbed her hand and sat her on one of the boxes of goods. "Calm down, lass. Who would want to do this to you?"

Morgan sat beside her.

Deirdre looked at the floor. She could think of a couple of enemies, neither of whom she could talk about. *But no, it couldn't be the Association, could it? It's been such a long time.*

She answered, "Not unless it is Walsh, himself. If he's in financial trouble, I mean."

Morgan checked her pulse, elevated, and worriedly looked at Tadgh.

"Is that likely, Deirdre?"

"Not from what I know of his business, Tadgh. He does, or did quite well, I think."

"I'm sorry that we have complicated this crisis by being seen in your establishment," Morgan said.

Tadgh knew that neither he nor Morgan could afford to be apprehended by the police. He wondered whether he could gain assistance from Michael Collins, who was likely just a block away on Crow Street. Unlikely, with these five burly sons. He wished he had his Luger that Aidan had brought him from Creagh, but he had left it hidden in their digs at Michael's that morning.

Tadgh got up and paced the small room before confronting the pub owner. "I have to say, unfortunately, that whoever set you up has done a very good job of it, Deirdre."

"I know, Tadgh. And I can't let you and Morgan be taken by the mongrel police. What can we do?"

"That's your decision, lass. This pub has been in your family for many years. You could mount a defense. Do you still have the note that summoned you to the Pelican last night?"

"Oh, no! I discarded it in the trash that was picked up yesterday. What about the fact that I have a laceration on the back of my head?"

Tadgh said, "They'll say you got disoriented while you were setting the fire and slipped and fell. That's why you didn't escape after finishing the deed."

"Well, then, did anyone in the street see you go in and save me?"

"No, I don't think so. I got to the pub before anyone else. It was after curfew, wasn't it? And we went out the back way into the alley. I used back alleys to avoid any police in the area while getting back here." Tadgh summarized the situation. "So you were there and photographed, and I can't vouch for you without being put back in the Joy for life."

Morgan looked at Tadgh with worry lines wrinkling her forehead.

Deirdre turned to Morgan. "We can't let Tadgh, or you be incarcerated again. I'll have to let it go for now, at least until we find out who set me up. The pub's only been in my family's possession for two generations."

Morgan grabbed for Deirdre's hand and said, "But it's yours and it's worth a lot of money."

Deirdre said, "That's all right, Morgan. If Walsh masterminded this calamity, we'll ferret him out, and I will have recourse. Meanwhile, I now have the grocery." She was thinking that her hibernated Templar role might demand more attention, and at least the grocery had normal eight-to-five business hours.

"What about the demand for you to leave Dublin?" Tadgh asked.

"I can't do that. I need to stay nearby until we sort this out."

"The way you dolled us up to slip by the bastards during the Rising, remember? Dressing us up like women," he laughed. "You should be able to figure it out, lass."

For the first time that morning, Deirdre smiled at Tadgh. "You and Peader didn't fool anybody, though you both looked quite comical with those skirts on, slipping past the police that time, remember?"

"But we were mere men." Tadgh lowered his voice to a whisper.

"You could be a very believable old grocery store proprietress. Does Walsh know that you acquired Gilroy's?"

Deirdre shook her head. "No one does."

Morgan looked pleadingly at Tadgh. "We can't let Deirdre lose her pub, Tadgh."

"Do you want to join me in the Joy . . . for life, aroon?"

Morgan shuddered. "God in heaven, no! Can't we overpower these men, Tadgh?"

Tadgh knew that his wife would never condone killing the Walsh family. "And then what? Deirdre will still be charged for arson and probably for assault and battery as well. There is the real perpetrator who presumably has copies of the photographs. We are all stuck in a bind here, together."

Deirdre stood up, staring at Morgan. "Tadgh's right. I have no alternative at the moment." She stood and knocked on the door.

Walsh looked impatient when he unlocked the pantry door. His sons still had their weapons when they rejoined the group. "Well? Are you going to deed me your pub?"

Deirdre stood her ground. "We believe that whoever gave you this fallacious and slanderous information, burned your pub down. They sent me a note to meet with you and hit me on the back of the head when I got there. I would have died if Mr. McCarthy had not pulled me out just in time."

"I don't believe a word of what you are saying, and neither will the police given that you've thrown in your lot with these murderers here," Walsh said, shaking his finger at the McCarthys. "What's the answer to my question?"

Tadgh edged towards the pantry door and the eldest son blocked his way.

Derek looked at Tadgh from the kitchen and McCarthy waved him off.

Deirdre continued her defense. "I was not to blame for the fire at the Pelican's Nest last night. I would never have risked my family's pub that my dead parents worked so hard for. And I never would have placed incriminating items where anyone could find them. Think, man! Who has much to gain? We both were doing fine."

Walsh wouldn't hear any more. "Enough talk, you Republican witch! What's your answer?"

Deirdre said something startling. "You have me over a barrel, Walsh. I will deed you my pub if you provide me with all the false materials that the perpetrator gave you, including the paper that he or she planted in my bar drawer. You must give me a signed written letter to state that I was not responsible for the fire in your pub and a separate document that states you will not reveal Mr. and Mrs. McCarthy's identity and whereabouts to the authorities, or else the pub ownership shall revert back to me. In return, I will agree not to press charges against you for blackmail."

Tadgh couldn't tell whether Walsh's reaction was a smile or a sneer.

"What about leaving Dublin to make sure you won't torch the Temple Bar Pub in another reprisal?"

"I will leave Dublin tomorrow, taking with me my personal belongings in my private residence, but you must agree to begin operations immediately so there will no disruption of service to my customers. You must also agree to continue to employ my chief server, Aileen."

Walsh's eyes lit up. "I knew you were guilty. I accept your terms."

Deirdre stomped her foot and crossed her arms in defiance. "I may agree to relinquish my establishment, but I am not guilty."

"Have it your way."

Tadgh said, "Let's make the agreement, now if we must."

"Who is this, your barrister?"

"If need be, Mr. Walsh."

Morgan thought, *Smart move. That way we can get the evidence before they get a chance to make copies if they haven't already.*

An hour later, the deed transfer signatures were in place. All Walsh had to do was take the document to be registered. Deirdre had the photographs, the fake threat sheet, and Walsh's signature on two documents that exonerated Deirdre and promised to leave the McCarthys alone. Despite the sons' presence, and burly sizes, Tadgh threatened all the Walsh men with death if they welched on the deal.

Deirdre made the same commitment.

As if realizing the full impact of this action, Deirdre snapped, "Now get out of my establishment until noon tomorrow when you can get the keys from me."

After the men left, the group huddled in Deirdre's upstairs parlor. Jack was livid and wished he'd been downstairs to help.

"There was nothing that you could have done, dear boys," Deirdre said to them as she held Jack's hands on the chesterfield. "They had strength in numbers, and their phony, so-called evidence."

Derek was ready to take revenge. "I know you can't get involved, Tadgh, but I can and will. They can all be eradicated."

Deirdre said, "You'll do nothing of the kind. I'll not have murder on my head. And besides, Walsh has undoubtedly gone directly to register the transaction."

"But all those years that you and your parents toiled to make this pub successful!" her cook and bodyguard lamented.

"Let it go, Derek, for now. You can investigate who really did this to us. That's who we have to expose and deal with. Some former adversary, likely."

Derek caught her drift. *The Association. Could they have done this? But if so, who? She's thinking ahead.* There is a bigger purpose even than avenging her father's death. "What are you going to do, Dee?"

"*We* are going to take my belongings and transfer them to the Grocery through the back alley tonight. The apartment there is empty. Tomorrow we will set up shop there. We're going to keep the name Gilroy's Grocery because of name recognition and to avoid suspicion. Derek, did the Walsh men get a good glimpse of you?

"No, I don't think so, boss."

Despite the terrible situation, Deirdre took command. "Good. You will work in the grocery getting the stock on the shelves, and Jack, you will help me manage the grocery. Morgan will help me fashion my disguise. And then Tadgh, you could help me pretend to leave Dublin."

None of them would deny Deirdre her urgent requests, given the circumstances. Tadgh realized that the past twenty-four hours had been cataclysmic for her, and she had come through them with dignity and clear pragmatic thinking. Deirdre had been duped into losing her pub by someone who must have been paying close attention, someone with access to the establishment. Who and why?

Tadgh's mind sprang into action. He wanted to find the answers to this mystery. If it turned out to be Walsh, himself, they would expose him and get Deirdre's pub back for her. And then there was the real arsonist who presumably still had the negatives of the pictures. He and Morgan would have to be doubly cautious in case Walsh decided not to abide by the agreement.

Then he realized that Mick's orders must take priority. He had to get back to Creagh. Derek would have to take care of his boss.

From the shadows of an alley across Temple Bar, Abbad watched the Walsh men go into, and later, come out of the Temple Bar pub. *Good. They look satisfied.* At least he disrupted Deirdre's operations, and she would be leaving the city if the pub owner had implemented his guidance. He would follow her, see where she settled, and take care of her there, where she would be more vulnerable. But damn that McCarthy for foiling what would otherwise have been a perfect plan.

Chapter Seventeen
Liffey

Sunday, November 28, 1920
Gilroy's Grocery, Temple Bar, Dublin

*T*hat pretty much takes care of the move, Deirdre," Tadgh said, as Derek and Jack sat for a minute to rest their weary bones. "It'll be light soon."

The tradesmen's entrance from the back alleyway had been directly east of the pub, and the north-south access lane behind the Fownes Street businesses that gave it access from Temple Bar down to Cecilia Street. Being late at night, no one else saw their moving activity through the back alleyway. The stairs at both ends had given them fits, but at least, in the alley between buildings, they were buffered from the windy night.

Morgan could see that the residence on top of Gilroy's Grocery was certainly not as polished as that of the Temple Bar pub, but it would be comfortable enough. They squeezed most of Deirdre's furniture into the wood-paneled parlor, Spartan dining area, good-sized kitchen, and four bedrooms, but her large hutch and two parlor chairs would not fit and remained above the pub. Given the number of smaller bedrooms, Morgan guessed Gilroy had a large family to help with his business. Deirdre said that his wife had recently died, and judging from the state of his home, he had clearly been having financial troubles. The walls needed a coat of paint. The God-awful faded green in the kitchen was enough to make a woman vomit.

In his hurry to vacate, Gilroy hadn't taken the time to fully clean the apartment. Morgan's attempt to do so had been interrupted by Deirdre's hastily necessitated move.

The store faced east on Fownes so that the kitchen in the upstairs residence would catch the morning sun. Being on the northeast corner of the block, one could glimpse the mighty River Liffey down the extension of Fownes Street from the north-facing kitchen window over the sink. And two of the three bedrooms overlooked the bustle of Temple Bar Street. It wasn't all bad.

There hadn't been time to properly pack the dishes, pots and pans, and contents of the drawers. They had been relayed over in a couple of open crates and lay strewn in the various rooms.

"I suggest that we go back to the pub and Derek can fix us breakfast before it opens," Morgan said. "We'll need our strength for the day ahead, especially since we've had no sleep. I will clean the empty pub residence later this morning."

"You will most certainly do nothing of the kind, my dear," Deirdre said. "Let that bastard Walsh and his sons do the dirty work. Did you commandeer a lorry to pretend to leave Dublin later today, Tadgh? I think that you, Morgan, and I should leave together. Walsh may be watching and have us followed."

"Or whoever really masterminded this disaster may be watching," Tadgh offered. "We must be very observant from now on. I'll go ask Mick for help with transportation."

They made sure that they left the grocery before dawn to ensure that no one saw Tadgh, Morgan, or Deirdre there.

While they were eating in the pub, Tadgh marveled at how organized and pragmatic Deirdre was under these very trying circumstances, especially since someone had almost murdered her only two nights earlier. Then that bastard Walsh, along with his five goon sons, had strong-armed her out of her pub that had meant the world to her. He was starting to believe that she was a good friend who had no ulterior motives when it came to the McCarthys. She had given up her pub in part to avoid having him and Morgan arrested.

After breakfast, Jack returned to the grocery to freshen the produce in the store with stocks that had come into the storage room two days ago, just before Gilroy had vacated. He decided that the job wasn't that much different from ordering and delivering all the provisions needed for transatlantic crossings on the Cunard liners. He could handle this. Morgan went with him to help until Tadgh arrived with the lorry.

Deirdre took Derek aside in the pub residence. "I have been thinking about that map that Jack found."

Derek scratched his head. "You're amazing, Dee. With all this turmoil, you had time to think about that? I thought your father established that the TR building was the Theatre Royal."

"He did. But we should research that theatre to make sure. We've always believed that the Temple residence was here at the intersection of Temple Bar Street and Temple Lane. But William Temple owned a larger plot of land here. Now that the McCarthys are snooping around, I want to be one step ahead of them. While we are gone on our ride out of Dublin, I'd like you to contact Lawlor and see if he has background information about that theatre."

"Certainly, boss, now that I don't have to cook for the pub." Derek sported a wide grin that spread his moustache out across his cheeks.

"When you get back, would you please help Jack with the heavy lifting over at the grocery?" Deirdre felt that they made a good team. And besides, if she could develop a more intimate relationship with Jack, Derek would be invaluable in pumping him for information vital to her crusade.

At eleven o'clock Tadgh arrived on Temple Bar Street at the pub in an unmarked lorry. He'd disguised himself as a dockworker. He and Deirdre moved what remained of her discarded belongings, along with quite a few empty crates for show into the vehicle.

Mr. Walsh showed up at precisely noon and Deirdre reluctantly gave him the keys.

She then went inside and introduced Aileen to her new boss and his boys who addressed her civilly. The younger Walsh appeared smitten by the waitress's obvious charms, and she seemed responsive to the attention.

Walsh himself presented quite a different persona to the world than they had seen the previous day. He seemed delighted with his acquisition as he and his boys took charge of the facility.

A jolly, rotund Italian woman, apparently thrilled with her new kitchen, began to inspect the provisions in the pantry.

When Deirdre was leaving, Walsh stuck out his hand. "No hard feelings, lass. You are honoring our bargain, and I will, too."

Deirdre declined his offering. "You forced me into this, falsely. I did not burn down the Pelican's Nest and I would never harm the Temple Bar. It has been my pride and joy all these years. Take care of it, or I and my friends will take care of you."

With that, she turned on her heel and clambered aboard the lorry where Tadgh was waiting. Morgan followed her lead. Then out the open window, she said, loud enough for everyone to here, "Farewell, Dublin. Tadgh, let's go to your part of Ireland where I can start a new life."

They set off heading west out of the city.

Abbad had been waiting in a vehicle of his own, further up Temple Bar Street. Seeing the lorry move out, he stayed behind at a distance.

Surprisingly, they encountered no resistance as they passed through Clane twenty miles east of Dublin where they had been stopped when running the guns on their way to Rossa's funeral five years earlier. Apparently, the Unionist forces were spread too thin as they struggled to address the guerrilla attacks throughout the south.

Tadgh did, however, notice an old Hudson as he turned south, before starting the return loop to Dublin. *Following us, I'd wager.*

There was one way to find out. He pulled over and stopped by the side of the road, got out and looked behind. Before he could get the bonnet open, he saw the trailing vehicle slow and stop some two hundred yards away. Tadgh fiddled under the hood, slammed the bonnet down, and pulled back out into traffic. The other car followed suit.

Tadgh said, "We're being followed, either by Walsh's stooge to see where we end up, or someone associated with the real arsonist. It's not the police or military."

Deirdre was in the left-hand seat with Morgan in between her and Tadgh. The women craned their necks to see behind them, but the truck bed blocked their view.

"What are we going to do about it?" Morgan asked.

Tadgh winked. "I have a plan. Ahead of us in Naas on the Dublin Road, the walls of old St. David's Castle run right up against the curving roadway. You'll see. Deirdre, I need you to be quick and observant when I pull behind the wall. Try to see who is driving as he or she goes by. Hopefully, we will lose them."

The sky darkened and rain started to fall.

Fifteen minutes later Tadgh sped up to gain temporary distance between themselves and their pursuer. Town buildings in Naas closed in around them and there ahead on the left was the old stone wall of the castle.

"Ready now. Here we go."

Tadgh took the sharp curve and then careened left at the end of the wall and stopped. Then he started to edge backward behind the wall so that they could see any vehicles continuing the curve ahead of them beyond the wall. The Hudson whizzed by the end of the wall as it sped through the curve.

Deirdre had a split-second to determine who was driving. *Damn. That's Abbad, I'd know that Moroccan anywhere. Why is the Association following us?"*

"Well?" Tadgh asked, looking left at the shop owner.

"He went by too fast, I'm afraid."

But Tadgh saw the look in her eyes and heard the hesitancy in her voice. "Are you sure, lass?"

Morgan eyed her, too.

"Yes, ah yes. Quite sure."

Tadgh started to wheel the lorry back out onto the road. "I'm going to follow that bastard and we'll get to the bottom of this."

Deirdre reached over and put her hand on the steering wheel. "No, Tadgh. You've done enough. I don't want to get you and Morgan into more trouble." She now realized that Abbad and the Association were behind the Pelican Nest fire with her as their target. She thought, *Damn them. They killed father but they won't get me. I'll kill them in the end.*

Morgan nodded her agreement. "Let's just continue with our plan to return Deirdre to Dublin, Tadgh, if we've given that fellow the slip."

Tadgh hesitated and Morgan prodded him in the ribs. "Tadgh!"

Reluctantly, Tadgh pulled out onto Dublin Road to the right, heading back the way they had come. Then a block away he turned right and headed back towards the city.

Abbad drove two city blocks before he realized he had lost them. He traveled on at high speed out of the town to catch up. Five minutes later, he realized that they had given him the slip. Due to traffic congestion on the narrow road, it took him three more minutes to turn around. Maybe their destination was Naas. He combed the streets of the town but saw neither hide nor hair of the lorry.

His plans had backfired. Wearily, he turned back for Dublin. He would keep vigil at the Temple Bar Pub to see if any of the three returned. Walsh should give him free stout for life. He pounded the steering wheel. Deirdre should have died, her body burned to a crisp.

They dropped the lorry at a Republican safe house on the outskirts of Dublin after Morgan helped Deidre into her disguise. What a transformation! Where before a young, beautiful close-cropped blond had stood, a spry, aging spinster with long stringy graying hair, plain ankle length dress, and matching shawl bent over on her cane. That was how she was going to have to be seen in public for the foreseeable future.

As pre-arranged, Deirdre used the tram system to return to Temple Bar while Tadgh and Morgan got a ride to the River Liffey, just opposite Fownes Street. They then joined Deirdre and Jack in the back of the grocery undetected. The McCarthys carefully avoided being seen in the grocery store itself from then on.

Jack was alarmed by the story that they were followed.

"It was probably just one of Walsh's men making sure that I left like I said I would," Deirdre said to calm him down. "I think we fooled them, so far."

Tadgh wasn't so sure, but he kept his opinion to himself.

Deirdre and Derek made a simple stew in the kitchen while her guests relaxed in the parlor. Exhausted, Morgan fell asleep in Tadgh's arms on the chesterfield while Jack busied himself down in the grocery. Derek told Deirdre that he was relieved to only cook now for family.

While he was paring the carrots, Derek said, "I was able to reach Lawlor at the college. We went to the customs house library. I have startling news."

Deirdre closed the door to the dining room and parlor before engaging in a conversation. "Yes?"

The Theatre Royal at the end of Crow Street at Cecilia was the second one. It was built by two thespians, Spranger Barry and Thomas Sheridan, and it opened in 1758. They had previously acted at the first Theatre Royal in Smock Alley that had been established in 1662 and had burned down in 1735, only to be rebuilt."

"Why is that startling? Wait a minute. Where do I remember that name, Sheridan?"

"I remember your father talking to you and your mother about your family history, lass."

"I remember, now. I was eight. When father was trying to explain what he knew of the old Temple residence, he said that the last of our ancestors to live there became mentally ill in his old age and that one of his only pleasures was hearing his good friend Thomas Sheridan quoting Shakespeare to him."

Derek was animated now. "That's right, Dee. I don't believe in coincidences, so we looked up the deed for the theatre property. You won't believe what I found."

Deirdre put her arm on the carrot scraper. "Quietly, now." She thought for a minute. "No, it can't be."

"Yes, it was, Dee. In his insanity, your ancestor willed the property on which the theatre stood to his good friend Thomas."

"That's interesting, Derek. But it could just have been a part of the land that he owned."

"We checked the city records further, lass. The only land owned by your ancestor in 1741 was the land on which the Temple residence itself stood. Also, we found a newspaper article from that year, that your ancestor Jonathan, who you'll remember was quite famous, had this somewhat dilapidated home demolished before he was taken over by guardians. It appears that it was quite the scandal at the time."

Deirdre was flabbergasted. "That means that the old house was situated where the Theatre Royal was located, not where the pub is."

"Aye, and it was demolished by your ancestor and not by the flood sixty-one years later."

"My God. That means that the iron chest could still be buried under the theatre. But wait a minute. There is no theatre there now. It's over on Hawkins Street, isn't it?"

"That's right, Dee. The Theatre Royal at the end of Crow Street was shut down in 1803. We read another article that said it was badly damaged in the flood of 1802. Apparently, a sink hole opened up under the theatre that had to be filled in and the theatre reworked. The theatre was never the same after that and closed a year later. That building was destroyed during the riot of 1814."

Deirdre thought for a moment before saying, "This is a marvelous development. You see, if Jack and the McCarthys hadn't pursued the meaning of the scribble Morgan found, we would never have unearthed this new path to our quest. We know more now than father was ever able to deduce. We've got to help our friends continue the search without alerting the McCarthys of our purpose."

Derek stroked his chin. "These McCarthys seem like decent people. Why don't you bring them into your Templar movement now that we have a trail, however slim?"

"No, I like Morgan, but I don't trust Tadgh. He's a fierce rebel and a soldier. There's no telling what he might do if the treasure were to be found. We can't let that happen. That's our ancient quest."

"As you wish, Dee. And I will have my revolver at the ready in the event that he gets too close to the truth. Can you imagine where this might lead?"

"Civilizations have sought the treasure over the ages, Derek. As the last Knights Templar, that we know of, we may be the ones to finally find and protect it."

That evening after closing and dinner, they organized the storage area and took inventory. Gilroy had left a list of his suppliers along with the journals, balance sheets, and ledgers.

Being a few feet larger than its neighboring establishments, the thirty-foot square Grocery at Number Forty Fownes Street Upper faced east on the corner of Temple Bar Street. The store itself took up two-thirds of the ground floor facing Fownes, with large glass windows for light and to attract customers. They sold perishables and dry goods. Jack could see that the wares could be displayed much more logically with a more appealing presentation. The window signs needed to be more eye-catching.

The staging area in the northwest corner of the building, with a service delivery entrance onto Temple Bar, took up two-thirds of what was left behind the storefront, with the last ninth being a hole-in-the-wall office for the manager. Liking his assignment,

Jack already had his office organized in his mind. He thought they should add hardware, tools, first-aid supplies and perhaps add a soda fountain for the patrons. That would be a big draw, especially in the summer.

"My, my, Jack. Aren't you the resourceful one!" Deirdre said, when they finally relaxed in the residence, away from prying eyes. She had doffed her granny clothes and was sporting a low-cut red shirtwaist with black trousers. "Who would have thought that you would make such a wonderful grocer."

"I love a challenge, Dee." He had already adopted Derek's nickname for her.

"There doesn't seem to be enough storage space behind the storefront," Morgan mentioned, while they were having evening tea.

"That's because there is a much larger basement storage cellar the full size of the building," Jack explained. "It goes down quite deep in order to keep the perishables cool all year round."

"Really, Jack?"

"The stairs going down are under the stairs to the residence, off the landing at the Temple Bar delivery entrance."

"I wondered where they went," Morgan commented.

"The only problem is that it smells damp and moldy down there because the lowest four feet above the dirt floor has hard earthen walls reinforced with timbers," Jack said.

"How deep is it below street level?" Morgan asked.

Deirdre responded. "About seventeen feet based on the number of stairs that run down the inside of the west wall. I inspected it this afternoon. It is deeper and larger than the storage area under the Temple Bar pub, you'll remember, below the pantry hole I stuffed you into, so long ago. That basement leaks every spring when the Liffey is high such that we had to move the storables. We'll have to do that here as well, I expect."

"It's like a mine, then. Does this basement leak here, Deirdre?" Tadgh asked.

"Likely. I've seen evidence of rats and former leaks have stained the wood. But not in November. The River Liffey is at generally low ebb after a relatively dry summer and fall."

Morgan scrunched her nose. "Why so deep?"

Jack answered. "There is a layer of rock crust about a foot thick down twelve feet. You can see it all around the perimeter of the building down there. The soil above it is soft river sediment so the building's foundation sits on it."

Tadgh was stroking his moustache. "Why go to the trouble to dig deeper than the foundation rock layer?"

"I suspect to keep the fresh produce colder to prolong its storage life," Jack said. "It is cooler under in the last four feet below that rock crust level."

Deirdre turned to Jack, her breasts flashing right under his eyes. "We'll have to do something about the condition down there, my boy. Line the walls completely and gravel or cement the floor."

Morgan said, "If there are rats down there, it must be made sanitary for the food." She saw Tadgh deep in concentration. "All right, I know that look. What are you thinking?"

Instead of answering his wife, Tadgh asked, "Do you know where the second branch of the Liffey was located back in 1600, Deirdre?"

"I was told it flowed west to east like the current river but to the south, between Cecilia and Dame Streets. That's the side where I noticed the damage to the timbers in the storage area," Deirdre said.

Now it was Morgan's turn to ask Deirdre, "Do you have that map of the area handy that Jack found?"

When Deirdre retrieved it from her bedroom drawer, Morgan spread it out on the table, pointing. "That's right where we're staying on Crow Street. That makes sense. The residence was on the original sand bar between the river branches."

Tadgh re-examined the map. "Deirdre, that iron chest you mentioned earlier, could it still be buried in the sand below where the house collapsed?"

"Wouldn't someone have found it?" Jack objected.

Derek started to say something, and Deirdre cut him off, saying, "Not necessarily, in the midst of a flood powerful enough to destroy the residence. They might well have assumed that the debris would be carried downstream."

Deirdre locked eyes with Derek who was now poring over the map.

"I had heard that the house was locked up some of the time when the Temples were in England. And the damaged residence was plowed under to build new buildings over the rubble, so I was told by my father," she said.

Tadgh continued. "That iron chest would likely have been heavy enough to drop like a stone and be swallowed up by the muck."

Morgan shook her head in frustration. "But we don't even know if that chest would have anything of value in it even if it *were* to be there, and the water would probably have destroyed the contents. Beyond that, the story about such a chest, as Deirdre said, is just hearsay."

Deirdre thought for a moment and raised her eyebrows in Derek's direction. He nodded inconspicuously. She asked, "How would you propose getting there, anyway?"

Tadgh used his thumb and index finger as a rule and measured the distance on the map from the grocery to T.R. before answering. "There are buildings on top of the residence now. It's about two hundred feet south by southwest of this grocery. That's short enough that we could excavate from the storage area!"

Morgan shook her head. "Surely, you are joking, Tadgh. It's too dangerous and would be like looking for an early vintage farthing in the Bank of Ireland."

Tadgh twirled the ends of his moustache. "I'm not so sure of that, lass. I became an expert in planning escape tunnels over the last three years, although those fantasy plans were only a way for me to keep from going crazy. I'd be willing to bet, with the evidence of past water seeping in, that we wouldn't have to tunnel all the way to where the residence was."

The shopkeeper broke in, "What do you mean, Tadgh."

"If I'm right, Deirdre, the southern branch of the river may have opened underground cavities over the years. We might just get lucky."

Although Morgan had originally been enthusiastic about the significance of the scribble in the book, it was now Tadgh who had gone overboard. She didn't like the idea of digging underground, since her excruciating experience in the hold of the sinking *Lusitania* had left her with a foreboding sense of claustrophobia. "I don't know, Tadgh. It seems like a longshot."

Tadgh turned to his companions, hopeful and lit with a purpose, a quest. "What do you think, Jack? If we move the stored goods out of the way, is the room big enough to store the dirt from a tunnel to try to reach where the residence once was located? We'd put the dirt back when we're finished."

"That depends upon how big a tunnel you would need, Tadgh."

"I don't know until I see the storage area. Let's go down and look."

After the five of them climbed down into the cavernous basement storage area, which took up the full dimensions of the building above, Tadgh said, "This looks like home, Morgan. I should talk to Mick about setting up a control center down here."

Deirdre shook her head. "Not on your life, Tadgh McCarthy! I've enough trouble without that."

"I was just joking, lass. It just reminded me of another control center, so it did."

Morgan drew her sweater around her and remarked, "It's pretty cool down here."

"I'd say about fifty degrees," Tadgh said. "But if we are digging and hauling dirt. we will work up a sweat, so we will."

Tadgh examined the south wall of dirt and timbers below the rock crust level and then paced the dirt floor. "Let's guess that we would need a tunnel of about a hundred feet if I'm right. Four feet high up to the underside of the rock crust. That would make the roof of our tunnel stable. Say three feet wide with reinforcing timbers to keep the side walls stable." He looked at Morgan who had been so mentally agile during the McCarthy gold hunt on the Rock of Cashel.

Morgan calculated. "Twelve hundred cubic feet of soil, Tadgh."

Tadgh looked around. "If we dig here at the southwest end of the south wall and store the soil along the east wall, how much of the storage area would be taken up?"

Morgan figured it out. "A lot. If we store it from the southern end a distance of twenty feet north that would leave ten feet for storage of the perishables along the north wall. Let's see. Say four feet high, that would mean the soil would stretch fifteen feet west from the east wall. That would allow maneuvering room around the west wall stairs and the mouth of the tunnel."

"So, half of the total area, right?"

"Yes, Tadgh."

"Enough space for all these goods, yes?" Tadgh said, sweeping his hand around in the direction of the boxes and crates on wooden shelves.

Jack said, "Maybe. But what if we had to dig the full two hundred feet, Tadgh? That would fill the entire storage area."

"But only four feet deep. I don't expect we'll need that length based on the moisture down here."

Always the pragmatic one, Morgan asked, "How long would it take to dig such a shaft, my tunnel expert?"

"That depends on how hard-packed the soil is," Tadgh said, going to the southwest wall location and pawing at the soil with his right hand. Despite having been stable since the grocery had been built, some of the material crumbled and fell onto the dirt floor. "It shouldn't be too difficult."

Jack spied a sizable wagon in the corner, evidently used to move the goods and containers around the storage area. Its bed was only a foot off the floor. "We would need a transport method for getting the soil out of, and later into the tunnel. How about using this wagon over here?" Jack rolled the vehicle out into the middle of the storage area.

Morgan was calculating when she said, "Good idea, Jack. Let's see, its bed is three feet long and about a foot and half wide. It would fit in such a tunnel. Its sidewalls to hold those storage boxes is a foot high. That makes two hundred and sixty-seven wagonloads to move all that soil. How long would it take us to move a wagonload, Tadgh?"

Tadgh saw a duplicate wagon under the stairs. "If we use the two wagons, let me see. Derek and I could spell each other digging and filling the wagon at the end of the tunnel. The other of us could be dumping the wagon and shoveling the soil onto the storage pile."

"What could I do?" Morgan asked.

"You could pull the wagon out, my dear. While one of us is filling a wagon, the other can be dumping the other wagon. I'd say one wagonload in about three minutes."

"I want to help," Jack said.

Tadgh beamed. "Fine, but with your back concern, I think you could help by cutting timbers for reinforcing the tunnel if you can scrounge some. Just four-foot lengths."

Morgan wiped her brow. "This process would take at least two days of hard work."

Deirdre looked at Derek again and said, "It seems like a lot of trouble for a slim possibility of finding a rumored chest, but if you want to make the effort, I suppose it is fine with me. Derek can help you after getting the shelves stocked early in the morning and I can tend the store in my disguise."

Tadgh grabbed Deirdre's hand and said, "Thank you. Let's plan on tackling this project starting tomorrow morning. All agreed?"

Derek nodded his head, followed by Jack and finally Morgan.

"Why don't you all stay here during this, ah, project?" Deirdre asked. "We have plenty of room and it looks like it's not going to be fit for man nor beast outside for a few days."

Morgan liked that idea. The rooms at Number Three Crow would be there when they needed them. For the time being, it would convenient to stay there. "Thanks, Deirdre, as long as we can help you get organized."

Deirdre laughed, "I think you'll be quite busy on your own."

They all agreed to get to bed and start early the next morning.

After the McCarthys and Jack had retired for the night, Derek chatted with his leader privately in her bedroom.

"I've always wondered about that chest, Dee. It was never found. Let them try and see what comes of it."

Deirdre went to the window and separated the drapes. The forecast storm was howling outside, rain pelting on the panes. She turned back into the room. "These are formidable foes, Derek. We may need to bring in the others if that time comes."

A flash of lightning momentarily lit the room, catching Deirdre in stark silhouette, followed almost immediately by a sharp clap of thunder.

"Understood."

Monday morning at seven o'clock, the adventurers, wearing outer garments against the elements, grabbed a muffin and coffee in Deirdre's kitchen before descending the stairs, down into the storage area. Outside, the storm continued unabated.

Derek proved to be a useful quartermaster. He had scrounged shovels, a pickaxe, and some wooden posts to use for shoring up the tunnel. By ten o'clock they had the stored crates moved to the east wall of the storage area away from the dig site. Tadgh had brought a tracing of the city map and they laid it out in the proper coordinates.

"Here's where we dig," Tadgh said, as he scribed a four-foot-high by three-foot-wide box on the south wall at its southwest corner just below the rock crust. "We need to mind the wooden foundation support beams and posts."

"Are you up to this, Tadgh?" Morgan frowned.

"Yes, aroon. We've been over this last night. If we're going to do this, we'd best get started."

Tadgh broke the surface of the wall with the pickaxe and started digging with a shovel, angling slightly to the west. The going was surprisingly easy after they got through the initial packed wall edging of the room. Once he got far enough in to begin the tunnel, they started the wagon process. Tadgh packed down the floor of the tunnel with his shovel, but Morgan found that rolling the wagon was difficult since the wheels sank into the soil. They wasted an hour while Jack and Derek scrounged up some long planks to use as a solid base for the tunnel. It would become Jack's job to move them quickly as the tunnel became longer in hopscotch fashion to keep the wagon on them as Morgan rolled it out. Additionally, Jack had brought a saw and started cutting the reinforcing timbers to the correct wedge length when necessary. Derek found that it was relatively easy to tip the wagon to get the soil out in the storage room, and then shovel it onto the storage pile.

They stopped periodically just long enough to reinforce the hole with timbers after they reached ten feet of tunnel length. This kept the soil from falling in on the sides. The roof of their tunnel wouldn't cave in because of the layer of rock above them. That limited the height of the tunnel, though. Tadgh looked like a dog scooping the dirt back through his legs after he picked and shoveled it out of the end wall. Working at a four-foot height proved to be more arduous than he expected, since he had to work in a semi-crouched position. He had long ago discarded the vest he had been wearing and sweat was pouring off his forehead and down his back.

At two o'clock they stopped for a breather, a snack, and to take stock. They had been excavating for three hours and the tunnel was about 18 feet long. The digging was going smoothly, as the rocks they encountered were generally small. There was some moisture in the dirt that made it easier to loosen up, yet heavier to dispose of.

The digger had but one kerosene lamp at the end of the tunnel, so they were essentially working in the dark as they got farther away from the storage area. The air smelled foul, and Tadgh realized that he was short of breath in there. Thoughts of his plan to dig to freedom came back to him, the harrowing, and sometimes deadly stories from the inmates of caved-in attempts at various prisons. Good thing he wasn't claustrophobic and that they had a solid rock crust ceiling above them.

From that morning's experience, Tadgh realized that it took four minutes for each wagonload extraction on average. He estimated that it would take about eighteen hours of extraction to dig out a hundred feet of tunnel length if they needed to dig that far.

Morgan could see that this job was taxing them all, except Derek, who looked as fresh as when they started. She felt concerned about Tadgh, given his long ordeal in jail, and Jack because of his earlier serious back injury. "I say we give up this endeavor, Tadgh. It was a crazy idea in the first place," she said, just as the boys were getting up to recommence digging. "What if we have to tunnel the full two hundred feet and there is nothing but more dirt greeting us there? Can't you see how enormous and likely futile the task is? Even if we tunnel for a hundred feet, the task to dig and then replace the soil will take four or five days."

Tadgh was undeterred. It was uncharacteristic for valiant Morgan to be giving up so soon. The idea of finding William Temple's documents was her idea in the first place. "We'll go as far as a hundred feet, aroon. If we don't find an existing underground passageway made by the covered over river, then we'll stop. Besides, it's raining so hard right now that we can't go outside anyway."

"Isn't your thinking being clouded by your recent history of wanting to break out of jail? Aren't you just fulfilling that fantasy?"

Tadgh picked up his shovel. "No, lass. I honestly believe that we will find an opening and that there is something important to find at the end of this search."

Morgan stood in his way to enter the tunnel. "How so, my love?"

"Intuition, aroon, just like yours. Or Divine intervention, call it what you will."

"You didn't see a vision of Sir Owain, did you?"

"No, aroon, just a hunch. But you did, right?"

As Tadgh started to coax Morgan out of the way, she asked the other men, "What do you think?"

Jack took every opportunity to agree with the unrequited love of his life and suggested that the search should be abandoned. He had work to do for Deirdre and she seemed more interested in getting the grocery up and running.

Morgan asked, "What about your back?"

Jack rubbed his lower back with the knuckles of his right hand before answering. He wasn't going to be the one to physically break down first. "All right, so far."

Even though Deirdre had feigned disinterest, Derek was under direction from her to do whatever necessary to search for the iron chest. "I agree with Tadgh, lass. We should proceed, at least for the time being."

Morgan understood how Tadgh felt. Temple's scribble in the Book appeared to be a sign she was meant to find after scholars had passed it over. Deirdre's story about the Temple history was intriguing. And more time spent in this basement meant more deferral from Tadgh having to fight his infernal war. Morgan stepped aside. "All right, Tadgh. Let's continue, for now."

The work grew all the more arduous as the time passed. Derek and Tadgh changed places frequently due to the air conditions in the tunnel. Finally, at eight-thirty they stopped for the night. Tadgh's back was aching from stooping over all day in that tunnel. Gingerly, he paced it off. They had been excavating for nine hours and the tunnel was fifty feet long with no opening in sight.

Back in the residence, Deirdre had supper ready. It turned out that she was a good cook in her own right. But she took one look at them all and ordered them to get cleaned up. "You all look like ragamuffins. No dinner for you until you wash up and change clothes."

During supper, they discussed the progress of their project and decided they would give it one more day before giving up. As they left the kitchen to go to a well-earned night's rest after the washing up, Deirdre asked Jack if he would wait behind to talk about the grocery.

"What do you think about this tunnel project, Jack?" she asked, as she patted the kitchen chair beside where she was sitting.

Jack sat down and answered, "I thought you wanted to talk about the business, Dee."

Deirdre rested her hand on his knee. "I'd like to talk about a lot of things with you."

He was startled when she undid the clip holding her blond hair in a knot, shook her head, and let her golden tresses tumble down around her neck. The sight mesmerized him.

"I like you, Jack, a lot. I've never been attracted to many men, but you excite me, so you do." Deirdre tightened her grip on his leg as she batted her eyelashes in his direction. While she had been washing the dishes, she had discreetly undone the top two buttons on her shirtwaist, exposing the cleavage between her ample breasts. As a result of the heat from the kitchen work, Jack could see beads of sweat trickling down from under her delicate throat.

"I, I like you too, Deirdre."

"How much?"

"You're a wonderful, accomplished woman."

"And what else, Jack?"

He turned his head away from Deirdre's intense blue eyes and realized he could drown in them. Then he spoke softly, almost a whisper. "I think you are a very attractive woman."

"Then you can touch me, Jack."

"It's been a long time, lass, since I let myself think in those directions. I was almost crippled with my back injury."

Deirdre moved her hand to his biceps. "Yet you are very strong, Jack, and certainly not crippled."

"Years of propelling myself with them in a wheelchair or on a crutch, lass."

"Well, you're a fit man now, that's certain. Why don't you stay with me in my room tonight? Yours is the smallest in the residence. I can give your back a massage."

Jack removed Deirdre's hand, kissing it gently and stood up. "I am truly flattered with your offer, but I must decline. I am rather tired from today's activities."

Deirdre gave a blank stare, trying to hide her disappointment. She had seen many men in her pub but had religiously resisted their charms. She had considered it to be good business management. And besides, none of them had gotten her heart fluttering like Jack did. This was going to become complicated yet, if she had her way, so rewarding. But not tonight. "I understand, lad. You've had a long day. We'll talk tomorrow."

As he walked down the hall to his solitary room, Jack wondered if he had just made the worst decision of his life.

The next day was Tuesday, November 30. The digging restarted at seven in the morning after a hurried breakfast. There was no time to relax or even read a newspaper. Morgan had questioned Tadgh's motives for continuing the project when they were alone in their room, and she could see his level of exhaustion, but he was insistent on continuing. It was truly as if he was tunneling out of jail.

They ran out of timbers around noon when the tunnel was at eighty feet. Jack had brought three more kerosene lamps to light the way in the tunnel. Deirdre had suggested using the free-standing circulating fan employed to aerate the vegetables in storage to blow fresher air into the mouth of the tunnel. Derek had found a long extension cord to power it. While they stopped for a snack of fruit and cheese, Tadgh said, "The soil is more moist, now. I'm hoping that's a good sign."

"It's a sign all right," Morgan lamented. "The wagon is much heavier to pull out of the tunnel. When are you going to call a halt to this madness, Tadgh?"

"As agreed, aroon. We will stop in another twenty feet."

Four hours later, at the end of the tunnel, Tadgh came upon more calcified rock in the soil. The digging became much harder. "Something's changing here," he announced. He hoped to hell that this project wouldn't end in hitting the proverbial rock wall. Ten shovelfuls later, he stopped digging and put his ear to the earth. Morgan was crouched behind him on the other side of the wagon, preparing to pull it down the tunnel after her husband filled it, as he had done several times before.

Tadgh exclaimed, "Morgan, can you hear that? There's water running nearby and it's colder in here now."

"It must be your imagination," Morgan responded. "I can't hear anything."

"Move back, lass." Tadgh lunged at the end of the tunnel with his shovel and the earth with rock gave way ahead. The blade of his shovel flew into the hole he had made. He skinned his knuckles on its rough edge. The water sounded like a roar. As Tadgh moved forward to look through, several rats leaped out of the hole close to his face and scampered down the tunnel past Morgan toward the storage room.

Morgan was stunned. Tadgh had been right.

Tadgh said, "Hand me that light, Morgan."

Tadgh took the kerosene lantern and thrust it through the jagged two-foot hole. "My God. The second branch of the Liffey is still strong underground, or maybe it is a third branch that was never found. It looks like it has diverted north and is flowing parallel to the main branch. It likely flows back into the Liffey underground."

He started chipping the rock back until he hollowed out a full four-foot hole at the end of the tunnel. Morgan returned from dumping off the dirt from the wagon and crawled forward to take a look. Their tunnel broke through at the top of a cavernous hole. Tadgh said, "No wonder there's evidence of water and mold. Look at that torrent flowing east."

They were looking into a much larger tunnel, a cavern really, roughly nine feet above its water line, running west to east. On the south side, in the dim light, they could see exposed rock and mud sidewalls. The rock crust they had found in the storage area that formed the ceiling of their tunnel extended as far as they could see into the underground river cavern as its roof. It was scraped bare of dirt as if the water sometime in the past had scoured its surface, likely during the flood of 1802.

Morgan exclaimed, "The second branch of the River Liffey must have carved this out ages ago after it was filled in."

By this time, Derek and Jack had crowded into the tunnel behind them to see what was going on. Tadgh noted the snide look on the cook's face, whereas Jack seemed astonished. Both were speechless.

Tadgh thrust the lantern as far in and down as he could without falling in. "How far down is the surface of the water?"

Morgan peered in past him. "I'd say five feet down and about sixty feet across to the south side. I can't tell how deep it is."

"Where do you place the end of the tunnel we dug, Morgan?" Tadgh asked.

She backed up and paced it off before returning. "We're in about ninety-five feet south and probably ten feet west of the western edge of the grocery. The floor of our tunnel is about seventeen feet below street level. Even with this one-foot crust of rock at its roof, I am surprised that the cavern hasn't caved in somewhere along the line over the years with those buildings above."

Tadgh held the lantern high. "It is one foot thick at the storage area but might be quite a bit thicker elsewhere, lass. But at least its ceiling appears to be level as far as I can see." He squinted into the gloom. "Now that my eyes have adjusted, I can see that the tunnel is quite a bit wider upstream to the west. It looks like the water coming from that direction must carve out a much wider swath of sand when its flow rate grows during spring storms."

"Well, we've got a doozy of a tempest going on outside, and it's November," Jack yelled from the tunnel behind them.

Derek looked past Tadgh, took the lantern, and thrust it further into the cavern. "I've got to tell Deirdre about this. It seems like this river is pushing farther and farther north over time. It could permanently flood the storage area and eventually undermine the grocery itself. Whether we find anything from the Temple residence or not, this has been a valuable exercise. All of Temple Bar area businesses need to know about this situation."

The group adjourned to the grocery and told Deirdre the tale of what they had seen.

"I hate the rats, Tadgh," Morgan announced in no uncertain terms. "Where did they run off to?"

"Waiting for you, love."

Morgan shivered.

Tadgh summarized the situation. "We have access underground to the vicinity of where the Temple residence stood before the flood. I think we have a chance of finding the mythical iron chest there."

Deirdre flashed a smile at Derek, both of them knowing that the demolition had been earlier than the flood. Now Deirdre was compelled to see this project through to its end. She had complete trust in Derek to protect her interests, come what may.

It was getting close to five o'clock and the men thought a libation was in order.

Chapter Eighteen
Secret Study

Tuesday, November 30, 1920
Gilroy's Grocery, Dublin

*U*p in the residence, Tadgh said, "There's no telling what lies on the other side of that underground branch of the Liffey, or if its water tunnel is stable."

"Except that it's been flowing down there since they reclaimed the land three hundred years ago, maybe before."

"Good point, Deirdre." Tadgh guzzled the B & C stout brought to him. "I guess our tunnel extends to roughly a hundred feet from the storage room, getting us approximately halfway to the location of the residence ruins. I suggest Derek and I take two lanterns and explore the tunnel this evening. We can decide what we will do tomorrow."

"If anything," Morgan added.

"Given your recent incarceration and all the digging you've done over the last two days, Tadgh, let me go with Derek on this underground exploration," Jack said, seeing Morgan's consternation.

"Remembering your physical condition after the *Lusitania* sank, I think it best if I go, Jack. You should back us up in the storage room tunnel."

Jack glanced at Morgan for guidance.

She shrugged. "I've never been able to stop my man from doing what he sets his mind to, Jack. He's made great progress in his recovery."

They all agreed and stayed in the residence for supper. Derek said he was happy to return to cooking duties for this one meal.

Before they set out after supper, Morgan took Tadgh aside. "You were right about that river. Perhaps you do have perceptive powers."

Tadgh kissed her cheek and laughed. "Well then, lass, it must have rubbed off from you, that's certain."

Morgan returned the laugh, then frowned. "You know that this is likely a wild goose chase, mavourneen. You're still somewhat weak, so don't take any chances."

"Don't fret, my love. I'm just going for a little midnight swim. I'll be back quick as a wink."

"You do that, Tadgh McCarthy. Then I promise I will remove your medical restrictions."

Tadgh reached out and pulled her in with a fierce kiss on the mouth.

"I'll hold you to that."

"I have no doubt of it. Get going if you must."

At the end of the tunnel they had dug, Tadgh and Derek prepared to explore the underground river. They donned leather vests and waders to ward off the cold. "I'll drop in and see the depth, Derek. You can fish me out if I go under."

"I'm concerned about the swiftness of the current, Tadgh, and the temperature of the water."

"I've been in colder in the Irish Sea, I can assure you."

"That may be, but not after a year in solitary confinement as Morgan told me."

"I'll be all right. Let's get going."

Tadgh thrust his bulk from their tunnel through the opening into the river channel and accidentally dislodged the vertical timber Jack had lodged at its edge. Dirt rained off the wall and partially blocked the way.

"Careful there, Tadgh," Derek shouted, as he grasped the timber and pushed it back into place. They spent the next few minutes clearing the way, realizing that their passageway was precarious.

"Maybe we should wait until tomorrow morning when we're fresh, Tadgh. This is a hazardous situation."

Shoveling the last of the blockage into the wagon and resting on his shovel, Tadgh responded, "I've places to go tomorrow so we need to get this done now."

"Have it your way, but with the torrid rain going on outside I don't think you'll be going anywhere soon."

"We're going ahead now." Tadgh left his lamp at the end of their tunnel and grasped Derek's hand for support. The musty smell of the river made the inside of his nose sting. Together they slowly lowered Tadgh into the torrent. At first, before his feet found bottom, the current started to drag him downstream. He would have disappeared had Derek not tightened his grip. The side tunnel's slippery mud-covered rock surface exacerbated his struggle. Finally, Tadgh found his footing against the surge. He felt the mud oozing up over his boots, the water mid-thigh.

"All right. The bottom is manageable with some rough form of solid material under the muck, but the water's damn cold. It looks like this underground river is flowing between two layers of rock. Pass my lamp, then come on down carefully, man."

Five minutes later, the two shivering men sat on a narrow rock ledge just above the water line on the south side of the tunnel.

"It looks like the base of this tunnel is higher over here on its south side," Tadgh said, examining the rock ledge material. "Something has carved it out lower to the north."

"Let's get moving before we turn into icicles," Derek suggested, getting up and brushing himself off.

"You should feel how brisk the Celtic Sea is in the winter, Derek."

"I was a mariner when you were still in britches, lad, before I became a prizefighter."

Tadgh's eyes narrowed. "Were ya, now?" That explained the older man's physique. *What other secrets does this close friend and employee of Deirdre have?*

"Look at all the rats scurrying about," Derek said in a low voice. "This must be where they all come from."

"Best to avoid them. They carry typhus and cholera, and God only knows what else."

"You seem skittish about such little critters."

"You would be, too, if you had spent three years in the Joy with them as your only companions, watching to be sure they didn't chew off your feet while you tried to sleep."

"Sorry, Tadgh. I see what you mean." Derek clapped him on his shoulder in sympathy.

They struggled upstream to the west on the ledge feeling as much as seeing their way along the slimy rock wall. With each step, they made sure something solid was under them.

The ledge widened as the wall peeled away to the south. Tadgh guessed that they were now about two hundred feet south of the storage area. They hadn't gone a hundred feet west in the gloom when they came to the corner of the wall opening to the south on their left. The river widened on that side upstream and was being diverted north around this rock corner because it ran into this obstacle.

Tadgh kicked the ground. "We're standing on a solid slab. I think there is a rock base to this tunnel. I wonder if this is some ancient lava tube formed millions of years ago and buried under centuries of river silt."

Derek was more interested in the sharp corner of the mud-covered wall. "This might have been where Temple built his house, on the strongest rock base of the sand bar between the rivers."

"On top of a lava tube, then, Derek."

Derek glanced up at the roof of the tunnel. In the gloom, it looked as if it had been scrubbed clean of earth and had the pebbled look of petrified magma. "I guess so. There are extinct volcanoes in Ireland, you know. I used to fish off Lambay Island in North Dublin County, as an example. Does it look to you that the water might have filled this tunnel sometime in the past?" He pointed up.

Tadgh raised his lantern above his head. "Could be."

Derek took his bearings. "We're just about at the T.R. point on that map Jack found, give or take."

Tadgh scraped away some of the mud on the corner above the waterline. "Could these walls be what's left of a fortified basement wall that sank through a weaker part of the crust when it was undermined during the flood of 1802? Look here. Mortar between these stones. This is a foundation."

Tadgh headed south from the corner, searching for a break in the wall but finding none. "Could this be the Temple residence, do ya think?"

Derek was following behind him, scraping away at the manmade wall with his knife. "There's only one way to answer that question. Find a way in and see what's inside, other than mud and water that is."

"Easier said than done, Derek."

"We'll have to climb up and over if there's a gap in the crust. This structure must be broken and can't go to street level. There are newer buildings up there off Cecilia Street now, I think."

"Unless this is the foundation of another existing building. It's getting late. Let's go back outside and determine what is above us here."

Later that evening, Tadgh and Derek paced off the direction and distance on the surface from the grocery southwest corner to where they thought the subterranean wall was located. This process was hampered by darkness, an intervening building, and incessant rain and wind. It was difficult to keep their kerosene lantern lit. The streets were flooding. Tadgh was not surprised when they stopped directly opposite the end of Crow Street in a narrow alleyway between one-story buildings on the north side of Cecilia Street. The building marked T.R. on the tracing had been located at this spot.

Tadgh kicked his feet on the alley cobblestones. "If we measured correctly, then that foundation wall could very well be the edge of the original Temple residence. That should be exciting for Deirdre given her interest in all things Temple."

"It certainly is a curious turn of events," Derek said, and thinking to himself, *You have no idea what can of worms you may be uncovering.*

Returning to Deirdre's residence, Derek and Tadgh reported their findings to the women who were waiting in the kitchen warming themselves with tea. Jack had headed to bed already.

Deirdre remained stoically skeptical, although her eyes were glued on Derek's mouth and body language as he told them what they had found underground.

Morgan, for the first time, was starting to get excited. 'Why would a portion of the residence be so far down in the ground, Tadgh?"

"I'm not sure, my love, until we explore some more. But I think, somehow its foundation or basement sank through the top crust of the water tunnel weakened during the 1802 flood and the house collapsed above it. There are two smaller buildings on the north side of Cecilia Street above this location now."

Deirdre said, "Derek?"

"I agree with Tadgh's assessment, Dee, although it's hard to navigate and see down there in the kerosene lamplight."

"Do you think it's worth pursuing further?" the shop owner asked.

Both men nodded their heads in the affirmative.

Tadgh and Morgan headed to their room for the night. The day had taken more of a toll than he realized. He fell asleep as soon as his head hit the pillow, leaving Morgan tossing and turning.

Morgan realized this wasn't going to be their first lovemaking after his incarceration, much as she would have loved it. She checked Tadgh's vital signs for any abnormality. His heart rate had been racing for a week after being sprung from jail, but that wasn't abnormal after a serious influenza infection. Generally, he seemed normal except now he still looked peaked. She had tried to get him to eat fresh fruits and vegetables now they were in a grocery.

Morgan couldn't sleep for hours. Too many unanswered questions. Maybe she had stirred up a beehive where there was no honey. The claustrophobic risks with subterranean exploration. Underground rivers right under the city. Insane. William Temple involved in the Clans Pact discovery seemed daft. And then the interest Deirdre and Derek were trying to avoid showing in the whole adventure. Not to mention the grocery owner's knowledge about the *Book of Ballymote* and Professor Lawlor.

Tadgh finally had to wake her up on Wednesday morning. The rain was pounding against the window panes on Temple Bar Street. "Up an at 'em, Morgan. It's six-thirty and we've got an iron chest to find."

Morgan yawned, and rolling over, and pulled the covers over her head.

"C'mon, woman. Let me help you up."

Morgan peeked an eye out from under the covers. "Come back to bed, mavourneen. I'll make it worth your while," she drawled sleepily.

Tadgh tore the bedclothes off the bed. "You're the one who started this little adventure, so you're going to help finish it. We have to go home tomorrow, whatever happens."

Morgan sat up in bed. "I had a dream."

"How did I know that you were going to say that, lass?"

"I was on . . ."

Tadgh pulled her up and threw her over his shoulder despite her protests. "You can tell me your story while you dress." He put her down and she started to wash her face in the basin.

"I dreamt I was on our hooker, adrift at sea. I didn't know where you were. Suddenly a big old whale breached and capsized the boat, throwing me overboard. Then the strangest thing happened. I was going down for the third time and the whale came up under me. I wasn't afraid and held on until that whale brought me to the surface where I grabbed hold of the boat. That's when you woke me up. What do you think it all means?"

Chuckling, Tadgh teased her, "I think it means that you think I'm a big old whale. Now let's get moving."

While she was dressing, Morgan asked about the details of what Tadgh found underground.

"Let's not dawdle, Morgan. You can see it for yourself, after breakfast."

Tadgh literally bumped into Derek coming out of Deirdre's room. The cook wondered if Tadgh had felt the Webley revolver that Deirdre had given him, concealed in his waistband, but McCarthy gave no indication of it. Derek said, "Dee wants to see you in the parlor, Tadgh, alone."

Morgan grabbed a cold breakfast and hot tea in the kitchen while Tadgh met with Deirdre.

After exchanging pleasantries, the shop owner said, "If we find anything from the Temples today, I want it understood it stays with me."

"But we started this investigation."

"Yes, but it pertains to the heritage of the pub. I may not own it anymore, but my father and mother worked it their whole lives, you know. In their memory, all right, Tadgh?"

"As long as we can make a copy of any materials found."

"Agreed, as long as you don't publish them."

"Agreed. You're not joining us?"

"No. Derek will assist you. I'm afraid of tight spaces. It was a frightful childhood incident. Good hunting and remember our bargain."

Tadgh decided that he would have to ask her about her experiences someday, since he had his own frightful childhood incident, the hiding during the murder of his parents.

The adventurers reached the end of their supply room tunnel at seven o'clock, dodging rats scurrying by. This time each member of the group carried a lantern. Jack had acquired an electric torch similar to the one Tadgh used at the National Museum adventure.

Tadgh surveyed the river cavern. "It's flowing faster than last night, I think, Derek."

"Definitely. We'd best get moving."

Morgan gasped when she saw into the river tunnel. "My God, Tadgh. We could be swept away. Why don't the buildings above fall in?"

"See the top of the tunnel? There's a rock crust."

"I think this is a fool's errand, Tadgh. We should stop right now. It's too dangerous."

"Nonsense, lass. We'll be all right. You'll see. And tomorrow we'll be on our way home."

Morgan hastily weighed the dangers of this adventure against the risks of fighting the British and decided it was better to be here with Tadgh where she could help him if need be. But she didn't like being underground in water. Too many terrifying memories. "All right, then. Let's get this over with," she exclaimed, as she pulled on the waders Tadgh had given her.

Tadgh lowered himself into the frigid water. He could hardly stand up. "It's running four feet deep now, Derek. Almost to my waist. C'mon down, Morgan. I'll catch you."

She started down and slipped, tumbling awkwardly into Tadgh's arms. He lost his footing and they both fell under the surface, the current carrying them downstream.

Pointing his torch out into the river tunnel, Jack could see Tadgh surface twenty feet to his left, but Morgan was nowhere to be seen. Tadgh dove and twenty seconds later came up with his sputtering wife fifty feet farther downstream.

"Do I constantly have to keep saving you from cold water, aroon?"

"Get me out of this, Tadgh!" Morgan shivered.

Tadgh waded to the far narrow rock ledge on the south side of the river, which was only a foot above the deluge now and hoisted her onto it. "Stay here, love. I'll be right back."

Backtracking from mid-river near the tunnel, he yelled over the roar of the water to Jack, "Give Derek that blanket you brought, then toss me the rope."

"But, Tadgh, I could help—"

"I think you should stay over there in the storage room tunnel, for when we need you, Jack."

Pushing past Jack at the end of the tunnel, Derek took the blanket and said, "Deirdre may need you if this river rises much higher."

Jack nodded his understanding and tossed Tadgh the coiled rope with the four-claw grappling hook that he had scrounged at his compatriot's request that morning on the riverfront. He was very happy with that dry assignment.

Derek deftly slipped the revolver into the blanket Jack gave him and held them over his head as he slid down into the torrent. The sure-footed ex-prizefighter landed squarely, navigating the water with ease. He calmly walked down to where Morgan sat, hiding the Webley in his trouser pocket. Then he wrapped the blanket around her shoulders.

"I'll get the lanterns and other equipment," Tadgh said, fording the river to where Jack could hand them down to him.

After two trips, Tadgh returned with two kerosene lights, the torch, and a shovel. Morgan was no longer shivering. "I don't think that water is very sanitary, Tadgh. With all the rats."

Tadgh looked back at the water level relative to the mouth of the storage room tunnel. "We need to move fast."

Packing their supplies, the trio inched in a southwesterly direction along the narrow ledge, finally arriving at the foundation wall corner buried in the silt. They rounded it on their left and stood looking up at its west side. The water level had reached its rock base.

Derek touched the moist wall and said, "Maybe the water filled this tunnel during the flood of 1802."

Looking east and shining the beam into the darkness higher on the west side of the wall, Tadgh said, "There's no mud up there. The water may never have reached that height."

Morgan looked concerned. "Or else it washed it clean." Abnormal for November, it had been pouring for two days. "Maybe this tunnel is completely filled during spring rains."

Derek said he thought so, too. He examined the wall at its northwest corner where the water turned. "There's no crack in this structure. It must have been built like a fortress." He scratched the mud away from the bottom of the wall. "Look here, where this bottom edge sits on the base rock. The stonework shows a stone floor to whatever this is. Could it be a sealed room?"

Shining the torch farther up along the vertical side of the structure, Tadgh could see where it disappeared through the roof of the tunnel. Rocks strewn on the riverbank at his feet showed him where this structure had likely plummeted through the mantel only to come to rest in the subterranean rock outcrop. "That must have been some cataclysmic event, with whatever was above suddenly breaking through and collapsing into the ground."

"Either due to the flood or afterwards when the area above was plowed under to build new structures," Derek said, glancing upwards to follow Tadgh's torchlight. He didn't want to tell them that he knew what had happened—that the initial demolition had occurred sixty-one years earlier than the flood. But the sink hole during the flood could have been caused by a subterranean collapse of an underground structure through the top crust of the river channel. "Let's follow the wall south and examine the roof of the tunnel."

The river was rising, now pounding against the base of the west wall. About twenty feet farther on, a large heap of rocks rested at the base of the wall, some now underwater. Tadgh estimated that about nine feet above, where the roof of the tunnel had crumbled, there was a gap between the wall and its edge.

"Up there!" Tadgh cried. He pointed the torch, at the opening in the rock. Stand back and hold the torch please, Morgan. "Let me try to hook the edge.

It took six attempts before the hook caught on the rock opening above.

He yanked to test the sturdiness of the connection. "Here's hoping it will hold my weight."

Derek held the rope taut at the bottom while Tadgh shinnied up to the tunnel roof clenching the torch in his teeth. Morgan was reminded of the night in the hole of Bull Rock when Tadgh tried to fix the top main mast hooker's lanyards. Tadgh was weaker now, and, once again, Morgan worried this crazy search might end in tragedy.

"Sweet Brigid!" Tadgh exclaimed, while struggling to hold the rope with his right arm, his leg entwined. He was using his left to raise the torch and scan the hole. He didn't like the clotted mud in the edges of the jagged hole.

"What do you see, mavourneen?"

"It looks like a fortified rock basement room below the rest of a house. I'm not yet at a level of the top of it because of a jumble of masonry, wood, and other house materials above it and to this side."

Tadgh pulled himself up until his head and shoulders disappeared into the hole. Holding himself partially on the edge of the rock crust, he shone the torch above the stone wall. Then he lowered himself back below the hole. "There is a rock crust to the tunnel roof at this point all right. It looks like a house was built above this heavy subterranean stone structure resting on the crust, until the flood. Then this structure caved through, and the house imploded above it. There's a space a couple of feet high above this opening to crawl around up against the wall of the structure. It looks like they just demolished the house above and covered it over. But the structure of the collapsed main floor is somewhat intact above this, held up by broken pieces of foundation."

Morgan called up, "That's enough, Tadgh. Come back down. This is getting too dangerous. We can come back another time." She had *déjà vu* feelings. Bad ones from the *Lusitania*. Most of her fellow passengers were dead, entombed in the destroyed liner at the bottom of the Celtic Sea. She was one of the few lucky ones.

As if he had been reading her thoughts, Jack yelled across the abyss, his voice echoing ominously down the cavern, "You all had better get back over here very soon."

"Okay, Jack!" Tadgh yelled. "Soon."

He shone the light along the top of the wall again, where the main floor attached. He saw a break in the flooring that he could squeeze through. "Just a minute. I need to explore." With that he hoisted himself up and was out of sight.

"Come back down!" Morgan shouted with no response.

Moments later, he dropped down below the tunnel crust and announced, "I saw above the flooring. There is a flat stone top to the structure at the level of the flooring. There probably was an underground room behind this wall. It isn't just a high foundation for the main house. Somebody wanted to have a fortified structure for sure. We need to continue, now." Tadgh did a calculation in his head and added, "The broken floor must be at least ten feet below street level I should think."

"How much open space above that broken flooring, Tadgh?" Derek asked.

"Well, it's full of a jumble of house materials and rotting contents, but I'd say a good three feet in places."

"Three feet? My God, Tadgh, that's nothing!" Morgan exclaimed.

Tadgh knew she must be frightened because of her previous trauma. "It's enough, though."

"What about any evidence of water?" Derek asked.

Tadgh hesitated but realized he needed to tell them the truth. "It looks from the silt on this opening in the crust that the water at some point in the past came up through this hole and excavated a small area under the broken floor."

Morgan held her lantern up to better illuminate Tadgh's face. "Do you think this is the old Temple residence?"

"I'd bet my life on it, aroon."

Morgan retorted, "If we're not careful you'll be betting all our lives on it." She pointed northeast across the river. "We should get out of here before the water reaches the height of the storage room tunnel. My feet are frozen. Please come down."

Tadgh obeyed, shinnying back down before he spoke. "Someone went to a lot of effort to build an underground stronghold. That's where I would hide an important iron chest. Unfortunately, if such a box is still in the upper house, then it is buried in jumbled and rotting building materials and dirt. We could never find it unless we could excavate the whole site from above."

"And that can't happen because of the buildings we saw last night on the north side of Cecilia Street," Derek added.

"Then let's get out of here," Morgan advised.

"But if it is in the basement room—?"

"The water is still rising, Tadgh. If we are going to do anything more it has to be now or much later," Derek said, pointing to the rushing river swirling at their feet.

Tadgh knew that it was now or maybe never. He had to get back to Creagh to join up with Tom Barry and his flying column. He looked up. "If the basement room can be accessed then there is a possibility it would be relatively intact." Tadgh pounded the stone with his fist. "I think we can access whatever's behind this wall."

"I can't pull myself up that rope, Tadgh."

"That's all right, Morgan. I'll hoist you if you can just hold on."

Derek assessed the danger. The underground river had risen about two feet since they first found it the night before. It was still seven feet below the ceiling of the tunnel but only three feet below the storage room tunnel. At that rate, they still had several hours before they would be trapped. The river speed was still navigable. He fingered the Webley in his pocket. "Let me go with you, Tadgh. Morgan can hold the bottom of the rope."

Morgan grabbed the rope taut. She knew there was no use trying to change Tadgh's mind. For some reason this tunneling project was some catharsis for him, like he was trying to reach freedom. Maybe it would help him to get over his recent emotional struggle. She warned them, "Hurry up, then, if you must. I don't want to be down here alone for long, with the rats and the river rising."

"We're on our way, lass." Tadgh was already halfway up the rope.

Then he disappeared, and Derek was scrambling up the rope behind him. Morgan hollered down the river tunnel to determine if Jack was still there. She needed the reassurance of a friendly voice. It was as if she was back on the port deck of the doomed ship with freezing water all around her.

A minute later, his voice came back, thin, and hollow. "You'd better hurry up or you might get trapped there for a while. I'm getting Deirdre's help to move the storage room produce and boxes up into the grocery in case it floods."

She called out, "The boys are scouting a stone fortress room over here. We should be coming back soon, Jack."

Looking down at the raging river that was rushing past no more than three feet below the bottom of the storage room tunnel, Jack was worried. The only other time he remembered Morgan's voice being so plaintive was when she was desperate to find her Byron as the *Lusitania* was sinking. "You do that, lass. You'll be all right if you can just come back here to safety." He wanted to add *to me*, but he bit his tongue.

Derek reached the top of the rope, the handle of his lantern in his teeth, fortunately avoiding breaking the glass and setting himself on fire. Tadgh noted he was a good ally to have as he took the lantern and helped him up through the hole. He could see that they were in a confined space with the flat stone wall directly in front of them. The ceiling of this somewhat open area looked like a jagged, rotting wooden floor held up by broken cement block pillars. He could also see some rusted metal fasteners where the flooring was anchored to the wall. Tadgh pointed to the hole in the flooring immediately above them and tied the rope off on solid-enough wooden beams.

"Let's climb up through the broken flooring to see if we can get on top of the room behind this wall." Tadgh snaked his way up and cleared the constricted path, all the while thinking what a terrible idea this had become. Yet he was intrigued about what they might find. It was Morgan's idea in the first place after all. Above the flooring, he looked up to see if there was any way out. As expected, it was a confined and jumbled mess with no daylight. He hoped the water below would stop rising soon.

Derek called up to check on his progress.

"There's a lot of rubble up here on top of a cemented rock-covered ceiling to this basement structure. It must have been a particularly important room, to have such a secure, almost impervious construction."

"How did they get into it, then?" Derek asked having climbed up to meet him.

Tadgh scraped away more debris. "Here's a horizontal metal trap door that looks like it may lead down into a fortified space. See the old hinges on one side. There's about three feet of open height to work in, just enough space to open it."

Derek announced, "Morgan is yelling—she wants you to hurry, Tadgh. The water's at her ankles."

"Tell her I will pull her up in a minute. I want to make sure there's something worth investigating before we bring her up and potentially lose our escape route. Surely the water can't rise this high, but we might have to wait until it recedes." Tadgh didn't bother to mention that air flow might become their main problem.

The cook ducked his head back down and conveyed the message. Tadgh heard Morgan's muffled voice from below admonishing them to come back down.

When Derek returned, he said, "We'd better decide. Your wife sounds desperate."

Tadgh was torn. As a risk taker, he was compelled to find out what was in this very curious structure, if anything. If they left now, back to Creagh, then Derek would solve the mystery.

"What do you think, Derek?"

"I think we need to find out what's in that storeroom."

Tadgh decided. "We've got time." He tugged at the debris. "Okay. Be careful you don't bring the rubble and dirt down on us."

Together they shifted three rotting beams that blocked the trap door and scraped away other debris until it was completely uncovered. They could smell the stench of rotting materials and the dust of ages clogging their noses. Fortunately, there was no dried mud at this height that Tadgh could see. Had they been claustrophobic, they would have panicked.

Tadgh examined the horizontal door. Not only was it padlocked, but it had crossed boards nailing it shut. It looked as if it hadn't been opened in centuries.

"What's this, Tadgh? Shine your torch."

Tadgh brushed the dirt off a faded brass notice bolted across the door frame.

Sealed by order of Jonathan Swift, Year of our Lord 1741.

"Damn. This has to be the wrong house, that's certain."

Derek eyes were beaming. "Don't be so sure."

They heard a crack like thunder and a faint cry for help.

"Morgan!" Tadgh cried and squirmed around to head back down to the hole in the crust. Shining the torch downward, he saw Morgan clinging to the rope. She had climbed halfway up it and the water was rushing at her heels.

"Help me, Tadgh. I can't hold on!"

"Don't let go, aroon. You'll be all right. I'll pull you up." *God. It looks like an underground dam has broken.* Tadgh had a sinking feeling, but there was no turning back now. If they descended into this maelstrom, they would all drown.

Tadgh pulled with all his might. Before Morgan reached the height of the hole, her right hand slipped. Tadgh couldn't reach down without letting go of the rope. Luckily, Derek came down behind him and took the rope. Tadgh grabbed Morgan's flailing right arm and yanked her up to safety.

There they all lay on top of the crust, spent, while the river boiled and rose below. When they looked down a minute later, the water level was only two feet below the hole.

Morgan shivered. "No wonder there is a huge tunnel. Look at

the power of that water." She realized, with the rushing sound of the deluge, that there was no way to communicate with Jack. It was too late anyway. The storage room tunnel would be flooded.

Tadgh pointed the torch towards the jagged opening above them. "We need to climb further, Morgan. Come see what we've found. Up there."

Morgan shook her head violently, her fists clenched at her side. "I can't do that, Tadgh."

"Yes, you must, aroon. The water may come higher."

"But the *Lusitania!*" Morgan eyes were wild.

Tadgh realized that the water and confined spaces must be torture for her and gently said, "Aye, lass."

"But how are we going to get out?" In her mind, she was back on the stairs of the sinking ship, trapped below decks by that mass of panicking humanity.

Tadgh wished to hell he hadn't let her come on this disastrous adventure.

"Close your eyes and pretend we are back home, aroon. You'll be all right. I'll lead you."

Morgan squinted shut and let Tadgh lead her through the constrictive jumble until they were sitting with their heads bowed on top of the trap door with a few feet of breathing space.

"You can open your eyes now," Tadgh said softly.

Morgan's lantern had been swept away by the underground river, but Derek had placed his among the debris. It gave off an eerie light among all the jagged beams, disintegrated walls, and wreckage of first floor belongings, now unrecognizable. She could see rats' eyes glowing in the light of the lantern. What were those infectious beasts waiting for? Human carrion to eat?

Tadgh pointed at the faded brass plate. "Apparently we are under Jonathan Swift's home. Look at that seal."

Morgan tried to force the terror out of her mind with rational thoughts. She asked, her voice quavering, "Wasn't he the Dean of St. Patrick's Cathedral back in the early 1700s?"

"Yes, Morgan," Derek said, wiping the seal with his sleeve. "And a major political activist against the English Queen Anne. They called him an Irish patriot when being that was likely to get your head lopped off. That's why he wrote in satire."

"I have no idea why Swift would be here since you boys say this was Temple's residence," Morgan commented, then added, "Be that as it may, let's get to it quickly and then find a way out of here before it's too late."

Tadgh ducked back down to the hole. The water was still rising. It was already too late.

Derek agreed, "But we need to break into this room. It was clearly important to Swift."

Tadgh wondered why their companion was more interested in a room of Swift's when they were in mortal danger. He knew more than he was letting on. Half an hour ago, they could have swum back to the storage room tunnel, but now they were trapped. They had to hope that the water wouldn't rise any higher.

There must be something important in there, but I have to be careful, thought Tadgh as he looked for an implement of leverage. Searching the rubble with the torch, he found an iron pipe attached under the flooring material. "Help me break this off, Derek."

Together they pried a six-foot section free by flexing it many times until it broke off at a joint creating a sharp edge. They used it to lever the sealing boards off the doorframe, one by one, until the only impediment remaining was the padlock.

Derek examined the latch and the lock. "This was a stout lock in its time, so let's try to spring its rusty latch hinge."

Tadgh inserted the pipe behind the padlock against the metal door and heaved without success.

"Help me again, Derek."

Together they strained against the barrier that was almost two hundred years old, without success.

"Try putting a rock near the lock but under the bar," Morgan suggested. She remembered Doctor Depage using a similar technique to force a compound fracture into place.

Tadgh found a large block of wood and placed it under the pipe. "All right. Let's try again."

On the second heave, the hinge sprang open, leaving a part still attached to the padlock. That freed the door.

"Thank you, aroon."

Morgan smiled for the first time since entering the tunnel. "As you said to Deirdre years ago in her pub, 'Elementary, my dear Tadgh.'"

The horizontal iron door resisted being opened. It took both men several attempts with their makeshift crowbar to open its hinges. At one point, Derek squirreled down to the hole and returned, announcing that the river was now up to the ceiling of the tunnel.

"Hopefully, it will stop there as the water rushes down the cavern," Tadgh said, hoping that this was just a surge after the dam broke. But he knew that increased pressure could force water up into this confined space.

Finally, once they levered the door partially open, the men managed to rotate it up and out with a mighty heave.

They were immersed in a pungent smell of moldy, rotting material. Tadgh shone the torch along the edge of the opening. "See here how it was sealed? It would have been watertight from above." He pointed the torch down the ancient stairs below the doorway and it flickered dim. "Damn." He pounded the base on the ground and the torch glowed brighter.

"I'm going down before I lose the light completely," Tadgh said, starting down the stairs.

"I'm coming with you," Derek said, bringing his lantern and following close behind. He put his hand in his pocket and felt for the grip on his revolver.

"Don't leave me behind in the dark," Morgan said, stepping last to the doorway.

Although the stairs were more than two hundred years old and rickety, they held their weight. Tadgh had been right. They saw a fortified bunker of about twenty feet square, the room presumably sealed off for more than a hundred and eighty years. It was a library of sorts or an office, with a heavy oak desk and built-in wooden shelves full of books behind the desk opposite the stairs. The books were giving off the putrid smell that caused them to gag. Water had seeped in at floor level over the ages, and what had been carpet was now a layer of mold. At least there were no rats.

Tadgh could see the similarity between this fortified space and his own bunker control room he personally hewed under his own home.

For a moment, being in a ten-foot-high room, Morgan's panic level dropped.

Derek put the lantern down on the desk. This had clearly been the private inner sanctum of Jonathan Swift, if not generations before him. A moldy copy of *Verses on the Death of Dr. Swift* dated 1741 lay on the desk. Beside it, on a paper in handwritten scrawl, a personal eulogy about the famous author, signed by the man himself. It read:

'Here is laid the Body
of Jonathan Swift, Doctor of Sacred Theology,
Dean of this Cathedral Church,
where fierce Indignation
can no longer
injure the Heart.
Go forth, Voyager,
and copy, if you can,
this vigorous (to the best of his ability)
Champion of Liberty.'

Morgan commented, "This man seemed obsessed with death."

"I heard that, too," Derek said, as he searched the bookcases, not stopping to examine the books.

Tadgh wondered what he was looking for.

"My God, Tadgh. Look at this." Morgan had found a metal box on the desk. Inside was a document titled, "Memoir of Sir William Temple," dated 1699, with the most profound handwritten words across the front— *'All that is good and amiable in mankind has died with you, dear Father.'*

She said, "Could this be the iron chest? At least we have a reference to William Temple at last. This must have been his residence, too. What was Swift doing here more than a hundred years after William died? Was Swift referring to the Father Almighty?"

"So many questions. I have no idea, Morgan. It's all very strange," Tadgh said, coming over to inspect the paper. "Wait a minute. That phrase is signed by . . . I can't make it out."

Morgan looked more closely. "Jonathan Swift."

Derek was watching the other two very closely and said, "We haven't got a minute to wait. That's not the chest."

How would he know? Looking down to examine the desk, Tadgh forced open the center drawer. Inside he found a lock of woman's hair wrapped in a paper bearing the words, *'Stella, Only strands of a woman's hair.'* How odd.

On the shelves, some of the book titles were still legible under moldy blotches of covers and spines. Books of poetry by Alexander Pope for instance.

While Morgan examined the books, Tadgh joined Derek in scrutinizing the bookshelves themselves. *Why were the shelves behind the desk set further out from the wall than elsewhere?* Then he saw it, a handhold between the first and second bookcase.

He reached out, and with a mighty jerk, the second bookcase hinge swiveled open revealing a cavity behind it, containing a large muslin-wrapped object coated in spiderwebs. He took his knife and slashed the ancient fabric. It crumbled away revealing a locked, wrought iron chest of about twenty-five cubic feet.

Chapter Nineteen
Iron Chest

*T*he rain had pelted the city incessantly all day, dropping more than a foot of water and setting a record for Dublin. At least the store was closed due to the storm. When Jack saw the water rising rapidly in the Liffey tunnel, he headed up to the grocery to inform Deirdre. She had come down to see and then started lugging crates up the stairs. Jack lent a hand in between monitoring the river and checking in on his compatriots' status.

Then, nearly an hour ago, water was seeping into the storage room tunnel and area. Jack worried his compatriots were in trouble. He couldn't look for them, the current was moving too fast. Soon, the storage room and river tunnels would be completely under water if it didn't stop raining. As he stood in a puddle at the foot of the storage room stairs, he heard the crack like thunder and the river water flooded through their excavation, overflowing it, and filling the area to a height of four feet. Mud exploded into the room and knocked Jack off his feet. The bottom of the stairs creaked, but held, and Jack scrambled up a few steps. Given the rock crust at the top of both tunnels, he thought that the river could rise no higher. But within minutes, the surging water had risen in the storage room another two feet and was not stopping. The thought of another flood like the one in 1802 that crippled Temple Bar entered his mind. He worried about the structural integrity of the grocery itself, even though the waters were still at least ten feet below street level.

Jack flashed back to the agony of his ship, the *Lusitania* sinking under him, his jumping overboard, and almost drowning with a broken back. Panic now set in, his legs shook, and he grabbed the stair railing to keep himself from falling down into the swirling water and muck. Then he realized that he could just ascend the stairs to the grocery and safety.

But what about the love of his life, Morgan? She must be trapped with no way out and frightened out of her wits. And he was powerless to help her, unlike his efforts on the dying ship. *God, no!*

Deirdre heard the crack from the residence. She descended the stairs and saw the deluge filling her storage room so far underground. The building was still safe but then she saw Jack below her, clinging to the railing for dear life. She reached down and grabbed his free hand, his frightened eyes fastened on hers.

"My God, Deirdre. Something broke upstream in the river and it's rising so much faster. They'll be trapped over there!" Jack cried, pointing towards the submerged tunnel. "I can't help them!"

Jack had seemed so self-confident to Deirdre before this. Perhaps the trauma of having been on the dying Lusitania and temporarily paralyzed was plaguing him. This vulnerability, so different from the other men she'd had to deal with, made her want him.

"Let me help you, Jack," she said calmly, as she led him up to the grocery. The stairs creaked again, this time swaying. She worried they might collapse. "I'm sure our friends will be all right. Let's go up now." That was a lie. Although she had confidence that her ex-prizefighting friend, cook, and bodyguard could weather most storms, she wasn't sure about this monster. There was nothing she could do to help him or the McCarthys at this stage. She reasoned that this search for the iron box was a gamble at best. The odds of finding that crucial Templar artifact, if it did exist, were a long shot. If the worst happened, she and Jack could just try to retrieve the bodies after the storm surge, if they hadn't flowed too far downstream, and seal up the storage room tunnel. She had faith that the ancient Templar crusade would survive, somehow, to fulfill its destiny.

What she could do was use this moment of openness to further her relationship with Jack when, she hoped, they did survive and continue their quest. And she truly liked this man, more than she knew. "Come on up to my residence and have some stew while we wait, Jack. We can't help them until the river subsides."

Cold and wet, Jack reluctantly followed her up and sat in the parlor on a sofa by the fire. Deirdre ordered him out of his wet clothes. He stripped sheepishly to his drawers and handed over his trousers and shirt. After laying them on a grate by the fire, Deirdre gave him a blanket, which he appreciated for modesty as well as warmth. She couldn't help but notice his rippling arms and chest muscles, created when he fought to regain his mobility after the *Lusitania* had sunk. His character and physique combined to warm her heart and loins for him. Maybe her strategy to get close to Jack to glean information would not be as sterile a prospect as she had first contrived.

Deirdre stood with her back to the fire and undid the top two buttons of her shirtwaist. "Is it hot in here?" She leaned over, stroking his biceps, her ample breasts straining out in front of his eyes. "You're a fit man, Jack Jordan."

Jack was temporarily distracted from the horror below. "You're a gorgeous lady, yourself, Deirdre. What's your surname, lass?"

"My friends just call me Dee."

When Deirdre brought him lamb stew and stout, she planted a slow, lingering kiss on his cheek. It set his nervous system on fire, not to mention his manhood. He thought how he had avoided feminine intimacy ever since the sinking and his accident, partly because of his perceived inadequacies, and also because no other woman could light a fire in his loins like Morgan.

He stammered, "What was that for?"

"Because I like you, Jack, very much." She disappeared into her kitchen.

A few minutes later, she returned with hot tea and apple pie and sat beside him on the sofa. She preened her hair while she watched him gobble down the dessert. Such a voracious appetite. Now he looked so much better under her care.

When Jack finished, she took his empty plate and set it beside her on the floor, then leaned over, wrapping her left arm around his shoulder.

Jack didn't move off the sofa. Instead, he wrapped the blanket tighter around his trunk and dropped his hands over his groin. Sure, he'd had sexual adventures as a young Cunard bosun on shore leave, but that was before the accident years ago on the *Lusitania*. Jumping off the stern of the doomed ship did more than break his spine, it had shattered his self-esteem, which was only now starting to re-emerge.

Deirdre lifted his hands gently. She saw more than his shyness. The bulge in his drawers, which she spied before he covered up, showed he was well endowed. Her strategy was to get close to this man, but it was also going to be stimulating, and enjoyable, that's for certain.

Deirdre used Jack's left hand to free her breast from her peasant shirtwaist, then used her own hand to trace it slowly and methodically, as he was obviously aroused.

He got up. "We need to get downstairs to see if the water is receding, Deirdre. This isn't the time for romance."

Deirdre grabbed his arm and held tight. "Nonsense, Jack. This is the perfect time to get to know each other better. You saw the flood level. It's still raining cats and dogs out. There's nothing we can do for now and we need to divert our attention to more pleasurable feelings." She tried to kiss him and missed as he broke free of her grasp.

Jack grabbed for his still-damp clothing and asked, "Aren't you worried for your cook?" The specter of the *Lusitania* drowning and sucking the passengers down with it seized him. He was deathly afraid for the McCarthys, especially Morgan.

Deirdre tucked her breast in and blocked his way. "I know Derek. He's resourceful. So are your friends. They'll have found a way out or a safe haven until the waters recede. You'll see. Sit down, Jack."

He tried to pull on his trousers and asked, "What about the storables, then?"

Deirdre wasn't going to let this opportunity alone with him go to waste. "The food is underwater, Jack, and the stairs are unsafe. Come and sit down. We'll deal with it later. Right now, I need you."

Jack saw she was right. Deirdre had been through a lot in her young life, including almost dying in a fire and losing her pub. Not that his own life had been easy, to say the least, but he had survived the sinking, barely. The nightmares of being under that cold water with a broken back, fighting the downdraft of the behemoth's death plunge, were subsiding. Deirdre had a cool head and could put things into perspective in dire times. That could help him with that. And the love of his life was unattainable.

He stepped out of his pants and laid them back on the grate.

"That's my boy," Deirdre cooed as she led him back to the sofa and loosed her breast once more. "They'll be all right."

Jack grabbed the blanket from the floor and sat down on the sofa. "But when the rain stops . . ."

Morgan opened up her shirt. "Of course, lad. Now where were we?"

He was mesmerized and inhaled deeply but dropped his left hand to cover his expanding manhood.

Her voice almost pleading, "Touch me, Jack, please." Her breasts were a creamy voluptuousness he had only imagined in the wet dreams of his youth. He wanted to see his hands fit around them, but he hesitated.

Deirdre reached down and pulled his hand up onto her exposed breast since he wouldn't do it himself, settling her other hand on his pulsing groin.

Jack couldn't help himself, his hands kneading.

She felt him quiver as his instincts took over. He leaned over and hungrily nuzzled and nibbled at her nipple as Deirdre's head fell back, exposing her neck.

Deirdre held his head to her bosom and stroked his hair with her other hand. "That's it, keep going, Jack," she purred.

The grocery front door swung open and crashed against the canned goods counter below them. Jack jerked his head back and Deirdre slipped her breast back into her shirtwaist, kissing him briskly on the lips. "Wait here. I'll be right back." She raced down the stairs and saw the water coming in the front door.

The floor was immersed in at least an inch of water. It would ruin the wood. Deirdre rushed out into the street to gauge the situation outside. The city drains were overflowing.

Moments later, Jack was by her side, having pulled on his clothing. "Get back inside, Deirdre. You're not dressed properly."

She realized she wasn't wearing her disguise and darted back inside. "Thanks for that warning. Shut and lock that door. I'd guess there hasn't been this much water since the flood of 1802. Let's get those potato sacks from the back room. Then we can block the doors. I'll start sweeping the water out through the tradesman's door at the back."

As Jack passed her by, she grabbed him and kissed him fiercely on the mouth, whispering, "You made me wet, you know."

Startled, Jack kissed her back and rushed off to get the potato sacks.

Tadgh and Derek dragged the iron chest out into the center of the study. Tadgh checked the locks. "This must be the chest Deirdre was talking about. But what's it doing in Jonathan Swift's old basement study?"

"Maybe the question, my love, is what was Jonathan Swift doing in the basement of William Temple's residence?"

Derek knew the answer as he ran his hand reverently over the object. "More importantly, what is in this chest?"

Tadgh noticed his companion's euphoria. There was more to this man than meets the eye. "I agree. It's not air-tight around the edge of the lid, but these three locks look formidable. Someone must have counted upon keeping the whole room sealed."

Morgan asked, "Can we carry it out of here and open it in the grocery, Tadgh? When the water subsides, that is."

Tadgh and Derek lifted the iron chest, straining with every muscle. "I don't know what's inside, but the box is too heavy to carry that far," Tadgh answered. "Whoever made it must have been planning for a long unattended storage period. Aside from some surface rust, it looks to be in fine condition."

"That pipe is too big to fit into the shackles. Let me get something to pry them loose," Derek said, looking around the furnished study. Seeing nothing of interest, he ascended the stairs with the kerosene lantern and was gone.

"What are you thinking, aroon?" Tadgh asked, in the semi darkness of the torch's faint glow.

Morgan mind was churning. The fact they found an iron chest meant they were likely within William Temple's study. The map showed T.R. *But why was Swift here?*

She answered, "The furniture in this room was very grand for its day, Tadgh. Certainly, earlier than the mid-1700s, more rustic. I'd bet this wasn't Jonathan Swift's home."

"William Temple's residence then?"

"Swift did refer to Temple, oddly, I thought."

"After all this effort, we can only hope that what is in this chest reveals PP's location."

Derek returned, empty-handed and winded. "It must be a hell of a storm above us because the river is up above the hole. If this keeps up, it could flood this basement now that the door is open."

Tadgh took the torch and rushed up the stairs to examine the door. "I'll be right back." The rusted hinges had been sprung. He tried to rotate the door closed. It wouldn't budge. He concluded the room could not be resealed. He snaked on his belly through the path they had cleared, back towards the hole. It was full of water cavitating and bubbling almost up to the flooring. He could hear rats clawing their way above him. He guessed the rate of rise about four feet an hour.

This was getting serious. He estimated the water level would only have to rise another foot to be above the study's trap door lip. If they couldn't climb up, they would drown another three feet above that if the river pressure kept increasing. Scrambling back to the door, he looked up above him. At first, it just seemed a jumble of debris in the dim light. Then he realized that the ceiling of this three-foot-high cavity was the irregular upper floor of the house, which had been crushed down as a result of the flood. Could there be a way out above it? How far underground were they? He estimated nine to ten feet. That would mean during the flood, the whole house collapsed and compressed by about one story through the crust. The torch light vanished. Banging it down did not revive it.

Tadgh descended the stairs into the study by the light of the lantern within and was met with worried stares. He did not have good news.

"The underground river is still rising. We probably only have fifteen minutes before it reaches this room. We can't reseal it."

Morgan looked stricken. "My God, Tadgh. What will we do?"

He could see she was panicking again. He remembered her telling him about being caught below decks on the sinking *Lusitania*, when they were sinking quickly into the sea. Now the sea was coming up to get them. Either way, they were trapped.

"If necessary, we're going to climb up, just like the rats."

Derek looked up from his examination of the chest lock, adding, "Fleeing a sinking ship."

Morgan's eyes darted from side to side. "But they're tiny creatures."

Tadgh said, "Not a good analogy, Derek. All right, here's what we are going to do. Derek, you go up and find a way up past the flooring while Morgan and I try to get the chest open. There is absolutely no way we are going to carry it out of here unless the river miraculously stops rising."

"I should stay to help you, Tadgh."

"Believe me, Derek. There's no way that Morgan can find out. You need to do it. I promise we won't disturb anything if we get the chest open before you return. I'll call to you if we do."

Reluctantly, Derek climbed the stairs. They heard him digging at the debris.

"Help me, aroon." Tadgh broke a chair leg off and handed it to Morgan. Then he pulled a long spike that he had ripped from the flooring out of his pants pocket and wedged it through the shackles of the first lock. "I want you to smash the end of this spike with the wooden leg while I hold the nail."

"I'll probably hit your hand."

"Just do it."

Morgan whacked as hard as she could. Although she hit the head of the iron spike, putting stress on the lock, it did not budge. After five smacks she stopped. "This is useless, Tadgh."

Tadgh was vainly searching for something more substantial like a hammer when Derek returned. "I see a way up. How are you two doing?"

"No progress, I'm afraid."

Derek hesitated for a minute and then pulled his revolver from his pants. "Stand back."

Tadgh was alarmed that the cook would be carrying a gun and concealing it from them. "Why did you tote a revolver on this hunt?"

"I always carry it with me wherever I go. With this war going on, one must be on the defensive."

Tadgh scowled. "If you're caught with that, you'll go to jail."

"I won't get caught. Let's get on with this." Derek aimed and his first shot ricocheted off the lock, denting it but not releasing the mechanism.

"How many bullets do you have in there, Derek?"

"Six, Tadgh, and I just used one." He aimed to shoot again.

"Hold on there." Tadgh examined the padlock again. Pointing to the side of the shackle where the mechanism opened, he instructed,

"Fire about half an inch below this interface."

The second shot was too low and failed to spring the lock.

"Give me the gun, Derek."

"No."

"You want to find out what's in here before it's too late, or not? We can just leave it here to become submerged. Whatever it contains will be reduced to mush. Your call."

"I can do it."

"So you've demonstrated. Give me the gun."

Water started to trickle down the stairs.

"We're out of time, Derek. Give me the gun."

This time Derek relinquished the weapon and Tadgh fired at his intended spot on the lock. It loosened but still would not open.

"Just three bullets left, Tadgh," Morgan whispered.

"I know, lass." Their feet were starting to get wet. Tadgh examined the matching imbedded flanges on the lid and top edge of the chest through where the lock shackles were looped. "Stand back. We have nothing to lose except the contents of the chest."

He stood at an oblique angle then fired at the base of the flanges on the first lock. The bullet shattered the flange on the top, and it broke away from the chest.

"You did it, Tadgh. Two more to go."

Two well-directed shots later and all three flanges were free. The water tumbled down the stairs and their ankles were awash. Tadgh handed the gun back to Derek, handle first. "Someday you'll have to tell me the real reason you felt the need to bring a gun to this shindig."

Derek took the gun but avoided Tadgh's gaze.

"Open it. Hurry," Morgan cried, her eyes darting back and forth from the stairs to the chest.

Tadgh tried to lift the lid, but the hinge was rusted shut. "Help me, Derek."

Together they heaved, and finally the lid cracked open so they could reach in. Tadgh tried the torch. No light. Its battery was still dead. "Bring the lantern over the chest, Morgan."

Several seconds later, the lantern illuminated the interior. They peered in and were shocked.

"What's this?" Tadgh reached in and drew out what looked like a Moorish cutlass, lethally curved, and wider at the blade than at the hilt. He tucked it down in his waistband.

"What else is in there?" Morgan pulled out an oilskin-covered object, bound by a leather strap. There was no time to unwrap it. Below were two faded documents. Only Tadgh could read the cover on the first. An excerpt from the *Book of Ballymote* preserved on vellum. The second was more substantial, a manuscript titled *Travels into Several Remote Nations of the World. In Four Parts.* The tome looked to be in better shape. He scooped them up.

There were other papers shoved farther down in the chest, documents that were quite moldy. Derek started to dig through them, but Morgan stopped him. She had been watching the waterfall coming down the stairs and was petrified. *Déjà vu.*

Tadgh realized they had to move. He grabbed the documents off the desk. If they stayed any longer, they would not be able to climb through the cascade. The water was up to their knees.

"Let's go." Handing Morgan all the documents from the chest, Tadgh said, "Keep these documents out of the water. Put them and the oilskin in that metal box you found on the desk and secure the lid."

It took them several minutes to climb up out of the study fortress. By then the room was more than half-full of water, and the cramped area above the open doorway was awash as well.

"Where's the way up, Derek?"

"Over here."

He hadn't found a pathway up, just a loose board in the flooring above. Tadgh hoped there would be a large open area above it.

Tadgh knew his wife's terror would lessen if he kept her busy. "Morgan, keep the box dry. Hold the lantern please. Derek, help me pry these boards off."

After they cleared debris out of the way, Tadgh took the cutlass and inserted it upwards into the loose board. Derek pounded the pommel with a piece of broken concrete, and the board popped up from the nailed joist without dirt pouring through the hole.

Tadgh announced, "Good. Means an air space of sorts up there."

Together they pounded the board nearest the next joist and the plank popped up. After three successful maneuvers, they were able to raise the loosened board up and off the joists, exposing a five-inch gap about three feet long.

Tadgh angled the cutlass, "Let's work the next plank."

Minutes later, they opened a hole in the floor above large enough to crawl through.

Tadgh grabbed the edges of the hole in the flooring and tried to pull himself up with both arms. He was shocked that he did not have the strength. "Give me a boost."

Derek pushed until the top half of Tadgh's body was above the flooring. The rebel was surprised his head had not bumped into any debris. Tadgh shifted sideways and sat down on top of the flooring with his legs dangling through the hole.

Looking down in the glow of the lantern, he could see that Morgan was struggling with the confinement. "Give me the lantern, please, aroon."

Morgan passed it up. Tadgh could see that she was having trouble keeping the documents above the water line.

"What do you see?" Derek asked.

Tadgh swiveled around with the lantern while still seated. "Another room of some sort up here. It's dry. I have about four feet of headroom above this floor. It may have been an upstairs bedroom that collapsed into the floor below."

He shone the lantern down through the opening. Morgan's face was panicked again.

"It'll be all right, my love."

"I can't feel my toes, Tadgh. With you up there, blocking my way, it's like being trapped by the boy with his foot caught on the ship that I told you about." The vein in her forehead was pulsing a mile a minute.

Tadgh got up on his knees and reached down through the hole. "Give me the box, and then I'll pull you up, lass."

Once Morgan was up with Derek's help, the ex-prizefighter pulled himself up. Then before turning his attention to their new environment, Tadgh held the lantern below the hole to survey their last refuge. The study room filled; they couldn't go back. The water level was surging up about two feet below their current floor level, rising fast in the cramped space.

Their new habitat was less confining than the area below the floor. The headroom was highest where they were seated at the hole. The floor that they could see occupied a space of about fifteen by twelve feet, with upper floor furniture debris and structure reducing the height at the periphery of three sides to nothing at the edge of their vision. On the fourth side, which Tadgh assessed as due south, the remains of a brick chimney held the roof of their enclosure two feet above the floor. The floor had also been held by the strong chimney as the building collapsed, and so it curved upwards about two feet from where they sat to the masonry rubble. A mangled brass bed frame sticking down through the jumbled wood top to their enclosure blocked their way to that chimney.

"Well, comrades. How do you like our luxurious accommodations?"

Morgan had her eyes screwed shut. "This is no time for joking, Tadgh."

"I'm just comparing it to solitary confinement at the Joy, don't ye know."

Tadgh examined the ceiling of their enclosure for any openings. It looked as if the roof of the building was squashed down above them. His heart sank. There would be no escape upwards. They were trapped, just like he had been for so long. After this house collapsed, they must have just plowed it under and covered it with dirt. He assessed their depth from street level at less than ten feet. It may as well have been a mile. Just enough for an impenetrable foundation for those buildings above this rubble. He had been hoping beyond hope the storm would end and the waters recede. Tadgh checked the height of water once again. Only one foot below the flooring now, and no sign of stopping. They would drown in a matter of minutes if they didn't suffocate from lack of air first.

For the second time in his life Tadgh felt completely powerless to save his loved ones. The first had been when he and Aidan witnessed their parents being murdered. Now, in his zeal for finding the iron chest he had put them all, including Morgan, in peril for their lives with a gruesome death only minutes away and no way to avoid it.

He dreaded telling Morgan the grim news but noted from Derek's countenance that he'd better be the one to tell her first. He wished there were still bullets left in Derek's gun. That would be less agonizing.

He leaned over and held her tightly before opening his mouth to speak.

Morgan knew the score from the look on Tadgh's face. She fought the renewed panic in her brain, and readied herself for the terror to come, just as she had on those frenzied stairs in the depths of the dying *Lusitania*.

THE END of Book Five
Book Six titled ***Fortunes*** is coming soon!

CAST OF CHARACTERS

North America—Historical

Johann von Bernstorff	German Ambassador, United States of America during WWI
John Devoy	Leader of Clan na Gael in America, New York
Heinrich von Eckhardt	German Ambassador, Mexico during WWI
Dorothy Finlay	Sam and Lil's Younger Daughter
Elizabeth Finlay (Lil)	Sam's Wife
Ernest Finlay	Sam and Lil's Elder Son
Norah Finlay	Sam and Lil's Elder Daughter
Samuel Stevenson Finlay	Artist & Director of Art at Riverdale High School, Toronto
Stephen Finlay	Sam and Lil's Newborn Son
Captain Jim McAllister	Captain of the Tugboat *Bronx Beauty*, New York Harbor
Joseph McGarrity	Leader of Clan na Gael in America, Philadelphia
Catherine McGillin	Owner of McGillin's Olde Ale House, Philadelphia
John Ross Robertson	Publisher and Editor-in-Chief, *Toronto Evening Telegram (Tely)*
Col. John Thompson	Chief Engineer, Remington Eddystone Plant
Woodrow Wilson	United States of America President, 1917

North America—Fictional

Jim Fletcher	*Toronto Evening Telegram*, News Director, Collin's Boss
Captain Josephson	Captain of the Freighter *Pretoria*

Cast of Characters

Collin O'Donnell	Young Irishman from Toronto
Kathleen O'Donnell (Kathy)	Young Irish Woman in Toronto, Collin's Wife. (née O'Sullivan)
Liam O'Donnell	Kathy and Collin's Son
Claire O'Donnell	Kathy and Collin's Elder Daughter
Shaina O'Donnell	Kathy and Collin's Newborn Daughter
Fiona O'Sullivan	Kathleen's Mother
Ryan O'Sullivan	Kathleen's Father
Henry Silvermann	Production Manager, Remington Eddystone Plant, USA

Europe—Historical

Tom Barry	O/C 3rd Cork West Flying Column, IRA
Harry Boland	Michael Collins' 2nd in Command
Cathal Brugha	Chief of Staff, Irish Republican Army (IRA), War of Independence
Sir George Carew	British Lord Totnes, President of Munster in 1601
Michael Collins	Adjutant General, Irish Volunteers, Director of Intelligence (IRA)
Robert Devereux	Earl of Essex, Queen Elizabeth I Favorite, Led Irish Campaign 1599
Sir Henry Dowcra	Governor of Derry after crushing the O'Donnell Irish Clan in 1602

Cast of Characters

David Lloyd George	Prime Minister, Great Britain during War of Independence
Molly Gleeson	Proprietress, *an Stad* Hotel and Pub, Dublin
Arthur Griffith	Founder of Sinn Féin Party and Leader in de Valera's Absence
John Edward Healy	Publisher, *The Irish Times*
Jan Janszoon van Haarlem	Murat Reis the Younger, Grand Admiral Republic of Salé
Reverend J.H. Lawlor	Professor of Ecclesiastical Studies, Dublin University Researcher of Ancient Gaelic Documents, including *Book of Ballymote*
Florence MacCarthaigh	Clan Chieftain until 1601, Arrested by George Carew before Battle of Kinsale in January 1602
Tomas Mac Curtain	Head of IRB for Cork, Tadgh's Commanding Officer Lord Mayor of Cork, Murdered by British
Terence MacSwiney	Lord Mayor of Cork, Died on Hunger Strike
Kathleen Markiewicz	Countess, Deputy Commandant Battalion #2, St. Stephen's Green, Irish Member of Parliament
Tonnaltagh McDonagh	Chieftain, recipient of the *Book of Ballymote*, 14th Century
Major Mills	British Leader, Croke Park Assassination, Bloody Sunday
Sean O'Casey	Irish Playwright, Tadgh's Literary Mentor

Peader O'Donnell	College Student, Later to be a Revolutionary Leader, "Peadar" O/C No. 2 Brigade, Donegal IRA During War of Independence
Niall Garve O'Donnell	Cousin of Red Hugh O'Donnell, Traitor selling out to the English
Red Hugh O'Donnell	Last Free Chieftain O'Donnell Clan until 1602, Battle of Kinsale
Rory O'Donnell	1st Earl of Tyrconnell, Red Hugh's Younger Brother Led Flight of the Earls to Europe in 1607
Hugh O'Neill	Clan Chieftain, Northeast Ireland. Compatriot of Red Hugh O'Donnell at the Battle of Kinsale, 1602
Paddy O'Reilly	IRA Leader of the Joy Prison Break, March 29, 1919
Sir Owain	Twelfth Century European Knight, Endured Entrance to Purgatory then Returned to Temple Castle, Now Ghost for Lost Souls there
Charlotte Perceval	Matron of Temple House, Ballymote Ireland
Jonathan Swift	Abigail's Son, Satirical Essayist (*Gulliver's Travels*) Dean, St. Patrick's Cathedral, Dublin
Martha Temple	William Temple's Wife
William Temple	4th Provost, Trinity College, Devereux Supporter

John Temple	William Temple's Son—Master of the Rolls, Ireland
Sir William Temple	John Temple's Son, Baronet, British Ambassador
Éamon de Valera	President of Dáil Éireann (Sinn Fein Party)
Edward Walsh	Owner of Grocery, Distillery, now called Temple Bar, (Temple Bar Pub) in 1920
Arthur Zimmermann	German Foreign Minister during WWI

Europe—Fictional

Deirdre	Owner and Barkeeper of the Temple Bar Pub, Dublin, Ireland, Owner and Shopkeeper of Gilroy's Grocery, Temple Bar, Dublin
Henry Hollingsworth	Graduate Student, Working for Professor Lawlor at RIA
Abbad Janszoon van Haarlem	Descendant of Jan Janszoon, Member British Israeli Association
Fazaar Janszoon van Haarlem	Descendant of Jan Janszoon, Lawlor Student
Flooren Janszoon van Haarlem	Brother of Jan Janszoon van Haarlem, Murad Reis the Younger

Cast of Characters

Jack Jordan	Third Bosun's Mate, HMS *Lusitania*, Manager, Cunard Operations, Queenstown, Ireland, Manager, Gilroy's Grocery for Deirdre, Deirdre's Lover
Aidan McCarthy	Tadgh's Younger Brother, Irish Volunteer
Tadgh McCarthy	Young Irish Revolutionary. Member of Cork IRB, Communications, and Transportation Specialist
Morgan McCarthy	Irish Woman Rescued by Tadgh McCarthy, his Wife (née O'Donnell)
Shaina O'Donnell	Collin's Mother, Murdered in Toronto
Maureen O'Sullivan	Journalist for *The Irish Times* Newspaper, Dublin, Ireland
Derek Slocum	Deirdre's Cook and Bodyguard, Ex-Mariner and Prizefighter
John Walsh	Edward Walsh's, (owner of Pelican's Nest, Dublin) strapping son
Jeffrey Wiggins	Transportation Leader, Beamish & Crawford (B&C) Brewery, Cork City, Ireland, and Tadgh's Colleague at B&C
William	Cunard Longshoreman Tries to Steal the Munitions at Queenstown.

HISTORICAL BACKGROUND

The purpose of this historical background is to illuminate the facts imbedded in Revolution: Book Five, particularly those associated with the Clans Pact Adventurers.

The Irish War of Independence was waged very differently from the Easter Rising Rebellion, where the Irish patriots occupied key locations in mostly Dublin and waited for the British to attack them in the open. As already discussed, the Rising was a heroic act of martyrdom intended to inflame the Irish people against the occupying British.

Primarily due to the inspired leadership of Michael Collins, the War of Independence was fought using the military methodology that had made the Clans so successful before the pitched battle of Kinsale in 1601, namely hit-and-run guerrilla warfare tactics.

As a result, there were many local skirmishes that confounded and enraged the British authorities. I have chosen several important battles and events that intertwine with my Clans storyline. Of course, there are also fictitious adventures that interact with the British as well.

Therefore, I have included a brief overview of the Irish War of Independence, and separately, a list of the historical events that are imbedded in my novel in this background section.

Ref.	Subject	Location
1.	Irish War of Independence - Summary	Author's Note
2.	War of Independence Historical Events in Revolution: Book Five	Author's Note
3.	US Enters WWI	Ch. 2, pg 43
4.	*Book of Ballymote* (*Leabhar Bhaile an Mhóta*)	Ch. 11, pg 222
5.	Poems of Denis Florence MacCarthy	Inspiration

1. The Irish War of Independence - Summary

This summary is a general overview of the history of the war that is used here, with modifications and additions by me for a more complete background. A source for more information about these events is Wikipedia.

The Irish War of Independence (Irish: *Cogadh na Saoirse*) or Anglo-Irish War, was a guerrilla war fought in Ireland from 1919 to 1921 between the Irish Republican Army (IRA, the army of the Irish Republic) and British forces—the British Army, along with the quasi-military Royal Irish Constabulary (RIC) and its paramilitary forces the Auxiliaries and Ulster Special Constabulary (USC). It was an escalation of the Irish revolutionary period into warfare.

In April 1916, Irish republicans launched the Easter Rising against British rule and proclaimed an Irish Republic. Although it was crushed after a week of fighting, the Easter Rising and the British response led to greater popular support for Irish independence.

Éamon de Valera, who commanded the battalion at Bolands Bakery during the Easter Rising, was uniquely spared execution because of his American birth. He became the political leader of the revolution, along with Arthur Griffith who had started the Sinn Féin political movement.

Michael Collins, who had served as aide-de-camp to Joseph Plunkett, one of the Easter Rising organizers at the Dublin General Post Office, emerged as the military leader of the War of Independence. Michael organized the guerrilla hit-and-run flying columns of the military Irish Republican Army (IRA) and employed an elite intelligence gathering and assassination team called 'The Squad' to confound the British forces in Ireland.

In the December 1918 general election, the republican party Sinn Féin won a landslide victory in Ireland. On 21 January 1919, they formed a breakaway government (Dáil Éireann) and declared Irish independence. That day, two RIC officers were shot dead in the Soloheadbeg ambush by IRA volunteers acting on their own initiative. The conflict developed gradually. For much of 1919, IRA activity involved capturing weaponry and freeing republican prisoners, while the Dáil set about clandestinely building a state.

In September 1919, the British government outlawed the Dáil and Sinn Féin, and the conflict intensified. The IRA began ambushing RIC and British Army patrols, attacking their barracks, and forcing isolated barracks to be abandoned. The British government bolstered the RIC with recruits from Britain—the Black and Tans and Auxiliaries—many of whom had survived the deadly trenches of WWI. They became notorious for being ill-disciplined and for their reprisal attacks on civilians, some of which were authorized by the British government (Winston Churchill). Thus, the conflict is sometimes called the Black and Tan War.

The conflict also involved civil disobedience, notably the refusal of Irish railway men to transport British forces or military supplies, refusal to obey the courts, and disruption of roads and communications systems.

In mid-1920, republicans won control of most county councils, and British authority collapsed in most of the south and west, forcing the British government to introduce emergency powers. About 300 people had been killed by late 1920.

The conflict escalated in November. On Bloody Sunday in Dublin, 21 November 1920, fourteen British intelligence operatives were assassinated in the morning by The Squad, plus one who died later. Then in the afternoon, the RIC opened fire on a crowd at a Gaelic football match at Croke Park, Dublin, killing fourteen civilians and wounding sixty-five. A week later, seventeen Auxiliaries were killed by the IRA in the Kilmichael Ambush in County Cork.

The British government declared martial law in much of southern Ireland. The center of Cork city was burned out by British forces in December 1920 in reprisal for Kilmichael. Violence continued to escalate over the next seven months, when 1,000 people were killed and 4,500 republicans were interned. Much of the fighting took place in Munster (particularly County Cork), Dublin, and Belfast, which together saw over 75 percent of the conflict deaths.

The conflict in north-east Ulster had a sectarian aspect. While the Catholic minority there mostly backed Irish independence, the Protestant majority were mostly unionist/loyalist. A Special

Constabulary was formed (USC), made up mostly of Protestants, and loyalist paramilitaries were active. They attacked Catholics in reprisal for IRA actions, and in Belfast, a sectarian conflict raged in which almost 500 were killed, most of them Catholics.

In May 1921, Ireland was partitioned under British law by the Government of Ireland Act, which created Northern Ireland. Both sides agreed to a ceasefire (or "truce") on 11 July 1921.

Michael Collins and Arthur Griffiths led the Irish delegation at these talks. Recognizing the British determination to retain its northern industrial center at all costs, with Winston Churchill threatening to destroy Ireland if this was not agreed, the Irish delegation accepted the split of Ireland between the six northern counties to stay in Great Britain, and the remaining 26 southern counties to form the new Republic of Ireland country. These post-ceasefire talks led to the signing of the Anglo-Irish Treaty on 6 December 1921, ending British rule in the Republic.

The Irish Free State awarded 62,868 medals for service during the War of Independence, of which 15,224 were issued to IRA fighters of the flying columns.

After a ten-month transitional period overseen by a provisional government, the Irish Free State was created as a self-governing Dominion on 6 December 1922, with British forces withdrawing from the new Republic of Ireland. Northern Ireland remained within the United Kingdom.

Revolution: Book Five covers the period from 1916, after the Easter Rising, until the period occurring after the Bloody Sunday events in Dublin in November 1920. *Fortunes*: Book Six continues the saga throughout the War of Independence until the ceasefire in July 1921.

Éamon de Valera and many followers did not agree that the country should be split in this way. Still the President of the Dáil Éireann, he rallied republican supporters who fought against the Irish Free State military in 1922-23 in the Irish Civil War. But that is the subject of the last novel in the Irish Clans series: *Revelation*: Book Seven in the Series of The Irish Clans.

2. War of Independence Historical Events in Revolution: Book Five

July 30, 1916
Black Tom Island Sabotage, New York Harbor.

December 24, 1916
Amnesty for many Rising prisoners.
Michael Collins released from Frongoch Internment Camp.

January 16, 1917
Zimmermann, Germany Foreign Secretary, sends a telegram to von Eckardt, the German ambassador to Mexico, with an offer to return Texas, New Mexico, and Arizona to the Mexicans when they agree to fight against the USA, that is, if the Americans enter the war against Germany and Germany wins the war. This is intercepted and decoded by the British.

January 31, 1917
Germany resumes unconditional submarine warfare. Ordered by Field Marshall Paul von Hindenburg and General Erich Ludendorff against the wishes of the civilian government and Chancellor Theobald von Bethmann Hollweg. They thought that the US could not mobilize in a year if they joined the war.

February 3, 1917
US severs diplomatic ties with Germany after the US Cargo ship *Housatonic* is sunk by the Germans.

February 24, 1917
Britain sends the Zimmermann telegram to Washington.

February 1917
Collins becomes Secretary of the IRB.

March 1917

5 US ships torpedoed by the Germans.

March 20, 1917

US Cabinet votes for war.

April 6, 1917

US Congress declares war on Germany.

April—Nov. 1917

Collins, Constance, (and Morgan) organize the Amalgamated National Aid Association for widows, orphans, and dependents of the Easter Rising participants.

June 1917

Éamon de Valera (ÉdeV) released from Lewes Prison.

October 1917

ÉdeV elected President of Sinn Féin and the Irish Volunteers (1917 – 1926).

March 1918

Collins elected Adjutant General of the Volunteers.

April 3, 1918

Collins arrested, posted bail, and thereafter, on the run.

May 1918

ÉdeV rearrested, put in Mountjoy Prison with other Dail members including Countess Constance Markiewicz.

August 1918

Collin elected Director of Intelligence of the Irish Volunteers.

January 21, 1919

First Dáil Éireann Meeting (rebel Sinn Féin Irish Parliament).

February 3, 1919

Collins facilitates ÉdV escape from Lincoln Gaol, with Harry Boland (Dressed as a woman.).

April 7, 1919

Collins assists 20 prisoners to escape from Mountjoy Prison. Tadgh is one of them, as is Piaras Béaslai (Gaelic scholar) both asked to edit *An tÓglach* (Irish Bulletin) newspaper. But Tadgh is detained.

June 1919

ÉdeV goes to America to gain support and money. Griffiths is in charge in ÉdeV absence.

September 12, 1919

Dáil considered illegal by the British

September 19, 1919

Founding of Collins' Intelligence Group, "The Squad" (counterintelligence and assassination).

November 24, 1919

British Cabinet rules two Irelands with two parliaments.

March 20, 1920

Tomas Mac Curtain, Lord Mayor of Cork, shot dead.

March 25, 1920

Black and Tans (B&T) arrive in Ireland to bring order.

April 5, 1920

POW hunger strikes begin in Mountjoy prison.

August 1920

Tom Barry starts the 3rd Cork West Flying Column.

August 9, 1920

Restoration of Order in Ireland Act (Martial Law declared).

August 12, 1920

Terrence MacSwiney—Lord Mayor of Cork arrested, Starts a hunger strike.

September 20, 1920

First soldiers killed in Dublin since 1916 Rising (3) B&T start burning towns and killing civilians.

Oct 25, 1920

Terence MacSwiney dies from hunger strike—Brixton Prison.

November 1, 1920

Arthur Griffith calls off Hunger Strike.

November 21, 1920

Bloody Sunday in Dublin. Collins orders 14 killed, 1 mortally wounded. Auxiliaries raid, Croke Park, killing 14—retaliation.

November 25, 1920

Arthur Griffiths and Eoin MacNeill arrested.

3. US Enters WWI

This summary is a concise overview of the history of the background for the United States of America deliberations and entry into the World War of 1914 – 1918, with modifications and additions by me for a more complete background. See Wikipedia for more information on this area of history.

The United States President, Woodrow Wilson, was a staunch advocate for maintaining neutrality from the War to End War for the two and a half years leading up to April 1917, when he finally changed his view and convinced his cabinet and the congress to declare war on the Central Powers led by Germany. Why, then, did he have this change of mind?

Let us examine the demographic conditions in that country before this change of heart. Early in the war, the Anglophile element urged support for the British, while the anti-Tsarist element, prior to the Bolshevik revolution of 1917, sympathized with Germany's war against Russia. Meanwhile, Irish, German, and Scandinavian Americans wanted neutrality. On top of that, church leaders, and women in general, opposed entry into the war.

However, Germany was viewed as the aggressor as they swept through Belgium inflicting atrocities on its citizens. Then the passenger liner HMS *Lusitania* was sunk by a German U-boat in April 1915 with 125 American citizens onboard. This caused a hue and cry in the citizenry but was not sufficient to change Wilson's mind.

He did, however put pressure on Kaiser Wilhelm III to stop torpedoing non-military shipping.

On May 6, the German government signed the so-called Sussex Pledge, promising to stop the indiscriminate sinking of non-military ships. According to the pledge, merchant ships would be searched, and sunk only if they were found to be carrying contraband materials. Furthermore, no ship would be sunk before safe passage had been provided for the ship's crew and its passengers.

American banks took advantage of the misfortunes of the Entente Powers and provided crushing loans so that Britain and their allies, including Russia, could procure sorely needed munitions, raw materials, and food from the United States.

With all these divisive factions, Wilson was narrowly reelected in 1916 on an anti-war platform. Bowing to his military, he did, however, authorize the build-up of the United States Navy.

Late in 1916, Germany still appeared to be winning the war in Europe, and their ally, the Ottoman Empire, was still in control of their empire in modern-day Iraq, Syria, and Palestine. However, the Entente economic embargo, and naval blockade, primarily in the North Sea, English Channel, in the Atlantic Ocean and Mediterranean Sea, were strangulating the Central Powers countries.

At the beginning of 1917, Germany realized that they could not win the war on two fronts simultaneously. They had been forced to shift military might to the Eastern front, leaving the European theater of battle at a stalemate in the trenches. They had to cut off supplies to the Entente countries and were therefore forced to resume unrestricted submarine warfare on February 1, 1917. The aim was to break the transatlantic supply chain to Britain from other nations, although the German high command realized that sinking American-flagged ships would almost certainly bring the United States into the war.

As a result, Germany made a secret attempt to ally with Mexico against the United States in an encoded correspondence in January 1917. They would help Mexico regain territories lost in the Mexican–American War, namely Texas, New Mexico, and Arizona, if Mexico would help them defeat the United States of America. The British intercepted and deciphered this message and transmitted it to United States officials. Publication of that communique, and the admission by the German Foreign Secretary Zimmermann in March that it was authentic, outraged Americans just after German submarines started sinking American merchant ships in the North Atlantic again. The Mexican government rejected Germany's offer.

Wilson was reluctantly convinced that the United States could not stay out of the war. He and his cabinet asked Congress for "a war to end all wars" that would "make the world safe for democracy." Congress voted to declare war on Germany on April 6, 1917.

U.S. troops began major combat operations on the Western Front under General John J. Pershing in the summer of 1918 and were a major factor in the defeat of the Central Powers led by Germany, and their capitulation on November 11, 1918.

4. *Book of Ballymote* (*Leabhar Bhaile an Mhóta*) *

In general, the Irish history was handed down verbally from pre-Christian times through the eighteenth century by wandering storytellers (seanchaí), the Google of ancient times. However, during the medieval period (1000-1500 AD), for a few wealthy Irish chieftains, religious scholars and scribes created written compendia of religious and secular history dating back to the Biblical flood. These were very valuable treasures in those days, and the few that remain in existence after the British purge in the 1600s are invaluable records of Gaelic Ireland held in libraries, including the Royal Irish Academy in Dublin.

The *Book of Ballymote* is one of the most valued and revered compendia. It was created in 1390 at the castle of Ballymote, Sligo, for Tonnaltagh McDonagh, who occupied the castle at that time. Manus O'Duigan was the primary scribe for most of this tome.

In 1522 this manuscript was purchased by Aeg Óg O'Donnell, prince of Tir Conaill, for the price of 140 milch cows. We can only imagine why the O'Donnell clan wanted this ancient collection of documents. It was in Red Hugh O'Donnell's possession during his reign as Chieftain, leading up to the Battle of Kinsale.

It remained in the hands of Rory O'Donnell until the Flight of the Earls in 1607. After that, its whereabouts was not known, until it was acquired by Trinity College before 1621. It stayed at Trinity until 1767. One can only assume that William Temple, 4th Provost of Trinity College from 1609 until his untimely death in 1627, would have had a hand in its acquisition. A Trinity scribe copied elements of the document in 1622.

In 1719 it was lent by the college library to Anthony Raymond, Vicar of Trim, and thence to other scholars. In 1785 the manuscript was presented by Chevalier Thomas O'Gorman to the newly formed Royal Irish Academy as its first acquisition for safekeeping. Apparently, O'Gorman acquired it from a millwright's widow in Drogheda for £20.

The Irish writing is in two columns with decorated capital letters of interwoven designs in red, black, green, vermilion and chrome. It is bound in leather with oak boards. The 251 vellum folios are 15.75 x 10.25 inches in size.

The table of contents that had been scribbled down by Professor Hugh Jackson Lawlor and passed over to Tadgh and Peader during the Rising is provided on the next page:

Book of Ballymote
Leabhar Bhaile an Mhóta)
Table of Contents

1. Drawing of Noah's Ark

2. History of the Lost Israelites—Migration from Israel into Europe to become Gaels and Anglo-Saxons

3. The Life of Saint Patrick

4. *Lebor Gabála Erenn* (*The Book of Invasions*) six civilizations, including Tuatha Dé Danann and Milesians

5. Instructions of King Cormac mac Airt

6. Triads of Ireland Including Customs, Law, and Behavior

7. Stories of Fionn MacCumhail (Finn MacCool) and Brian Borumh (Brian Boru).

8. Genealogies of clans and kings of Ulster, Leinster, Connaught, and Munster

9. Irish Versification

10. *Auraicept na n-Éces* (scholar's primer) Including In Lebor Ogaim, a rare treatise on the Ogham language

11. The *Lebor na gCeart* (Book of Rights)

12. Various Greek and Latin fragments on the fall of Troy— including part of the *Aeneid*

* last leaf is a faded vellum fragment.

Book of Ballymote
Folio Example
Courtesy Royal Irish Academy

5. Poems of Denis Florence MacCarthy

Denis Florence MacCarthy,* a prolific Irish poet, translator, and biographer, was born in Lower O'Connell Street in 1817, and died in Dublin in 1882. During his life, he lived in Dublin, continental Europe, and London. In 1846 he was called to the Irish bar, but never practiced law.

He was a prolific translator, notably of Pedro Calderón de la Barca, the Spanish Shakespeare, and he edited notable poetic compendia such as The *Poets and Dramatists of Ireland* and *The Book of Irish Ballads*. He greatly admired Percy Bysshe Shelley and published *Shelley's Early Life* while living in London.

Denis's own *Ballads, Poems, and Lyrics* was published in 1850. One poem with an excerpt quoted in the novel is included below in its entirety.

* (Reference: Wikipedia Sources and http://www.gutenberg.org/ebooks/author/4460)

Cease To Do Evil—Learn To Do Well
by Denis Florence MacCarthy

Oh! thou whom sacred duty hither calls,
Some glorious hours in freedom's cause to dwell,
Read the mute lesson on thy prison walls,
"Cease to do evil—learn to do well."

If haply thou art one of genius vast,
Of generous heart, of mind sublime and grand,
Who all the spring-time of thy life has pass'd
Battling with tyrants for thy native land,
If thou hast spent thy summer as thy prime,
The serpent brood of bigotry to quell,
Repent, repent thee of thy hideous crime,
"Cease to do evil—learn to do well!"

If thy great heart beat warmly in the cause
Of outraged man, whate'er his race might be,
If thou hast preached the Christian's equal laws,
And stayed the lash beyond the Indian sea!
If at thy call a nation rose sublime,
If at thy voice seven million fetters fell,—
Repent, repent thee of thy hideous crime,
"Cease to do evil—learn to do well!"

If thou hast seen thy country's quick decay,
And, like the prophet, raised thy saving hand,
And pointed out the only certain way
To stop the plague that ravaged o'er the land!
If thou hast summoned from an alien clime
Her banished senate here at home to dwell:
Repent, repent thee of thy hideous crime,
"Cease to do evil—learn to do well!"

Or if, perchance, a younger man thou art,
Whose ardent soul in throbbings doth aspire,
Come weal, come woe, to play the patriot's part
In the bright footsteps of thy glorious sire
If all the pleasures of life's youthful time
Thou hast abandoned for the martyr's cell,
Do thou repent thee of thy hideous crime,
"Cease to do evil—learn to do well!"

Or art thou one whom early science led
To walk with Newton through the immense of heaven,
Who soared with Milton, and with Mina bled,
And all thou hadst in freedom's cause hast given?
Oh! fond enthusiast—in the after time
Our children's children of thy worth shall tell—
England proclaims thy honesty a crime,
"Cease to do evil—learn to do well!"

Or art thou one whose strong and fearless pen
Roused the Young Isle, and bade it dry its tears,
And gathered round thee ardent, gifted men,
The hope of Ireland in the coming years?
Who dares in prose and heart-awakening rhyme,
Bright hopes to breathe and bitter truths to tell?
Oh! dangerous criminal, repent thy crime,
"Cease to do evil—learn to do well!"

"Cease to do evil"—ay! ye madmen, cease!
Cease to love Ireland—cease to serve her well;
Make with her foes a foul and fatal peace,
And quick will ope your darkest, dreariest cell.
"Learn to do well"—ay! learn to betray,
Learn to revile the land in which you dwell
England will bless you on your altered way
"Cease to do evil—learn to do well!"

The title is an inscription on the front of
Richmond Penitentiary, Dublin, in which Daniel O'Connell
and the other political prisoners were confined in the year 1844.

ACKNOWLEDGMENTS

Once again, the author is indebted to Manzanita Writers Press, in San Andreas, California, for its tireless support in editing, producing, and marketing of these novels. Of particular note are its founding director and creative editor Monika Rose, editors Kati Rose, Michael Murray, and Joy Roberts, as well as book designer Joyce Dedini, who took me under their wing to wrestle my manuscripts into shape. Thank you, ladies, and gentleman!

There are two readers who have given me constructive feedback for *Revolution*—Bob Kolakowski, and Kathy Archer. Thank you both.

I would like to express my appreciation to Mr. Martin McGrinder, a well-known, accomplished Northern Ireland artist, whose *Legacy of Music Collection* of paintings depicts the effervescence of Irish music and dance so beautifully. But it is his fine painting of an ambush during the Irish War of Independence, which he painted specifically for the front cover of this novel, that illustrates the hit and run skirmish nature of this war of attrition. Thank you, Martin.

The image of one folio from the magnificent *Book of Ballymote*, which is presented in the historical background section and on the back cover [2] is reproduced by permission of the Royal Irish Academy. Thank you.

Also, Map #2 is the Temple Bar portion of "A New Plan of Dublin," prepared by Mr. Samuel Byron, Dublin City Surveyor in 1793, and published in *The Gentleman's and Citizen's Almanack*. I wish to thank the Board of Trinity College, Dublin, and its magnificent library, for allowing the use of this map in my novel.

Most of all, I wish to express my undying love and appreciation to the woman who, for over thirty-five years, has been the wind beneath my wings, my darling wife Kathy. Without her constant encouragement and nurturing guidance in all aspects of our life together, I would have given up on the quest to complete this multi-novel tale of The Irish Clans long ago. Her loving support during this decade-long journey is all the more remarkable because this is my dream and not hers. I try to tell her each day, as the song goes, *You are my sunshine, my only sunshine. You make me happy when skies are gray.*

AUTHOR'S NOTE

Michael Collins was the young adjutant to Joseph Plunkett during the martyrdom of the Easter Rising in 1916, where the rebels confronted the British in an entrenched, pitched battle. After the last-minute loss of the German weapons, these tactics were not meant to defeat the enemy, just cause them to be so tyrannical that the Irish people would subsequently rise up to throw the British out of Ireland. Michael remembered that this method of fighting also resulted in the Clans being defeated in 1602 after centuries of successful guerrilla warfare.

Michael helped the main General Post Office contingent fight their way out of the GPO when it was destroyed by British artillery at the end of the one week Rising. He survived the battle and was interred in Frongoch Internment Camp in Wales with many of the rebel fighters whom he trained for the War of Independence conflict ahead in 1919-1921[1, 2].

Éamon de Valera was the American-born commandant of #3 Battalion at Boland's Mill during the Rising. A twelve-man contingent of his battalion, led by brave Malone at the McKenna Bridge on the Northumberland Road entrance to East Dublin, held off hundreds of British soldiers. De Valera's contingent, however, saw little action. He was the only leader of a battalion to escape execution due to his American heritage.

These two men, Collins, and de Valera, were to become main leaders of the Republican War of Independence three years after the Rising. Collins excelled in military and intelligence prowess, whereas de Valera became the Sein Féin political leader of the rebel movement.

Michael realized that the rebel Volunteers needed to return to the guerrilla warfare tactics that had been so successful for their Clan ancestors before 1600. He set up Republican flying column battalions thirty to a hundred Volunteers strong throughout Ireland who used hit-and-run tactics to disrupt British operations and infrastructure starting in 1919. They attacked RIC police stations to kill the enemy and commandeer weapons. They attacked trains, post offices, telephone communications lines, and destroyed roads and bridges. They refused to allow the judicial court system to function.

Probably the most effective method Michael employed to confound the British was to establish an intelligence network to attack the British spy and intelligence system within Ireland during this War of Independence. He had his own spies within the British Castle stronghold in Dublin who helped him ferret out the British agents.

As Michael Collins stated at the end of the war,

"Without her spies England was helpless . . . Spies are not so ready to step into the shoes of their departed confederates as are soldiers to fill up the front line in honourable battle. And, even when the new spy stepped into the shoes of the old one, he could not step into the old one's knowledge . . . We struck at individuals, and by doing so we cut their lines of communication, and we shook their morale."

In 1919, Michael established a twelve-man assassin team called the Squad to eliminate the British spies who would otherwise help defeat the Republican nationalists. Members of the Squad included Mick McDonnell, Liam Tobin, Vinny Byrne, Paddy Daly, and Jim Slattery.

They singled out members of the "Cairo Gang" of British intelligence officers. The Squad systematically eliminated them after giving them fair notice. All the while, Michael and his executioners were on the run, in plain sight in Dublin, not meeting or staying twice in any one place, except for their Crow Street residence.

One of the major events in this war was the execution of fifteen British agents by the Squad on the morning of November 21, 1920. Michael would have targeted more British agents except for the restraints imposed Cathal Brugha, IRA Minister for Defense. Michael's comments on that Bloody Sunday were, "There is no crime for detecting and destroying in wartime the spy and informer. They have destroyed without trial. I have paid them back in their own coin."

This military event was made more infamous because the British forces, in retaliation that afternoon, opened fire on Irish spectators and players at the Dublin vs Tipperary football match at Croke Park in Dublin. Fourteen innocent people were killed, and dozens injured in this vengeful attack, which became known as Bloody Sunday – Dublin. From that point onward, the attacks and killings on both sides became more vicious and spiteful.

This guerrilla war was raging in Ireland, with Michael and his Irish Republican Army (IRA) of Volunteers risking their lives daily in 1919 and 1920. Meanwhile, Éamon de Valera, who had been broken out from Lincoln Jail by Michael and his trusted friend Harry Boland in February 1920, spent this time in safety in America, drumming up support for the revolution. He returned to Dublin and became President of the Dáil Éireann rebel parliament in December 1920, just in time for the British Government of Ireland Act separating North from South, an act he was dead set against.

Michael and Éamon's fate, along with the entire IRA movement, will be become clearer in Books Six and Seven of this series, in a reversal of what you might expect. As a result, it is Michael Collins who history remembers as the savior of the Irish nation. But that is a story for later in the series.

As Éamon wrote later in life, "It is my considered opinion that in the fullness of time history will record the greatness of Michael Collins and it will be recorded at my expense."

After consultation with my editors, I decided to separate the lead-up and early stages of the War of Independence, culminating with Bloody Sunday in Dublin on November 21, 1920, in *Revolution: Book Five*, from the latter stages of this war, including the Custom House Burning and ceasefire, plus the search for the hidden O'Donnell fortune in *Fortunes: Book Six*. This results in manageable length novels and means that the series will now have seven books in total.

I hope you enjoy the continuing adventures of the McCarthy and O'Donnell Clans in *Revolution: Book Five*, as they try to use McCarthy Gold to fight for freedom in the Irish War of Independence[1] and search for their rightful O'Donnell treasure to support the revolution.

INSPIRATION

Cease To Do Evil – Learn To Do Well[5]
by Denis Florence MacCarthy (1817 -1882)

Oh! thou whom sacred duty hither calls,
Some glorious hours in freedom's cause to dwell,
Read the mute lesson on thy prison walls,
"Cease to do evil—learn to do well."

If thy great heart beat warmly in the cause
Of outraged man, whate'er his race might be,
If thou hast preached the Christian's equal laws,
And stayed the lash beyond the Indian sea!
If at thy call a nation rose sublime,
If at thy voice seven million fetters fell,—
Repent, repent thee of thy hideous crime,
"Cease to do evil—learn to do well!"

Or if, perchance, a younger man thou art,
Whose ardent soul in throbbings doth aspire,
Come weal, come woe, to play the patriot's part
In the bright footsteps of thy glorious sire
If all the pleasures of life's youthful time
Thou hast abandoned for the martyr's cell,
Do thou repent thee of thy hideous crime,
"Cease to do evil—learn to do well!"

"Cease to do evil"—ay! ye madmen, cease!
Cease to love Ireland—cease to serve her well;
Make with her foes a foul and fatal peace,
And quick will ope your darkest, dreariest cell.
"Learn to do well"—ay! learn to betray,
Learn to revile the land in which you dwell
England will bless you on your altered way
"Cease to do evil—learn to do well!"

The title is an inscription on the front of Richmond Penitentiary, Dublin, in which O'Connell and the other political prisoners were confined in the year 1844, yet it could aptly describe Michael Collins and his revolutionary Volunteers in the years 1919 –1921 during the Irish War of Independence.

ABOUT THE AUTHOR

Stephen Finlay Archer

The author writes Irish historical fiction. His latest seven-novel series, *The Irish Clans*, covers the Irish revolutionary period from 1915 to 1923. This Irish family saga full of swashbuckling characters and page-turning action tells the true story of Ireland's conflict with England.

It is also a personal portrayal since the fictitious story involves his own ancestral family as they are drawn into the conflict of their Irish homeland, while in his birthplace of Toronto, Canada.

Archer lives in Northern California with his wife Kathy. He is a member of Writers Unlimited in California Goldrush Country and the North American Historical Novel Society. Before his retirement, he was an Aerospace Manager directing large-scale, delivery-in orbit, satellite systems for the U.S. Navy and NASA/NOAA.

Stephen Finlay Archer's books are available on Amazon.com and directly from the author and publisher. Stephen can be reached at:

> Email: stephenfinlayarcher@gmail.com
>
> Website: www.stephenfinlayarcher.com
>
> LinkedIn: (Stephen Finlay Archer)
>
> Twitter: @SFinlayArcher"
>
> Blog: www.StephenFinlayArcher.com/blog

Revolution: The Irish Clans: Book Five

Dee Marley, CEO and Reviewer at The Historical Fiction Company ★ ★ ★ ★ ★

. . . *the author does a remarkable job of revealing the actual history of the time period, the passion and the patriotism fueled in the fiery hearts of Ireland's Gaelic heritage . . . In one quote from the author , he states that 'readers who are interested in Ireland's struggles for freedom and its storied but often mythical history will enjoy The Irish Clans series. Readers who enjoyed Da Vinci Code, National Treasure, or Outlander will be enthralled by my stories.' I have to concur with this statement, for the essence of all three of those books resonates in just this one book alone, and now I am intrigued to start with book one and read them all.*

. . . *This is Ireland's story, and the implications echo across generations and across oceans. 'Man's inhumanity to man' screams loud in this book, the sacrifice, the blood, the bravery, and desperation for justice. . . I am left on the edge of what is to come, and I look forward to continuing the saga with Tadgh and Morgan McCarthy.*

Amazon Five Star Reviews ★ ★ ★ ★ ★

McCarthy Gold: The Irish Clans: Book Four
<u>Fascinating Irish History and Great Storyline</u>

J. Pierce, March 26, 2020

Verified Purchase

Enjoyed this book four in the Irish Clans series. The story is engaging and there is so much action. Keeps me turning the pages! Plus, I enjoy the Irish history. It is obvious that there has been quite a bit of research done. Can't wait for Book five!

McCarthy Gold: The Irish Clans: Book Four
The Latest in this Historical Action Adventure Delivers
The Bors Family, November 23, 2020

Our own clan continues to be entertained and impressed by this most ambitious multi-book saga by Stephen Finlay Archer. After meeting (and learning to care greatly about) the many inter-woven characters in the initial books leading up to the Rising, McCarthy Gold sees the protagonists and villainous rivals through a race to recover a clan's ancient treasure and avenge past and ongoing evil doings. The author's creativity abounds in this tapestry of well-spun adventure, romance, and actual history.

The Irish Clans Series
Carlo Pietro Sanfilippo, *It's the Journey Podcast Episode 41,* 9/21/21@ //Carloblog.com/podcast

The series called The Irish Clans is Irish historical fiction that dives into the fascinating and interesting Irish history as well as his (Stephen's) family history. If you like fiction you'll love it. If you like Irish history or you have Irish roots you'll really love it. You can really, really feel Stephen's love of Ireland jumping off the pages.

The Irish Clans Series
R. Kolakowski

From the beginning of the Searchers through the ending of McCarthy Gold I have been captivated with this story. McCarthy Gold was the latest of a tale with all the twists and turns heading to what can only be a fantastic finish. Each novel has its own flavor, McCarthy Gold leads the reader closer to the conclusion. Great storytelling.

The Irish Clans is an epic story immersed in the tumultuous Irish revolutionary period of 1915 through 1923, while the world is embroiled in the Great War and its aftermath. The once mighty McCarthy and O'Donnell Clans, overthrown in ancient times, are not extinct. They are linked on two continents by a medieval pact entwining military history and religious mythology. Divine intervention plays a pivotal role in unearthing the secrets of the Clans' treasure and heroic exploits. The patriotism and passion of Celtic heritage lies at the heart of this intriguing story.

Other novels in the series:

A tragedy at sea sets in motion the search for life's true treasures, both in 1915 Ireland, when the funeral of Fenian Rossa fans the flames of revolution, and in America, where the clans begin a journey toward their destiny in **Searchers**, *the first book of the series.*
Published March 2016

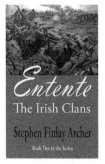

The mysteries of an ancient Clans Pact deepen beneath the horrors of WWI as Irish Rebels march toward revolution in **Entente**, *the second book in the series.*
Published May 2017

Irish Republican martyrs rise against overpowering British forces to spark the revolution in the 1916 Easter Rising, while the Clans search for unity and treasure to honor the Clans Pact of their ancestors in **Rising**, the third book in the series. **Published January 2019.**

In the aftermath of the Easter Rising, the Clans and murderous Head Constable Boyle seek each other and the McCarthy treasure, while Collin searches for his missing sister in **McCarthy Gold**, the fourth book in the series. **Published January 2020**

The mysteries of the O'Donnell Clan are explored in **Fortunes**, the sixth book in the series, set in the last year of the Irish Revolution's War of Independence upheaval, leading to the Anglo-Irish Treaty of 1921.

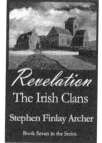

The Clans, while supporting the Irish Civil War in 1922 – 1923, seek to unravel and unearth an ancient religious mystery that has confounded civilization for centuries in **Revelation**, the seventh book in the series.

Made in the USA
Las Vegas, NV
04 April 2022

46815773R00223